BEN JONSON'S PLAYS

Knowledge is the action of the *Soule*; and is perfect without the *senses*, as having the seeds of all *Science*, and *Vertue* in its selfe; but not without the service of the *senses*: by those Organs, the *Soule workes*:

Discoveries, 811–814

But, because some, sweete *Madame*, can leape ditches,
Wee must not all shunne to goe ouer bridges.

The Devil is an Ass IV.i.8–9

Ben Jonson's Plays

An Introduction

by

ROBERT E. KNOLL

UNIVERSITY OF NEBRASKA PRESS · LINCOLN

Publishers on the Plains
UNP

Manufactured in the United States of America

For Virginia,
yet once more

Foreword

THIS BOOK is a critical study of Jonson's plays by one of their admirers. Criticism is a modest calling, useful as it returns its reader clear-eyed to the art which gives it excuse for existence; and I hope this book will do that. Since each section contains information or judgments that have not been put down before, it may sharpen a reader's understanding of the plays. I have not tried to be startling on every page, because I would rather be conventional than wrong; and I have leaned on my betters where I could. This book will not replace theirs, but it might supplement them. My task has been to define Jonson's dramatic ideas by close examination of the structure of the plays and to deal with some of the principal scholarly controversies touching them. Though partisan, I have tried not to be blind. In clarifying each play's principle of unity, I have compared the more successful to the less, and Jonson himself to his lesser—and greater—contemporaries: Jonson's are not the only plays deserving notice. And I have tried to be brief.

When I started this study, I had no axe to grind. I had no preconceived notions that I was prepared to defend. As I have read these plays over the years, several generalizations have forced themselves upon me; and the individual sections of this book, though having independent integrity, are nonetheless closely related to the convictions. In the interests of clarity they should be stated at the outset. Jonson's plays strike me as more indigenous than classical, for they are elaborations of the Tudor morality drama. They are not one-dimensional, however. The characters in them may be of the surface, as Eliot says—I think he means that their motives are uncomplicated and obvious—but the total plays in which they exist have more than surface significance. Jonson enriches the simplicity of his drama by setting his contemporaneous world within a mythic one. The majority of his plays are written against some explicit, fabulous background, and their full meaning is available when we recognize it. The Venetian foxes and Bartholomew Fair puppets thus inhabit several worlds simultaneously. Jonson strives to show the timeless implications of his characters' problems in this way.

The narrative—that is, the dramatic action—is not Jonson's chief interest, nor is it the chief concern of the morality writers from whom he descends. Both are essentially concerned with "sense," the term Jonson uses for "meaning." "In all speech, words, and sense, are as the body, and the soule," he wrote in *Discoveries* (ll. 1884–1887), his manual of critical precepts. "The sense is as the life and soule of Language, without which all words are dead." To understand this "sense" we may profitably give our attention to the story behind the action, the fox tales in *Volpone*, the parable of the talents in *The Alchemist*, the devil fables in *The Devil is an Ass*. The plays which are most successful use native, Christian stories, and those plays in which Jonson draws on classical literature have worn least well. When he equates the contemporaneous situation to the classic prototype, the resulting Roman play is rather algebraic. The "satyricall comedies" strike the modern reader as silly, and dated besides. In the other plays, the native English materials are richly provocative.

As I have studied these plays I have come to recognize how thoroughly Jonson is a humanist. Even more, I have come to see how fully he is a Christian humanist. He was never given to theological speculation, and whatever inclination to religious mysticism he may have had does not show itself in his plays. But the plays, however rational they strike us, are ultimately religious. Jonson's common sense told him that by standing straight he might reach full height, but by taking thought he knew he could not add one cubit to his stature. The old morality drama was not simply a formula to him; it was no empty vessel into which he poured his Roman ideas. Form and content were no more separable for him than for any other playwright. His dramatic vocabulary determined what he could say. By the time he had reached maturity his classical learning had been assimilated into his English body, and his sophisticated morality plays preached Christian sermons. In his hands Terence became a Londoner, the old Vice a frequenter of St. Paul's, and both lived together in plays that are neither classical nor medieval but Jonsonian.[1] When one considers Jonson's drama as a whole, surveying it from beginning to its end, one finds that Jonson reiterates certain dramatic situations and attacks a single range of vices. But by his middle years he is less harsh in his judgments of the vices; understanding more fully, and growing more fatigued, he partially forgives what he formerly castigated.

In my study of the plays I have had a good deal of scholarly and critical help. Herford and Simpson's massive edition of Jonson's works, which contains more information than any one writer can possibly assimilate, was finally completed in 1952. Perhaps because of this edition, in the past

1. See H. A. Mason, *Humanism and Poetry in the Early Tudor Period* (London: Routledge and Kegan Paul, 1959; New York: Barnes and Noble, 1959), "Epilogue, The Humanist Heritage," pp. 255–289.

two decades more detailed criticism of Jonson has appeared than in all
the previous century. Unhappily the plays have seemed exotic ever since
the Romantic Revolt, and almost all the nineteenth- and early twentieth-
century studies were biographical and narrowly historical. Gifford,
Jonson's editor, in 1816 felt compelled to defend him against a host of
detractors; and later critics, Swinburne apart, have been less than
openhanded in their praise.

Fresh analysis is necessary. Modern criticism really begins with T. S.
Eliot's essay in *The Sacred Wood* (1920), but most students are equally
indebted to L. C. Knights's *Drama and Society in the Age of Jonson*
(1937). That book awakened a whole generation of readers, including
me.[2] Since the Second World War a number of helpful monographs have
appeared. Freda L. Townsend (1947) examined the structure of the
comedies to show that the indigenous *Bartholomew Fair* is more closely
akin to the classical earlier plays, *Every Man in his Humour* and *The
Alchemist*, than had generally been acknowledged. Mrs. H. W. Baum
(1947) studied the "satiric and didactic in Jonson's comedy," and A. H.
Sackton (1948), in the first of a number of such studies by several hands,
analyzed the rhetorical patterns in Jonson's dramatic language. Occa-
sional writers like D. J. Enright, Ray Heffner, Jr., J. A. Bryant, Jr., and
S. Musgrove have clarified various aspects of several of the plays. More
recently some useful general criticism has been published. John J. Enck
(1957) has searched for a central "comic truth" in the plays; Edward B.
Partridge (1958) in a particularly helpful book has scrutinized the imagery
of the major comedies; Jonas A. Barish (1960) has discussed the prose;
and C. G. Thayer (1963), surveying the whole corpus of the dramatic
work, has sought to explicate themes and arguments.[3]

2. Eliot's essay is included in *Selected Essays, 1917–1932* (New York: Harcourt,
Brace and Company, 1932), pp. 127–139. Knights's book has had an American edition
(New York: Barnes and Noble, 1957).

3. Freda L. Townsend, *Apologie for Bartholmew Fayre* (New York: Modern
Language Association of America, 1947); Helena Watts Baum, *The Satiric and the
Didactic in Ben Jonson's Comedy* (Chapel Hill: University of North Carolina Press,
1947); Jonas A. Barish, *Ben Jonson and the Language of Prose Comedy* (Cambridge:
Harvard University Press, 1960) and "*Bartholomew Fair* and Its Puppets," *MLQ*,
XX (1959), 3–17; Edward B. Partridge, *The Broken Compass: A Study of the Major
Comedies of Ben Jonson* (New York: Columbia University Press, 1958); John J. Enck,
Jonson and the Comic Truth (Madison: University of Wisconsin Press, 1957); D. J.
Enright, "Crime and Punishment in Ben Jonson," *Scrutiny*, IX (1940), 231–248, and
"Poetic Satire and Satire in Verse: A Consideration of Ben Jonson and Philip Mas-
singer," *Scrutiny*, XVIII (1951–1952), 211–223, reprinted in *The Apothecary's Shop:
Essays on Literature* (Philadelphia: Dufour Editions, 1957), pp. 54–74; Ray Heffner,
Jr., "Unifying Symbols in the Comedy of Ben Jonson," *English Stage Comedy* (English

The body of Jonson criticism is thus clearly growing. One can only wonder that it has flourished so late and that its flower is still so small, but readers can be grateful for all of it. Teachers of Elizabethan and Jacobean drama have often had trouble working up student enthusiasm for Jonson's comedies, and the tragedies have seemed beyond recovery. Marlowe strikes home and so do Webster, Greene, Middleton, and even Kyd. But Jonson does not. These plays are *sui generis*; readers have to be taught all over again what to find in them. Perhaps the Romantic sensibility which we in the twentieth century have willy-nilly inherited makes Jonson difficult to respond to. Perhaps we cannot easily shuck off our predilections for passion and our fears of absolute moral judgments. It may be that the cult of personality has thrust Ben himself between us and his work. Be that as it may, in this generation one can detect the beginning of a shift in sensibility. A start to an appreciation of Jonson's excellence has been made. He may even yet be rescued from the great storehouse of unread classics, and it is my purpose in this book to indicate some ways this might be done.

Institute Essays, 1954), W. K. Wimsatt, Jr., ed. (New York: Columbia University Press, 1955), pp. 74–97; Joseph Allen Bryant, Jr., "The Nature of the Conflict in Jonson's *Sejanus*," *Vanderbilt Studies in the Humanities*, R. C. Beatty, J. P. Hyatt, M. K. Spears, eds. (Nashville: Vanderbilt University Press, 1951), pp. 197–219, and "The Significance of Ben Jonson's First Requirement for Tragedy: 'Truth of Argument,'" *SP*, XLIX (1952), 195–213, and "*Catiline* and the Nature of Jonson's Tragic Fable," *PMLA*, LXIX (1954), 265–277; S. Musgrove, *Shakespeare and Jonson*, The Macmillan Brown Lectures 1957 (Auckland University College, Bulletin No. 51, English Series No. 9, 1957). See also Una Ellis-Fermor, *The Jacobean Drama, An Interpretation* (London: Methuen and Company, 1936; rev. 1953), esp. pp. 98–117; Evelyn M. Simpson, "Jonson and Dickens: A Study in the Comic Genius of London," *E&S*, XXIX (1943), 82–92, Percy Simpson, "The Art of Ben Jonson," *E&S*, XXX (1944), 35–49, reprinted in his *Studies in Elizabethan Drama* (Oxford: Clarendon Press, 1955), pp. 112–130; M. C. Bradbrook, *The Growth and Structure of Elizabethan Comedy* (Berkeley and Los Angeles: University of California Press, 1956), esp. pp. 138–165. *Ben Jonson: A Collection of Critical Essays*, Jonas A. Barish, ed. (Englewood Cliffs: Prentice-Hall, Inc., 1963), reprints a dozen pieces of general interest. C. G. Thayer, *Ben Jonson: Studies in the Plays* (Norman: University of Oklahoma Press, 1963) has recently appeared.

Contents

List of Illustrations

BEN JONSON'S PLAYS

List of Abbreviations

ALL REFERENCES to Jonson are to *Ben Jonson*, C. H. Herford, Percy and Evelyn Simpson, edd. (Oxford: Clarendon Press, 1925–1952), 11 vols., referred to in text and footnotes as Herford and Simpson. Harry Levin edited *Selected Works* (New York: Random House, 1938). The Everyman Library edition of *The Complete Plays* (London: J. M. Dent and Sons; New York: E. P. Dutton and Co., 1910, 2 vols.) is a reprint of the nineteenth-century Gifford edition and thus is far below modern critical standards. *The Yale Ben Jonson*, Alvin B. Kernan and Richard B. Young, gen. edd., is under way at Yale University Press, with each play occupying a single volume.

The following list of the plays, with the dates of their first publication and production, also gives the abbreviations that appear throughout the text and footnotes.

	A Tale of a Tub (F1640) acted 1633. Written 1596 or 1597/1633.
	The Case is Altered (Q1609) acted 1597–1598?
EMI:	*Every Man in his Humour* (Q1601; F1616) acted 1598 (revised for F1616).
EMO:	*Every Man Out of his Humour* (Q1600; F1616) acted 1599.
CR:	*Cynthia's Revels* (Q1601; F1616) acted 1600.
Poet:	*Poetaster* (Q1602; F1616) acted 1601.
Sej:	*Sejanus His Fall* (Q1605; F1616) acted 1603.
	Eastward Ho (Q1605 "Made by Geo. Chapman. Ben: Ionson, Ioh: Marston") acted 1604.
Vol:	*Volpone or The Fox* (Q1607; F1616) acted 1605/1606.
SW:	*Epicoene, or The Silent Woman* (Q1612?; F1616) acted 1609.
Alch:	*The Alchemist* (Q1612; F1616) acted 1610.
Cat:	*Catiline his Conspiracy* (Q1611; F1616) acted 1611.
BF:	*Bartholomew Fair* (F1631; F1640) acted 1614.
D is A:	*The Devil is an Ass* (F1631; F1640) acted 1616.
	The Staple of News (F1631; F1640) acted 1626.
NI:	*The New Inn* (Q1631; F1692) acted 1629.
ML:	*The Magnetic Lady* (F1640) acted 1632.
	The Sad Shepherd (F1640) fragment not acted (date of composition unknown).

Montimer His Fall (F1640) fragment not acted. "It is clearly early work."

The major plays are to be found in the following volumes of Herford and Simpson: III—*Every Man in his Humour*; V—*Volpone*; *The Silent Woman*; *The Alchemist*; VI—*Bartholomew Fair*.

Other abbreviations in the text and footnotes are:

E&S :   *Essays and Studies* by Members of the English Association
JHI :   *Journal of the History of Ideas*
MLQ :   *Modern Language Quarterly*
MLR :   *Modern Language Review*
MP :   *Modern Philology*
PQ :   *Philological Quarterly*
PMLA :   *Publications of the Modern Language Association*
RES :   *Review of English Studies*
SP :   *Studies in Philology*
TLS :   *Times Literary Supplement*

CHAPTER I

On Reading—and Misreading—the Plays

IN MANY RESPECTS Ben Jonson, like Dr. Samuel Johnson, was his own worst enemy. For generations Dr. Johnson stood between his books and his readers; only in recent times has his work, as opposed to his conversation, come into its own. Something of this is true for Ben Jonson. He was so commanding as a person that he too has been more talked about than read. To be buried in Westminster Abbey is a distinction that did not come even to Shakespeare. But one recalls how a passerby dictated and paid for the chiseling of the epitaph—"O rare Ben Jonson"—before one remembers his plays. His quarrels with Inigo Jones have gone down into literary anecdotage though their joint masques have not. "Painting and carpentry are the soul of the masque," Jonson protested. But the protest is heard still more frequently than his verse. It is well known that Jonson once fought a duel with a theater colleague, one Gabriel Spencer, and killed him; Jonson's old mother brought poison to the prison that he might escape public execution should his special pleading fail. He escaped by "benefit of clergy"—a legalistic trick that earned him a branding on the thumb, but with a cold iron apparently. Gabriel Spencer was not the first man Jonson had killed; he had seen service in the Low Countries and, killing a man behind enemy lines, proved his considerable courage. Jonson had spirit. It is no wonder that the details of his life have entered the gossip of literature, but perhaps it is better to be remembered for the wrong qualities than not remembered at all.[1]

The stories about his literary activity are no less persistent than those about his extraliterary experiences. Like Dr. Johnson, he was a clubman; he was a formidable eater and drinker. His poem "Ben Jonson's Sociable Rules for the Apollo" takes us to the Apollo Room in the Devil Tavern: wit, gaiety, and old Ben officiating.[2] A literary dictator, he sat enthroned,

1. All the standard factual information about Jonson is conveniently assembled in Herford and Simpson: "the whole of the extant and accessible documents bearing upon Jonson are reproduced *in extenso*" (I, v) in this edition, and vol. I contains a "Life."

2. See Katherine A. Esdaile, "Ben Jonson and the Devil Tavern," *E&S*, XXIX (1943), 93–100.

surrounded by his "Tribe of Ben." Herrick later wrote of him in the
London taverns:

> Ah *Ben*!
> Say how, or when
> Shall we thy Guests
> Meet at those *Lyrick* Feasts,
> Made at the *Sun*,
> The *Dog*, the Triple *Tunne*?
> Where we such clusters had,
> As made us nobly wild, not mad;
> And yet each Verse of thine
> Out-did the meate, out-did the frolick wine.[3]

We catch a glimpse of the man in a verse letter which Francis Beaumont
wrote to him:

> What things haue wee seene
> Done at the Mermaide? heard words that haue beene
> soe nimble, and soe full of subtill flame,
> as if that euery one from whom they came
> had meant to putt his whole witt in a Ieast
> and had resolu'd to liue a foole the rest
> of his dull life . . . (45–51)[4]

Like Falstaff, Jonson seems not only to have been witty in himself,
but the cause of wit in other men. It can be no wonder that his personality
survives the centuries.

The most celebrated contemporary account of Ben Jonson compares
him and Shakespeare in conversation. Thomas Fuller writes (1662):
"Many were the *wit-combates* betwixt him and *Ben Johnson*, which two I
behold like a *Spanish great Gallion*, and an *English man of War*; *Master
Johnson* (like the former) was built far higher in Learning; *Solid*, but *Slow*
in his performances. *Shake-spear*, with the *English man of War*, lesser in
bulk, but lighter in *sailing*, could turn with all tides, tack about and take
advantage of all winds, by the quickness of his Wit and Invention."[5] One
could wish that Ben Jonson had had a Boswell; but if he had, his plays
would be even more eclipsed. Unfortunately Fuller's account of their
conversation is frequently taken as a comparison of the work of Shakespeare and Jonson. It is, rather, an account of their social deportment.
However Jonson may have talked, his plays were anything but solid

---

3. Quoted in Herford and Simpson, XI, 416.
4. Quoted in Herford and Simpson, XI, 375–376; I have expanded the contractions.
5. Quoted in Herford and Simpson, XI, 510.

BEN JONSON

From the portrait by an unknown artist in the National Portrait Gallery. By courtesy
of the National Portrait Gallery, London.

and slow, bulky and heavy. Though he wrote carefully (to the amusement of the contemporary hacks) and carried with him a great ballast of learning, *The Alchemist* and *Bartholomew Fair* are very little like Fuller's "Spanish great Gallion." The most notable characteristic of *The Alchemist* is surely its swift movement and its darting, incisive action. Its careful construction, the result of artful planning, does not show any more than the careful planning of the shipbuilder. If in conversation Jonson was like a Spanish galleon, in his plays he was swift as a sloop. And the plays were as indigenous as they were swift moving. *Bartholomew Fair* gives a full picture of seventeenth-century London, crowded with masses of local detail. It belongs to London as surely as Jonson himself, and it is more English than Shakespeare, by far. Cicero's elaborate oration in the fourth act of *Catiline his Conspiracy* may be slow and artful and perhaps the learning in *Sejanus* bulks too large. But this is debatable. Even the tragedies move with wit and, though constructed solidly, ride with grace. Fuller's gossip is not literary criticism.

Not only does Jonson's personality get between us and his plays, but his learning intrudes too. In the margins of his printed tragedies he carefully cites his sources, and in his critical remarks he insists that we note his high antecedents. "He was not only a professed Imitator of *Horace*, but a learned Plagiary of all the others; you track him every where in their Snow," Dryden said long ago (1668); and this opinion has been repeated ever since. "He invades Authours like a Monarch, and what would be theft in other Poets, is onely victory in him," Dryden said a moment later.[6] Jonson's insistence on his learning has invited us to look at his plays from the wrong angle. Too frequently we become so obsessed with the sources, we pay such close attention to the writers from whom he borrows, that we fail to regard the finished work as a thing independent of its genesis. Critics begin by deploring Jonson's method, which they take to be rather like mosaic work: the fitting together of bits and pieces brought from the ancient Greek and Roman world. They proceed to a specification of the rules he professed to write by, and they end by condemning his incomplete use of stolen classics and his infidelity to cited rules. Encouraged by Jonson himself, the critic-scholars have postulated a classical standard and have then deplored any deviation from it. The

6. *Essays of John Dryden*, W. P. Ker, ed. (Oxford: Clarendon Press, 1899, 1926), I, 43, 82. Quoted in Herford and Simpson, XI, 513, 515. Cf. William Hazlitt, *Lectures on the English Comic Writers* (1819) in *The Complete Works*, P. P. Howe, ed. (London: J. M. Dent and Sons, 1931), VI, 38: "Ben Jonson is a great borrower from the works of others, and a plagiarist even from nature; so little freedom is there in his imitations of her, and he appears to receive her bounty like an alms. His works read like translations, from a certain cramp manner, and want of adaptation."

result is a critical paradox. The much praised writer of correct comedies is seen to deal fast and loose with the rules.[7]

It is next to impossible to examine Jonson by classical precepts, for we can hardly separate his announced classicism from his indigenous heart; Jonson thought of himself as writing with Horatian aims. He expected his plays to be *dulce et utile*, pleasing and (morally) useful; and his distinction between "great noble wits" and "poetic elves" is on a didactic basis. Late in his career (1625) he wrote, for instance,

> Great noble wits, be good vnto your selues,
> And make a difference 'twixt Poetique elues,
> And Poets: All that dable in the inke,
> And defile quills, are not those few, can thinke,
> Conceiue, expresse, and steere the soules of men,
> As with a rudder, round thus, with their pen.
>
> *The Staple of News* (Prologue for the Stage, 19-24)

At first glance, Jonson's poetic seems solidly classical. But his central conviction, that drama is didactic, is not so much Roman as Christian and medieval. It is an assumption of the religious drama. The writers of the interludes, not to speak of the mystery cycles, had every intention of instructing their audiences, and they entertained in order to hold their attention. Horace may or may not have intended to instruct. He certainly did not mean what Jonson and Philip Sidney thought he meant when he said that poetry was *dulce et utile*: sweet and useful. He did not mean that the poet was *sweet* in order to be *useful* or that all utility was didactic. Horace was more urbane than that. He knew that preachers were not the only useful members of society. Ultimately, of course, the morality and classical traditions are not altogether separable. *Gammer Gurton's Needle* has its kinship with both Roman and native farce, and Kyd's *Spanish Tragedy* looks in two directions at once. Apologists for both use ethical arguments. The problem of indebtedness is one of degree. But insofar as they can be separated, Jonson's insistent didacticism places him in the native tradition. Nobody would have doubted it except for Jonson's insistence on his Roman affinities.

There is a touch of the Johnny-come-lately about Jonson's learning. He parades it like exotic finery. But on close examination much turns out to be commonplace.[8] *Every Man Out of his Humour* was designed

7. Cf. Freda L. Townsend, *Apologie for Bartholmew Fayre* (New York: Modern Language Association of America, 1947), p. 34. Chapter I of this book contains a convenient and rather elaborate history of Jonson criticism.

8. Cf., for example, Allan H. Gilbert, *The Symbolic Persons in the Masques of Ben Jonson* (Durham: Duke University Press, 1948), p. 14: "[Jonson's] erudition is not strikingly greater than that of Chapman or Heywood."

to be such a play as other plays should be; it was, he says, "somewhat like *Vetus Comoedia*" (Ind. 232). The term *vetus comoedia* (old comedy) is usually assumed to refer to the ancient comedy of Greece; Jonson seems to be claiming that his play is in the Aristophanic tradition. But when we examine the summary history of comedy which he conveniently provides in the Introduction to *Every Man Out of his Humour* we find no clear *vetus comoedia* to which this play might be compared. He seems to be using *vetus comoedia* as an honorific term with which to put off his critics. He wants to borrow the dignity more than the substance of classicism. As a matter of cold fact in Jonson's time the term is not indisputably a reference to classic drama at all. Jonson's erstwhile collaborator Thomas Nashe used it, perhaps ironically, in *The Returne of the renowned Cavaliero Pasquill of England* (1589) to refer to an allegorical interlude. Later (1619) Jonson himself used it in connection with a morality play.[9] To see Jonson as a follower of Aristophanes because he employs this term is more than a little daring.

Jonson's attitude towards his precursors—not his betters—was always independent. He claims for himself the same magisterial independence of rules which he professes to find among the ancients. "I see not then," he said, "but we should enjoy the same licence, or free power, to illustrate and heighten our invention as they did" (*EMO*, Ind. 266–267). Of course one can find certain parallels between Jonson's and ancient comedy: all giants are tall. But that is another matter. Jonson bowed to the ancients, but he asserted his right to sit in their company. To be of their quality is not necessarily to be of their kind.

In several ways, then, Jonson is his own worst enemy. His personality is so commanding that he sometimes seems to overshadow his own work. Very much a man of his own time, he seems to invite us to find topical comment in his plays. Few dramatists make so many contemporary references as he; and looking into the influence of ancient theatrical feuds on the plays O. J. Campbell and others have illuminated a chapter in literary history.[10] A concern for theatrical history is likely to take us off the highways of art, however, and into extraneous historical matters. Jonson's classicism also misleads us. Because of his insistent profession of it scholar-critics have looked for Roman simplicity where simplicity is quite

9. *The Works of Thomas Nashe*, Ronald B. McKerrow, ed. (London: Sedgwick and Jackson, 1910; rev. F. P. Wilson, ed. [Oxford: Basil Blackwell, 1958]), I, 92, 100. *Conversations with Drummond*, 409–415 (Herford and Simpson, I, 143–144).

10. Josiah H. Penniman, *The War of the Theatres* (Boston, 1897); Roscoe A. Small, *The Stage-Quarrel between Ben Jonson and the so-called Poetasters* (Breslau, 1899); Oscar J. Campbell, *Comicall Satyre and Shakespeare's "Troilus and Cressida"* (San Marino: Henry E. Huntington Library and Art Gallery Publications, 1938).

beside his purpose.[11] For all this, Jonson is himself at least partially responsible.

Jonson is his own chief enemy. Shakespeare is his next worst. Since we often do not find the qualities in Jonson that we admire in Shakespeare, we are blind to some of Jonson's excellences. His plays, unlike Shakespeare's, do not lend themselves to the detailed psychological analyses that post-Romantic critics are so fond of making. Ever since Morgann (1777), drama criticism has tended to be a search for personality, either of the dramatist or of his creations. When E. K. Chambers, for example, writes, "art is before all things the expression of the personality of the artist," he speaks not as the great Elizabethan scholar but as a modern post-Romantic critic.[12] This interest in personality extends to the characters in the plays and leads to a misunderstanding of Jonson. His dramatis personae do not suggest unfathomed depths and hidden motives. Jonson did not inquire into the working of the mind out of simple curiosity, for the machinations of motives were not of ultimate concern to him. An overwhelming interest in psychology is one of the defining characteristics of the modern, not the Renaissance, world. Marlowe and his friends disputed the existence of God; Auden and his group, the complexity of the human psyche. And that "wisest fool in Christendom," James I, was learned in theology, not psychology. Divine philosophy was queen of subjects in Jonson's day. It is not irrelevant that the word *psychology* first appeared as late as 1693, according to the *Oxford English Dictionary*, and that the proliferation of words containing *psyche-* is a nineteenth-century phenomenon.

One can assert the pre-eminence of psychology in modern times in the face of the fact that throughout his career Ben Jonson harped on a theory of humours. To the end of his life he spoke of his plays as comedies of humours, almost as though they were case studies, almost as though he had, in Auden's words, "committed/A social science."[13] But Jonson was interested in the humours as moral types; he was making observations about man's moral, not his psychic, nature. Theories of humours and of passions were branches of ethics then. When we in our time read Tennessee Williams and identify a character as schizophrenic, we have reached

11. C. H. Herford, "Introduction," *Ben Jonson* (Mermaid Series, London, 1893–1894), Vol. I, is an excellent summary of a traditional view of Jonson. See also J. B. Bamborough, *Ben Jonson* (Writers and Their Work, No. 112; Published for The British Council and The National Book League by Longmans, Green and Co., 1959).

12. E. K. Chambers, "*The Merchant of Venice*" in *Shakespeare: A Survey* (London: Oxford University Press, 1925), p. 108.

13. "Under which Lyre: A Reactionary Tract for the Times" in *Nones* (New York: Random House, 1951).

the limit of our diagnosis. The disease is our concern. When we identify a Jonson character as sanguine, we are led then to ask how this kind of man injures himself and how he offends against divine law. For Jonson, the identification of humourous types is only the beginning—and this is fortunate, because his dramatis personae, humourous or not, are often rather uninteresting. They are not enveloped in the half light of suggestion. We understand exactly what they are doing every minute we observe them; and we know what they are doing when they are off-stage too.

It is almost accidental that Jonson's contemporary, Shakespeare, offers the psychological complexity modern men search for. It is easy to exaggerate its importance, as the last two generations of Shakespearean critics have attempted to show. The serious Renaissance artist sought to illustrate moral wisdom, not scientific, or pseudo-scientific, knowledge. He held a mirror up to nature, "to show virtue her own feature, scorn her own image, and the very age and body of the time his form and pressure."[14] On this, at least, Shakespeare and Jonson were agreed and on this they differ from James Joyce and even T. S. Eliot. Jonson and Shakespeare were after bigger fish than psychological observations. This is not to suggest that we should ignore the very real psychological complexity of Cleopatra and Hamlet and Brutus: whatever one can find in the lines is surely there, even if the author did not knowingly put it there. I mean only that Shakespeare's plays allow inquiry in a direction which Jonson's forbid, and Shakespeare's popularity has caused readers to search for undiscoverable values in Jonson's plays.

There is another important basic way in which Jonson (especially the early and middle Jonson) differs from Shakespeare. In Jonson the major characters do not learn from their experience. Given the chance, Volpone would return to his old habits when the play is over; and we are not convinced that once he is thrown into prison he is done with scheming. When Lovewit comes home, Face is sure to continue in his old habits. Bobadill is immune to change. In Shakespeare, on the other hand, the characters learn; the action educates them. Katharina, in *The Taming of the Shrew*, ends wiser than she began; and because of what befalls him, the Duke in *Twelfth Night* is cured of his melancholy. For these Shakespearean persons, life is growth. Not so for Jonson's. For them life is a game, and if you know the rules you can win. ("*I know* no disease of the *Soule*, but *Ignorance*," Jonson wrote.[15]) Neither Volpone nor Face nor Sejanus has been shrewd enough. They have failed to take all details into consideration. There is nothing about themselves nor about the machinery

14. *Hamlet*, III. ii. 25–29.
15. *Discoveries*, p. 801 (Herford and Simpson, VIII, 588).

of the world that is not available to them, if they are clever enough to find it out. Or so they think. Indeed part of the laughter that these plays earn comes from the integrity of the characters and the simplicity of their world. In the late plays, *Bartholomew Fair* and *The Devil is an Ass* and *The New Inn*, the characters find that the world is not so simple as they had thought. In these last plays some of the dramatis personae seem to have learned their lessons. At the end of his career Jonson's protagonists discover that the world and they are less knowable than they had assumed. Jonson's laughter is now less at his characters' expense.

In a larger sense, the difference between Shakespeare and Jonson is the difference between discovery and exposition. In most of the plays of Jonson there is no development of character, situation, or philosophy. There is, rather, the exposition of a settled philosophic system. The values are set forth in the first scene of the first act and repeated and reiterated throughout the rest of the play. They are never in doubt. From Volpone's first words, we know the ostensible theme of his play, and we understand what our reaction ought to be. Volpone appears before us, and says:

> Good morning to the day; and, next, my gold:
> Open the shrine, that I may see my *saint*.
> Haile, the worlds soule, and mine. (I. i. 1–3)

Immediately we know that this play is about the substitution of a false god for the true God, about worshipping at a golden shrine and exulting in a false religion. This play is to be about avarice, first, and beyond this, impiety. The entire play is an elaborate embroidery on this announced theme.

In Shakespeare the construction is of quite a different sort. The Duke appears in *Twelfth Night* saying,

> If music be the food of love, play on,
> Give me excess of it, that, surfeiting,
> The appetite may sicken, and so die. (I. i. 1–3)

We know immediately that love is the subject of this play, and if we are clever we may even be able to deduce that it deals with sentimentality. But no man is clever enough to detect from this beginning that the play will turn out to question the necessity of conventions—if indeed it does. It is only in retrospect that we are able to perceive the idea which combines apparently disparate elements in its action. The theme develops as the play proceeds, drawing more and more to a central core which yet remains an enigma. We await its meaning throughout the play. No single scene contains its epitome. The action is a gradual revelation of the play's significance. The suspense comes in part from this ambiguity in the meaning of the action. In Jonson's plays, on the other hand, we always understand the significance of each situation, and we understand the alternatives confronting any character. The suspense comes not from asking, What does this mean? but, What will happen next? We always know what a character is morally bound to do, for we know what is right and what is wrong. We may sympathize ironically or sardonically with the rascals rather than with the abused, but we know where one's duties lie. In Shakespeare we are not sure what ought to be done, for the questions posed are ticklish.

One wonders often if Shakespeare knew precisely where he was going when he started a play. A central action, certainly, but he drops hints and leaves undeveloped fragments of plot which suggest that their implications appeared to him as he wrote. One might say that the play was for him, as for us, an act of discovery; he found what he wanted to say as he said it. Each play contained all he knew, and he did not know what he knew until he read what he had written. I don't mean to suggest that he was given to automatic writing. He often followed rather closely a story line which he had picked up someplace or other. When he started a play he may even have known what he would put in each act. But the significance of it, what for the lack of a better expression we call his view of life, or more elaborately his philosophy, must have been little thought out independent of the drama. He was not a systematic thinker. One can almost imagine Ben Jonson saying to him, "Will, pray, what view have you of the place of romantic love in the world's affairs?" and Shakespeare replying, "Mark Antony thought . . . Now there's a subject for a play. . . ." And the play would be the answer.[16]

16. Mark Twain's observations concerning his experience with the creative process is relevant: "A man who is not born with the novel-writing gift has a troublesome time of it when he tries to build a novel. I know this from experience. He has no clear idea of his story; in fact he has no story. He merely has some people in his mind, and an incident or two, also a locality. He knows these people, he knows the selected locality, and he trusts that he can plunge those people into those incidents with interesting results. So he goes to work. To write a novel? No—that is a thought which comes later; in the beginning he is only proposing to tell a little tale, a very little tale, a six-page tale. But as it is a tale which he is not acquainted with, and can only find out what it is by listening as it goes along telling itself, it is more than apt to go on and on and on till it spreads itself into a book. I know about this, because it has happened to me so many times.

"And I have noticed another thing: that as the short tale grows into the long tale, the original intention (or motif) is apt to get abolished and find itself superseded by a quite different one. It was so in the case of a magazine sketch which I once started to

But this is fanciful, though, I think, sound. Before he put quill to paper Jonson had thought out his views on a given subject; the play which resulted was the exposition of them. Shakespeare worked from deeper resources. Perhaps Jonson's greater popularity in the seventeenth and eighteenth centuries[17] derived from a general confidence in those far days that the reason had a major share in making truth clear; and that truth, once defined, needed only to be stated to be recognized by reasonable men. Shakespeare's great popularity in more modern times may be a result of a general conviction that truth is not everywhere the same; that it must be discovered individually and explained tediously, and sometimes irrationally. For us the map of the universe has been lost, and we live our lives out in a pathless wood. Shakespeare seems to be one of us, for his characters discover each day what that day they have to do. Jonson's always know, and their duty remains the same, now and forever. For Jonson a play is not a discovery. It is a statement. Shakespeare is in this sense modern, and Jonson is not. This does not necessarily make Jonson the less worth reading.

Until now I have been speaking of how Jonson ought *not* to be read, the kinds of approaches to his plays which have misled readers generally. I want now to suggest some approaches to the plays which are more profitable. In his recent book on *Jonson and the Comic Truth* Professor Enck is right to suggest that in Jonson's plays one's first concern may be with general patterns of action.[18] With Dryden we may observe that "the beauty of the whole be kept intire, and that the variety become not a perplex'd and confus'd mass of accidents." Then we will find it "infinitely pleasing to be led in a labyrinth of design, where you see some of your way before you, yet discern not the end till you arrive at it."[19] If

---

write—a funny and fantastic sketch about a prince and a pauper; it presently assumed a grave cast of its own accord, and in that new shape spread itself out into a book. Much the same thing happened with *Pudd'nhead Wilson.* I had a sufficiently hard time with that tale, because it changed itself from a farce to a tragedy while I was going along with it—a most embarrassing circumstance." "Author's Note to *Those Extraordinary Twins*" (1894), conveniently reprinted as an appendix to *The Tragedy of Pudd'nhead Wilson* (New York: Signet Classics, The New American Library of World Literature, and Harper and Row, 1964).

17. Gerald E. Bentley, *Shakespeare and Jonson: Their Reputations in the Seventeenth Century Compared* (Chicago: University of Chicago Press, 1945), 2 vols. Robert Gale Noyes, *Ben Jonson on the English Stage, 1660–1776* (Cambridge: Harvard University Press, 1935).

18. John J. Enck, *Jonson and the Comic Truth* (Madison: University of Wisconsin Press, 1957), p. 16.

19. Ker, ed., I, p. 73; Herford and Simpson, XI, 514.

we take a dispassionate, even intellectual, delight in form for its own sake, we can enjoy the machinations of plot for the sake of machinations, rather as we enjoy watching tight rope walkers perform their impossible feats. There is of course an element of bravura in all art. The greatest statues are of the hardest materials not only because they are the most enduring, but because they are the most difficult to work in. The drapery on Michaelangelo's *Pietà* pleases because here hard stone is made to resemble soft cloth. One likes to see difficulty overcome. Perhaps what gratifies us is that here convincing evidence is given that we can, after all, triumph over intransigent nature and that we are not totally at the mercy of the physical universe. Every art attests to such triumph; the greater the difficulties, the greater one kind of delight. In reading Ben Jonson we may be particularly pleased. The tricks that he is able to play are spectacular. His is brilliant theater.

A full delight in his plays requires a kind of double consciousness. We submit temporarily to the spell of the moment and at the same time know that we are submitting. This double consciousness is not confusing, though perhaps less fully used by other writers. When we read Jonson we have an ironic montage in our minds: the idea of the thing represented and the representation itself. We are not laid asleep in body to become a living soul. We do not yield to the moment nor do we lose our sense of ourselves. Jonson asks us to bring our critical intelligence to his plays. Unlike Housman, he does not suggest that we avoid shaving while reading his lines, nor does he try to take the top of the head off, as Emily Dickinson thought all poetry ought. Our emotional life remains our own business and none of Jonson's, and his plays do not invade our privacy. Having been to the movies one distrusts the irresponsibility of the lachrymose glands and thus welcomes his respect for us. Jonson asks us to remain in the market place where men's similarities can be observed. He does not take us to the confessional booth for intimate revelations nor to the boudoir for vicarious satisfactions. He is a rational man speaking to other rational men.

Indeed when we are reading these plays, we must be consciously aware that we read plays, not narrative fiction (I say *read*, for few of us have much opportunity to see these plays performed). One does not read drama as one reads fiction, if one wants to get full measure for his effort. Music does not exist until it is played, and plays do not exist until they are acted. The skillful musician learns in time to hear the music as he reads the notes, and it is a truism that the skillful student of drama must constantly visualize the drama on the stage, if he would understand it. Marston speaks for Jonson and to all of us when he directs his "equall

Reader," "*Comedies* are writ to be spoken, not read: Remember the life
of these things consists in action."[20] Every reader of Jonson must think
of himself as a director and producer, with all technical facilities at his
disposal. He must decide how entrances are to be made, how exits might
be arranged, where actors stand, how the lights can heighten the point
of a scene, how the actors should be costumed, how the lines might best
be read, how fast the scenes ought to be played. He must supply stage
business which is only implied in the lines. Not to do so is to read the
play as a novel and thus to misread.

Though Jonson provides fewer directions for his actors, and thus less
help in visualizing the action, than modern playwrights like Shaw, he
gives more assistance than Shakespeare. In editing his texts for publication, he sometimes arranged them for our edification. He prints some
speeches in double columns on his pages in *The Alchemist* in order to
indicate which lines are spoken simultaneously, and in the late comedies
he gives rather elaborate indications of stage business. Jonson's plays
constantly imply elaborate dramaturgical byplay. In the first scenes of *The
Alchemist* if we fail to visualize Dol Common running between the
quarreling Face and Subtle, we miss a well-planned joke. If we do not
picture Mosca shouting into Volpone's deaf ear, or Ursla's piglike appearance, or Bobadill brandishing his bedpost like a weapon, much of the fun
of these plays is lost. Jonson writes farce, a type of drama not often of
sufficient merit to deserve close literary study. He gives intellectual
content to a form which by definition "makes no intellectual appeal"
and surprises us by dignifying the common.[21]

If we are to understand the patterns of the plots, we must be aware of
certain recurring dramaturgical forms. Unlike Shakespeare, Jonson must
be read horizontally. Shakespeare must be, and is, read vertically.
Falstaff is what he is in large part because of his relationship to the other
figures in his play. Hotspur's talk of honor illuminates Hal and in turn
illuminates our understanding of the King. The incidents and characters
in Shakespeare's plays are intricately interdependent; that is why cutting
Shakespeare is so dangerous. The characters and actions of Jonson's
plays are not interdependent; they duplicate rather than complement
each other. In *The Alchemist* we meet successively Dapper, Drugger,

20. "To my equall Reader," *The Fawne* (1606), *The Plays of John Marston*, H.
Harvey Wood, ed. (Edinburgh and London: Oliver and Boyd, 1934–1939), II, 144.

21. M. H. Abrams, ed., *A Glossary of Literary Terms* by Dan S. Norton and Peter
Rushton (New York: Rinehart and Co., 1957), p. 14. A more extended and a relevant
definition is contained in Ian C. M. Maxwell, *French Farce and John Heywood* (Melbourne: Melbourne University Press, 1946), p. 47.

Sir Epicure Mammon, Ananias, and Kastril; each mirrors the character and action of the others and each strives illicitly for a single goal: worldly wealth. They are not related to one another in action. They meet in a single scene, but then as a collection, not as an association. The richness of Jonson is in his clever variations on a simple theme.

We are conscious of various plot lines—the horizontal development of the play, as it were; in reading Shakespeare, we note the vertical development, the interrelationship of the various parts. Jonson's plays are like neat brick walls; no single brick is indispensable to the whole and the wall will stand without any individual item; Shakespeare is rather like a mortarless wall of miscellaneous field stones, irregular in shape and held in place by the seeming accident of size and position. Remove one pebble and the whole intricate structure comes tumbling down.

The structure of a Jonson play may be profitably compared to Bach, Shakespeare to Beethoven. Bach and Jonson are both polyphonic and must be listened to horizontally. In both we have early a statement of a theme followed by its development and repetition. Both attempt to exploit or even exhaust its implications. Both are logical and expository. Both remain contrapuntal to the end, for even their finales isolate the various themes from one another; they are harmonic only incidentally. Shakespeare and Beethoven, on the other hand, are harmonic. We listen here to clusters rather than lines of sound. We hear the progressive development of relationships rather than the expository filling out of stated intentions. In Beethoven and Shakespeare both, we hear a series of chords. The comparison may be carried further. The finales of Beethoven symphonies and Shakespearean plays are climactic; the finales of Bach suites and Jonson plays are not. Unforeseen relationships and interrelationships are explored fortissimo in these Beethoven-Shakespeare conclusions; in Bach-Jonson, the finales are restatements of the original ideas; they are not appreciably more complicated than the previous actions. Beethoven and Shakespeare ask us to submit—which we do, willingly; Bach and Jonson ask us to observe. It is for this reason that Bach and Jonson are often called "intellectual"; they do not make a direct attack on the passions of the heart.

Though all plays ought to be read as plays, not all can be read either "horizontally" or "vertically." Indeed Jonson's plays are not everywhere as horizontal as The Alchemist and Volpone, nor are Shakespeare's as vertical always as Twelfth Night; in the sense I have described, The Tempest is a rather horizontal play, and Jonson's latest plays are more nearly vertical than the earlier. But Jonson tends toward the one kind, Shakespeare toward the other, and the differences are more illuminating than the similarities. If we examine Jonson's plays in order of their writing, we can see the changing and developing methods and ideas as he matures and grows old. Through them all we must remember constantly that in these plays Jonson is a man speaking to men, that it matters to him that he be understood; that he is addressing an unlearned audience, however learned he himself may have been. He does not conceive of himself as a man separated from society, different from other men. He is not above making little private jokes with his friends, for what person of the theater does not love trade jokes? But his plays were written not for the amusement of his master Camden but to instruct mankind. He saw himself as the spokesman for the accepted vision of generations; and if the plays sometimes strike us as didactic, this is because they are didactic.

Jonson's chief rewards are of his own kind. He gives few peculiar psychological specimens; he offers no interesting stories, no detachable observations about life; little romance, less passion, no sweep of history. Jonson has no truck with moods, even blessed moods when sweet thoughts bring sad thoughts to the mind. To understand his plays we need to track their action closely. Jonson shows us the rational connections between things. It is to the connections we constantly return. In these plays we can escape from the indulgence of our own feelings. We can delight in wit, in bravura. We can recognize an intellectual's shrewd analysis of men and society and we can be informed by his revelation of the root cause of human frailty. We can be entertained by the cleverest intrigues in literature, and we can be amused by the realistic detail transmogrified into art. We can rest secure in poetry that never falls into bathos and that sometimes rises into an elegance unmatched even by Shakespeare. These are plays for those who like the inexpressive in art, for those who prefer sanity to disease and order to chaos, for those who do not choose to dwell on the eternal sadness of things even while they do not ignore it. In short, these are plays for civilized men.

CHAPTER II

The Earliest Plays

IN 1616 JONSON published his *Works*, a folio volume that contained all the plays written before 1612 which he wished to claim. He was the first English playwright with the audacity to name his plays his "works", and his contemporaries laughed. Men of the theater in those days made no artistic claims. Jonson alone publicly professed himself to be more than a hack and his theater more than a means to notoriety and money. This great volume of 1616 did much to dignify the drama. One wonders if Heminge and Condell could have brought out the First Folio of Shakespeare's plays in 1623 if Jonson had not set a precedent. One can speculate concerning the part Jonson played in the production of the Shakespeare First Folio, too.

Though eleven of Jonson's plays had previously been printed in quarto, he included only nine in his *Works* of 1616. The two omitted plays were *Eastward Ho* (printed 1605), a joint effort with Chapman and Marston which was brilliant theatrical journalism; and *The Case is Altered* (printed 1609), a piece of juvenilia excluded presumably on aesthetic grounds. *Bartholomew Fair* (1614) was completed too late for inclusion; the 1616 Folio was in the press for a very long time. Jonson had written several more plays. He told Drummond that "the half of his comedies were not in Print" in 1619;[1] and though none of the tragedies earlier than *Sejanus* (1603) are extant, Meres in 1598 lists Jonson among the playwrights of the time "best for Tragedie."[2] We know that early in his career he had constructed plays or parts of plays for Henslowe,[3] but if any of them have survived, the scholars have been unable to identify his hand in them. His relation to the theater in the 1590's was rather like the relation of the Hollywood script writer to movie companies. What he produced was an expendable commodity to be used or misused at the discretion of the

1. *Conversations with Drummond*, 393 (Herford and Simpson, I, 143).
2. Quoted in Herford and Simpson, I, 17.
3. The portions of *Henslowe's Diary*, W. W. Greg, ed. (London: A. H. Bullen, 1904–1908), 2 vol., relevant to Jonson are conveniently quoted in Herford and Simpson, XI, 307–308.

business managers. Jonson clearly disapproved of this system. He thought that the artist should be master, not servant, in the theater.

Three examples of Jonson's earliest work—one probable and two certain—have come down to us. *A Tale of a Tub* offers a problem in dating. It was probably an apprentice piece, written before 1598, in an original, lost form. The text as we have it was acted in 1633, years after its initial production, and it gives evidence of thorough revision. The style of some of the verse is immature, and the structure and tone are experimental and uncertain. Some other scenes are in Jonson's late manner. *A Tale of a Tub* is included in the 1640 Folio, presumably with its author's blessing; but it does not appear in the 1616 Folio. Jonson seemed willing to own it only after retouching. The comedy is valuable to students because it contains some of his earliest work.

Unlike *A Tale of a Tub*, we have two others of Jonson's earliest plays substantially unrevised. *The Case is Altered* is the first of these. Printed in a 1609 quarto in reaction to the great success of *Volpone* (acted 1605/1606), it was excluded from the 1616 Folio. Jonson probably had no part in the carelessly printed quarto of 1609 even though his name appears on its title page. *The Case is Altered* was incorporated into the corpus of Jonson's work only in 1756, in Whalley's seven-volume edition. Like *A Tale*, *The Case* is important for those who want to watch the curve of Jonson's development. Further, it is a jolly play, more intrinsically interesting than Jonson admitted and quite worthy of inclusion in any collection of representative Elizabethan comedies.[4]

In addition to *A Tale of a Tub* (1596? revised by 1633) and *The Case is Altered* (1597?), we have a third very early play: the Italian version of *Every Man in his Humour*. Produced in 1598 with great success, it was published subsequently in quarto (1601). It was revised, Englished one might say, some years later. A comparison of the early and the later versions of this play can help us discover the direction of Jonson's developing interests during this first decade of his maturity. Looking closely at the three plays, *A Tale of a Tub*, *The Case is Altered*, and the two versions of *Every Man in his Humour*, we can catch a glimpse of what he was like when he wrote for hire and by what process he became so "restrained," so "classical," so "Jonsonian."

1. *A Tale of a Tub*

Much of the limited discussion of *A Tale of a Tub* in the past three hundred years has been concerned with the satire of Inigo Jones that it is

4. See John Palmer, *Ben Jonson* (New York: Viking Press, 1934), pp. 257–258; John Addington Symonds, *Ben Jonson* (London, 1888), 188–189.

supposed to contain.[5] In 1633 Jonson finally lost his long quarrel with Inigo Jones. From the early years in the century the two of them had produced poetic extravaganzas for the Court, Jonson supplying the texts and Jones the sets and costuming. They quarreled presumably over the credit each deserved for the joint ventures; both were too much individualists for indefinite collaboration. When Jonson set out to write, or rewrite, *A Tale of a Tub*, he took this opportunity to satirize his old collaborator. These sections were cut when the play was submitted to the censors, "exceptions being taken against it by Inigo Jones, surveyor of the kings workes, as a personal injury unto him."[6] The revised play was licensed for Queen Henrietta Maria's Men on May 7, 1633 and performed in London during that year. It was acted at Court on January 14, 1633/ 1634, when Sir Henry Herbert, Master of Revels, recorded it was "not likte."[7]

The text we possess is the play as it was revised subsequent to the censor's cuttings. In this version the character In-and-In Medlay replaces the excised character Vitruvius Hoop. W. W. Greg has suggested that Jonson met the censor's objections by simply changing Hoop's name to Medlay.[8] An affected rustic speaking a clownish dialect, for the greater part of the play In-and-In Medlay is hardly distinguishable from the other clowns—Diogenes, Scriben, To-Pan, Rasi' Clench, Hannibal Puppy. Symonds has called the part a "savagely satirical caricature,"[9] but most readers do not find it so. It seems rather mild to them. When the play was presented in the city it must have been reasonably popular or it would not have been taken to Court, but one can see why it was "not likte" at Court. It attacks one of the Court favorites with insufficient charm to challenge accepted opinion. Indeed it seems rather astonishing under the circumstances that the play was tried at Court at all.

More important than the circumstances of its original production is the question of the date of the original play. One should like to be able to separate the early Jonson from the late. Distinguished scholars have held various views of the matter and the question is still open, but all the critic-scholars are fairly well agreed on the evidence that must be evaluated. Greg and Bentley not less than Herford and Simpson find that the play contains "traces of an earlier style" than Jonson's habitual manner

5. See, for example, Herford and Simpson, I, 275–301.

6. Sir Henry Herbert's office book is quoted in Herford and Simpson, III, 3.

7. See E. R. Brown, Letter, *TLS*, May 10, 1928, p. 358, who denies that the play was ever staged at Blackfriars as suggested by Herford and Simpson.

8. W. W. Greg, "Some Notes on Ben Jonson's Works," *RES*, II (1926), 129–145, especially 133.

9. Symonds, p. 188.

of 1633.[10] In some scenes—indeed in most—the style is colloquial, racy, easy, the work of a very practiced hand. In others there are passages of much less fluency, with the woodenness characteristic of novice work. The following two speeches by a single character will illustrate the differences. The first is satisfactory dramatic speech. Tub says:

> A testie Clowne: but a tender Clowne, as wooll:
> And melting as the Weather in a Thaw:
> Hee'll weepe you, like all *Aprill*: But he'ull roare you
> Like middle *March* afore: He will be as mellow,
> And tipsie too, as *October*: And as grave,
> And bound up like a frost (with the new yeare)
> In *Ianuary*; as rigid, as he is rusticke. (I. i. 77–83)

Compare this with Tub's speech in another place:

> *Turfe*, I am privie to thy deepe unrest:
> The ground of which, springs from an idle plot,
> Cast by a Suitor, to your daughter *Awdrey*—
> And thus much, *Turfe*, let me advertise you;
> Your daughter *Awdrey*, met I on the way,
> With Justice *Bramble* in her company:
> Who meanes to marry her at Pancridge Church.
>
> (III. iii. 3–9)

Where the first passage is easily colloquial, the second is self-consciously stage talk. The first has movement, the second is rather flat. In the first the verse-line does not interfere with the flow of the sentence; in the second the lines are frequently end-stopped. The two styles exist side by side throughout the play, the stiff in much less quantity than the fluent. All the critics have agreed that these two styles must be accounted for.[11]

There are "traces of an earlier style" in more than the versification.[12] A real countrywoman is the center of this action, and in the 1590's country-girl heroines had a vogue that they did not long enjoy. Margaret of Fressingfield in Greene's *Friar Bacon and Friar Bungay* (1589) may be the most famous of them. Awdrey of *A Tale* and Margaret do not have the same appeal, but they are sisters. Their stories are essentially romances, and their major theme is love. Margaret, it is true, appears at the

10. G. E. Bentley, *The Jacobean and Caroline Stage* (Oxford: Clarendon Press, 1941–1956), IV, 632–636; Herford and Simpson, I, 275–301; Greg, 134.

11. For further discussion see Ben Jonson, *A Tale of a Tub*, Florence M. Snell, ed. (London: Longmans, Green and Co., 1915), pp. xiv–xxviii; Herford and Simpson, IX, 271–273.

12. Bentley, IV, 634.

beginning of the fashion, and Awdrey at its end. The charm of Elizabethan romance was running thin by the time of *A Tale*, and the rather ludicrous Awdrey is the kind of character that one would expect the critical Jonson to create. Shakespeare, reacting against the romance, created his own Audrey in *As You Like It* (1600). During the first three acts Medlay is hardly distinguishable from the other rustics. He and all the bumpkins are like those to be found in *The Case is Altered* (1597?) and plays by other hands in the '90's.

Altogether the dramatis personae of this play are farcical country folk and not representations of ideas. After 1600, emblematic city types engaged Jonson's attention, and he satirized urban rather than rural fools. His last, fragmentary, play, *The Sad Shepherd* (printed posthumously from a manuscript in 1640), is pastoral, as are some of his masques, but pastoral drama is not rural drama. Hannibal Puppy, John Clay, Clench, and the others smell of horse dung, as Jonson would say, not of remote Sicily or legendary Sherwood Forest; and Awdrey is a milkmaid, no shepherdess. The characters as well as some of the style point to early composition.

Baskervill long ago suggested that the persons of this play are descendants of the conventional Vice and fool and clown.[13] As such, they are not sharply different from those found in other Elizabethan romances. He thought the play belonged in the tradition of the morality play, and it seems to me that he was right. Jonson returned to the morality play in his maturity; *The Devil is an Ass* (1616) is a deliberate utilization of it, and so are others of his plays, as we shall see; but his use of the tradition in his maturity and his use of it in his apprentice days differ. In *A Tale of a Tub* the connections with the older drama are unexploited, even unstated; in the later work they are self-conscious. He may or may not have been fully aware of the affinities of this early play. The difference between his early and his late indebtedness is the difference between writing in a tradition and adapting that tradition to a calculated purpose. *The Devil is an Ass* is sophisticated where *A Tale of a Tub* is historically innocent. They represent two different attitudes toward the indigenous drama. Neither Baskervill nor any other critic touches on this important distinction.

A Tale of a Tub is, then, a thoroughly Elizabethan drama. It seems unnecessary to find in it a "dexterous handling of the Terentian intrigue."[14]

13. Charles Read Baskervill, *English Elements in Jonson's Early Comedy* (Bulletin of the University of Texas, Humanistic Series, No. 12, Studies in English, No. 1, 1911), p. 89.

14. Freda L. Townsend, *Apologie for Bartholmew Fayre* (New York: Modern Language Association of America, 1947), p. 35.

ELIZABETHAN STREET SCENE
From the *Roxburghe Ballads*.

How thoroughly un-Roman it is can be seen by comparing it to a contemporary Terentian comedy, George Chapman's *All Fools* (1599). *All Fools* is an adaptation of two plays, the *Heautontimoroumenos* and the *Adelphi,* and its intrigue is markedly successful.[15] Rinaldo succeeds in reconciling Gostanzo to his son's marriage while he at the same time marries off Gostanzo's daughter to an unwelcome suitor. The action divides itself neatly into two parts; in the first, Rinaldo deposits the four young people for whom he schemes in Marc Antonio's house; in the second, he puts them all in Gostanzo's house. The play ends with Gostanzo reluctantly agreeing to general amnesty. There is one underplot. Jealous Cornelio finally gives up his suspicions of his wife's fidelity. In *All Fools* the plot lines are sharply separated. One episode is completed before another is introduced; the jealous-husband theme acts as counterpoint, and the action is lucid. In Jonson's play, unlike Chapman's, four or five intrigues are carried on simultaneously. They are inter-related, rather like the un-Roman intrigues of *A Midsummer Night's Dream* (1594).

There are other differences. Though *All Fools* was adapted from a Roman to a London audience, it almost entirely lacks the kind of references with which Jonson "stuffs out" his play. Dariotto and Claudio are Elizabethan courtiers and an Elizabethan page parodies euphuism, but there are none of the native detail and domestic types that enliven *A Tale of a Tub.* Chapman's play is orderly, but rather thin; Jonson's is disorderly, but promises wealth. Chapman's is localized Latin comedy; Jonson's is two steps from folk drama on its way to native art. Gazetta in *All Fools* is an English adaptation of the courtesan of Terence; Chapman's fathers and sons are all English versions of Latin originals. Jonson's Canon Hugh is a descendant of Dikkon; Lady Tub is a neighbor of Gammer Gurton, and Awdrey has a dozen sisters in Sussex. Chapman is smooth and clever and amusing; Jonson has an Elizabethan gusto only slightly disciplined by Latin masters. If Tudor comedy owes a debt to Roman drama, by the time Jonson wrote, the drama had been thoroughly Englished. Jonson uses Terence and Plautus to sharpen English comedy.

A Tale of a Tub is what one would have expected Jonson's destroyed juvenilia to have been: English, lively, vulgar, with only a casual relevance to the Roman classics. Its faults and its virtues are the faults and virtues of the contemporaneous theater. In time he refined his virtues and developed faults of his own kind. When he rewrote *A Tale* for presentation in 1633, he retained the dramaturgical form of the apprentice work. Only

15. See *The Comedies of George Chapman,* Thomas Marc Parrott, ed. (London: G. Routledge and Sons, 1914), Introduction, pp. 701–712.

the style was corrected, and that incompletely. He added a few scenes, like Act IV, scene ii, which he calls a "scene interpolated," the attacks on Inigo Jones, and the Prologue. In this Prologue he apologizes for its weaknesses and pretends they are self-conscious archaisms in a new play. Its peculiarities of style and subject can more easily be accounted for by seeing it as an apprentice comedy thoroughly revised.

Even in this very early play Jonson exhibits certain qualities that he retains throughout his career. There is much in it which would delight the lover of medieval fabliaux and the comedy of John Skelton and John Heywood. Here we are in the world of Eleanor Rumming and Syr Johan the Priest. The scene in which Hannibal Puppy discovers a devil in the barn (IV.vi), for example, is funny in the way the Reeve's Tale is funny; and the scene in which Lady Tub and Dido Whispe attempt to kiss the unwilling Puppy (III.iv) recalls Heywood. Puppy's sputterings, confusions, and simple stupidity look backward to the clowns of *Respublica* (1555); and they look forward to John Daw of *The Silent Woman* and Cokes of *Bartholomew Fair*. Here we are in the vulgar, English world of *The Alchemist* and the revised *Every Man in his Humour*. *A Tale of a Tub* has the *sine qua non* of much popular literature: a sense of life. Whatever its shortcomings, in every scene one detects a delight in the world similar to the ebullience of the low comedy of Chaucer, Shakespeare, and to a lesser degree Dickens. This poor play cannot take its place with the work of the masters, but it partakes in small of the zest that Chaucer and Shakespeare have in quantity. It is no play for the Aristotelian or the formalist, but for one who looks in literature for life, and that most fully, it has its merits. It is Jonson's first quarrying in a rich vein: the tradition of the vulgar farce.

The chief limitations of the play can be traced to the same vulgar source. In gathering his bumpkins together, Jonson fails to give their actions unity. Any general significance is sacrificed to immediate laughter. The component elements are not subordinated to a theme. Canon Hugh recalls the joking parsons of the popular traditions and presages such types as Parson Palate in *The Magnetic Lady* (1632). He deliberately neglects his divine duties for money and the fun of a practical joke. He suffers no unhappy consequences. On the other hand, when Tobie Turfe tries to be a good High Constable, he is gulled. Squire Tub wants to marry beneath him; Lady Tub, his mother, is determined to restrain him. Awdrey Turfe, who is sought by all the young men, seems not to care whom she marries, so long as she marries somebody. John Clay, her principal suitor, turns out to be incapable, perhaps, of the virile responsibilities of a bridegroom. These plot elements lie side by side, unrelated at any level other than action. That they might have been unified we know from Jonson's greater plays, like *Bartholomew Fair*. Perhaps he attempts too much. It would have been safer for him to use only half his subject matter and make a neater play; but caution was not a quality Jonson cultivated. He was gambler and this time he lost. The Prologue suggests that he knew it. He wrote:

> . . . acts of *Clownes* and *Constables*, to day
> Stuffe out the *Scenes* of our ridiculous play. (Pro. 2–3)

Even if Jonson was punning learnedly in these lines (*Satura*, one etymology of *satire*, means stuffed with many things), to "stuff out" is not to "build up." *A Tale of a Tub* wants art.

The popular tradition contributes to Jonson's particular *joie de vivre*, and the popular tradition contributes to his dramatis personae also. His standards of character development were the current ones. Consistency was not a primary concern for any of the Elizabethans, and it was not Jonson's either. "It is the rarest thing outside Shakespeare to find the gradual modification of character by character or experience," F. P. Wilson has said,[16] and this is true of *A Tale of a Tub*. Squire Tub is a simple country fool who is tied to his mother's apronstrings, or so we are told. But he is bright enough and independent enough to engineer the most complicated plots. He sends his "governor," Hilts, to masquerade as a robbed captain; he discovers Preamble's plot and exposes it. Even until the last minute he schemes to get Awdrey delivered to him disguised. For a bumpkin he is pretty quick-witted. Lady Tub is even more inconsistent. In some scenes she appears to be a kind of doting mother; in others she is a lusty widow, determined to find her Valentine. The qualities of lustiness and maternal devotion, though hardly inconsistent, demand reconciliation which is not provided. The other characters in the play are not clearly drawn. Justice Preamble is so hazy that his youth is a surprise when we discover it. The rustics are never individuals as, say, Bottom and his fellows are; and Awdrey herself is scarcely more than a pawn. We do not understand why everybody wants to marry her; perhaps this is part of the joke. In his mature plays, Jonson can create a character in half a dozen lines and allow him ludicrously consistent behavior thereafter. Here he focuses his attention on the farcical incident, for the quick turn of laughter.

In part Jonson does not yet have the skill to build characterization and episode simultaneously. In his youth he had greater ambitions than his

16. Frank Percy Wilson, *Elizabethan and Jacobean* (Oxford: Clarendon Press, 1945), pp. 101–102.

craft could sustain. He puts necessary exposition into the mouth of Canon Hugh in the first act because he is unable to dramatize it. His discussions of poetry in the same act recall similar digressions in *Every Man in his Humour* (1598). They are irrelevant to his present purposes. The third act contains passing burlesques of popular romances, legal jargon, and prophetic miracles which need to be digested into the action. And yet in spite of the disparate nature of the plotting, one can see Jonson feeling his way toward his later manner. In the great plays each figure has singleness of purpose from which he does not deviate. The gulls in *Volpone* each want to be the single heir; the gulls in *The Alchemist* each want power. In *A Tale of a Tub* each character sets out after a single goal, but he gets sidetracked and ends pursuing another course of action. Tub, for example, wants to rescue Awdrey from Clay but spends most of his time forestalling Bramble, and, incidentally, refurbishing Clay's chances. Bramble and his man Metaphor conclude their marriage plot by the middle of the third act and in the second half of the play are forced into new action. In *A Tale of a Tub* the lines of plot are not clear. They interfere with one another. Others of Jonson's dramaturgical devices make an early appearance in this play. In the mature comedies, Jonson relies very heavily on surprise. He leads his audience to expect one kind of denouement only to provide them with another. The plot of *The Silent Woman* hangs on this trick. Though Jonson strives for the same kind of joke in *A Tale*, he does not bring it off. His timing is wrong. But the plot, the characters, the dramatic devices all anticipate in their rough Elizabethan way the polished perfection of the later plays.

2. *The Case is Altered*

The Case is Altered was originally produced ten or twelve years before it was printed in 1609. Thomas Nashe in *Lenten Stuffe* (1599) makes an explicit reference to its popularity.[17] One can see why it was popular. In addition to its charm, it was modish. As Baskervill observed long ago, it "exhibits nearly every current that is apparent in the drama around 1597."[18] Here Jonson was going his competitors in the popular theater one better: he demonstrates that he can improve on everything the hacks were about. Some time after 1598 *The Case is Altered* received some alterations and additions, including personal attacks on Anthony Munday,

17. *The Works of Thomas Nashe*, Ronald B. McKerrow, ed. (London: Sedgwick and Jackson, 1910; rev. F. P. Wilson, ed., Oxford: Basil Blackwell, 1958), III, 220.

18. Baskervill, p. 105; see also Alexander H. Sackton, *Rhetoric as a Dramatic Language in Ben Jonson* (New York: Columbia University Press, 1948), p. 55.

an Elizabethan journalist whose translations were to receive Jonson's contempt on other occasions.[19] The Children of the Blackfriars presented it "sundry times" in 1609 or thereabouts. Though since produced only once or twice, it has never been without its admirers.[20]

Until recently much of the critical and scholarly attention it has received has dealt with its classical sources.[21] For the first and only time in his career, Jonson drew on Plautus for his situations. From the *Captives* he borrowed the story of the stolen son. According to Jonson, Count Ferneze lost his four-year-old son Camillo in a battle nineteen years before the play opens. Now he regains him. At first he does not recognize his own, not only because of the length of time they have been separated but because Camillo and his friend Chamont masquerade as each other. The second major plot of *The Case* is concerned with a miser who disguises himself as a beggar. It comes from another Plautine comedy, the *Aulularia*. In Jonson's adaptation a miser, Jaques de Prie, has a beautiful daughter who is sought in marriage by several worthy men. Ultimately she is found to be the stolen sister of Chamont. Though the two Plautine plays are of widely different kinds, the one being a romance and the other a satire, Jonson combines them and gives his play a unified English tone. The raw material, derived as it is from ancient Rome, under his hand is absorbed into folk romance. Long-lost heirs, mixed identities, faithless friends, jolly cobblers, avaricious Jews, irresistible and innocent heroines, all have their prototypes in Elizabethan story. The most remarkable element of *The Case is Altered* is thus not its source but its unity. Of the same kind as its predecessor, *A Tale of a Tub*, it shows a considerable dramaturgical advance. Though both draw on indigenous types and homely situations, the earlier play is miscellaneous and without theme. It is juvenilia. The new play is more nearly mature; structurally and thematically, it foreshadows Jonson's later work.

This early comedy is similar to *The Magnetic Lady*, Jonson's last comedy. In both plays a lady attracts to herself an assortment of interesting people: Rachel de Prie is a young Lady Loadstone. Lady Loadstone's niece, Placentia, like Rachel, is marriageable, and the young men seek

19. See *S.W.* IV. i. 56; *Alch*, IV. vii. 40; *N.I.* I. vi. 125; "An Execration vpon Vulcan," 29.

20. "A Study of Ben Jonson," *The Complete Works of Algernon Charles Swinburne*, Edmund Gosse and Thomas James Wise, eds. (London: W. Heinemann Ltd., 1926), XII, 8. S. Musgrove, *Shakespeare and Jonson*, The Macmillan Brown Lectures 1957 (Auckland University College, Bulletin No. 51, English Series No. 9), p. 52.

21. See, for example, Herford and Simpson, I, 305–327. *The Case is Altered*, William E. Selin, ed. (Yale Studies in English, LVI [1917]), Introduction, pp. xlvii–lxvi.

them out. All the action of both plays comes home to the feminine center. Something of this organization was hinted at in *A Tale of a Tub*, in which all the men sought Awdrey. The great plays are centripetal, like *The Magnetic Lady* and *The Case is Altered*. In *Volpone* the old fox is the center on whom all the various lines of action converge. In *The Alchemist* Subtle draws all the gulls in town like a magnet. In *Bartholomew Fair* all the kinds and types of London assemble, attracted to Smithfield. In this early play Jonson is already reaching toward the unique organization which allows him to present a panoramic view of society and its depravities. He is, in short, already attempting to deal in ideas. *The Case is Altered* is an Elizabethan play with all the Elizabethan clichés freshly touched up, but it is also the play of a craftsman interested in the manipulation of plot for intellectual purposes. One can find in it certain thematic considerations foreign to such contemporaneous comedies as *The Shoemakers' Holiday* (1599/1600). It is worth noting that in passing Jonson hits at Dekker's other celebrated romance, *Old Fortunatus* (I.ix.24).

In the great plays Jonson makes his intellectual points by duplication. Corvino, Corbaccio, and Voltore all represent different aspects of a single vice; Dapper, Drugger, and Sir Epicure Mammon seek material advantage over their fellows. In *The Case is Altered* Jonson has not yet developed this repetition with variation to its later perfection, so he establishes not only a series of close parallels, but a series of complements as well. Every important dramatic situation has at least one mirror image to explain it. This is not true in the later plays. For example, the theme of male friendship is dramatized in the Paulo-Angelo story. Paulo, in going to the wars, leaves his Rachel in the care of his friend; scarcely has he left than Angelo courts Rachel on his own. Angelo's faithlessness is contrasted to Gaspar's fidelity. When Gaspar and Chamont are captured by the Milanese, Gaspar masquerades as Chamont so Chamont may escape to the French forces. Though Paulo has been "a traitor to [Paulo's] trust" (V.viii.66), Gaspar asserts *ad nauseam* his willingness to suffer for his friend. The faithlessness of Angelo is contrasted further with the low comedy characters, Onion and Christophero. Onion too is in love with Rachel; but instead of helping Onion to win her, the steward Christophero says, "This wench wil I solicite for my selfe" (II.ii.49). Christophero in turn goes to his master Ferneze for help in suing for Rachel's hand, but Ferneze says to himself, "I must sue, and seeke her for my selfe" (II.vi.45). The Gaspar-Chamont fidelity is thus contrasted with a series of situations dramatizing infidelity. Parallelism of situation reappears often as a dramatic device in later plays; we see complementarity of situations too, but less often.

There are other contrasts in the play. Aurelia and Phoenixella, the daughters of Ferneze, represent opposing points of view which are close to the intellectual heart of the play. Phoenixella is a virtuous woman who, we are repeatedly told, is "a most rare creature" (I.ix.91). She conveniently gives us her credo:

> It is the excesse of either [griefes and pleasures] that I striue
> So much to shun in all my proou'd endeauours.
> Although perhaps vnto a generall eye,
> I may appeare most wedded to my griefes,
> Yet doth my mind forsake no tast of pleasure,
> I meane that happy pleasure of the soule,
> Deuine and sacred contemplation
> Of that eternall, and most glorious blisse,
> Proposed as the crowne vnto our soules. (II. iv. 30–38)

Phoenixella speaks like a Christian saint who has been reading the classics. She seems to be a Christian humanist. Her name has Christian overtones: the phoenix is one of the emblematic representations of Jesus Christ. Perhaps with all her generosity and self-restraint she is a bit smug and pontifical, but Jonson at least does not satirize her as he does other virtuous ladies. He simply denies her charm. She is not very interesting except as the representation of an important point of view.

Aurelia is constantly contrasted to her sister Phoenixella. She has more charm though she is considerably less virtuous. A light woman who cannot resist a male, in her virginal youth she promises lustiness in age. Unlike her sister, she swears by that "sweet Queene of loue" (IV.xi.74); .when Chamont departs, she prays Venus to

> Hasten *Chamounts* returne, let him affect me,
> Though father, friends, and all the world reiect me.
>
> (IV. xi. 80–81)

Aurelia has only one subject. It is love, romantic love, love as described in Petrarchan poems and narrated in chivalric tales of high deeds. She cannot imagine a fraternal affection of the kind her sister feels when she sees her long-lost brother, Gaspar.[22]

In this play the contrast of characters suggests a contrast in ideas. The admirable characters (Phoenixella, Paulo, Maximilian) share certain qualities, and the unadmirable ones share other qualities. Jonson contrasts not only fidelity with infidelity; he contrasts the life of pleasure, appetite, and passion with the life of judgment, responsibility, and restraint.

22. See John J. Enck, *Jonson and the Comic Truth* (Madison: University of Wisconsin Press, 1957), pp. 21–33, for a different reading of this play.

Maximilian, a kind of choric figure, urges Ferneze to restrain his passions, and Paulo describes his father as "wayward":

> ... affections in him, are like powder,
> Apt to enflame with euery little sparke,
> and blow vp reason ... (I. vi. 88–90)

Phoenixella says "my fathers rage/Is too extreame, too sterne and violent!" (IV.xi.52–53). And the old man, in a remarkable speech of self-revelation, indicates that love, or "fancie," forces him to act against his best judgment (II.vi.35–48). The contrast is insistence. Rachel passes verdict on all her various, unfaithful suitors and points up the major theme of the play:

> ... ô heauen, can it be,
> That men should liue with such vnfeeling soules,
> Without or touch of conscience or religion,
> Or that their warping appetites should spoile
> Those honor'd formes, that the true seale of friendship
> Had set vpon their faces? (V. viii. 14–19)

Appetite is the cause of infidelity. The rage which Ferneze feels toward Gaspar when he thinks his son Paulo cannot now be ransomed is only one aspect of the self-indulgence which leads away from reason.

But virtue is not entirely the result of reason. Good men have intuitions which are not available to the self-indulgent. Phoenixella, Paulo, and Maximilian all have perceptions to which they give various degrees of credence. Paulo has an irrational premonition that his friend Angelo cannot be trusted. "My thoughts cannot propose a reason,/Why I should fear" (I.vi.9–10), he says. Phoenixella on seeing her brother has a "strange affection" (IV.xi.59) for him; she, unlike Paulo, trusts it. And Maximilian, on discovering that Gaspar is actually the long-lost son of Ferneze, says: "I will hereafter giue more obseruance to my visions, I drempt of this" (V.xii.55–56). Merit shows itself immediately and undisguised to good men. "Natiue honour sparkles in thine eyes," Chamont says to Gaspar (IV.iv.22) before he knows of Gaspar's noble birth. The rewards of a reasonable life are sensitivity to merit. Even from this first play Jonson shows himself to be a conservative. Nobility, he thinks, is a quality more frequently found in the well-born than in the base, a quality which shows itself to those with eyes to see. It cannot be obtained by purchase. To attempt to rise above one's station is to be ludicrous, and Onion and Juniper are ludicrous when they put on borrowed clothing and courtesy. The story of Gaspar and Chamont complements the story of Paulo and Angelo and dramatizes the theme of friendship; the story of the rediscovered son complements that of the aspiring clowns and dramatizes the theme of inherent nobility. The contrasted episodes lead us to intellectual conclusions.

The Case is Altered anticipates some prominent characteristics of the later comedies, but it is not a finished play. Stylistically it contains many elements that Jonson discarded by the time he matured. Jonas A. Barish has recently pointed out certain elements of "verbal dandyism" in the prose of the play that "within a year would have aroused only the most stinging contempt from Jonson."[23] Its elaborate rhetoric in both prose and verse, like its story, is characteristic of the 1590's. The decorated extravagances of such lines as these belong to Elizabethan drama:

> And happy was that foote, that first could presse
> The flowry champagne, bordering on *Verona*. (I. ix. 79–80)

and

> . . . these legs should rot with irons,
> This body pine in prison, till the flesh
> Dropt from my bones in flakes, like withered leaues,
> In heart of *Autumne*, from a stubborne Oke. (IV. i. 33–36)

The wordplay with the name Onion, the malapropisms with which Juniper indulges himself, and the burlesque of courtly language are Elizabethan. The artifice of some of the language contrasts with the colloquial fluency of the rest. Jaques's speech reflects his nature as closely as Sir Epicure Mammon's reflects his. Like Corvino, words rush from his mouth, in their impatience to be heard repeating themselves. "Tis safe, tis safe," he says. "Sir, Gods my life, sir, sir, call me sir?" (III.ii.12,14). When he discovers his gold stolen, he cries in an ecstasy of grief which reflects his sensual, unrestrained nature: "My gold, my gold, my life, my soule, my heauen . . ." (V.xi.1). Jaques's language is more than impatient. Syntactically it has a Hebraic parallelism. Like the versification of the Psalms, his impassioned pleas are made up of balanced half-lines which rise to a rhetorical climax. Jonson no place identifies Jaques as a member of Shylock's tribe, his style does. In these speeches, Jonson is in total control of his medium:

> (My gold is in his nostrels, he has smelt it,
> Breake breast, breake heart, fall on the earth my entrailes,
> With this same bursting admiration!
> He knowes my gold, he knowes of all my treasure,)
> How do you know sir? whereby do you guess? (III. ii. 21–25)

23. Jonas A. Barish, *Ben Jonson and the Language of Prose Comedy* (Cambridge: Harvard University Press, 1960), p. 96.

But for all the excellence of his language, Jaques is not, finally, a totally convincing character. A thief who kidnapped the daughter of his master

> Because it lou'd me so, that it would leaue
> The nurse her selfe, to come into mine armes,
> And had I left it, it would sure have dyed. (II. i. 38–40)

does not convincingly demand that the girl, now grown to maturity as his daughter, be tortured to reveal the hiding place of his stolen gold. Jonson strives to create a complicated character. He does not quite succeed. His effort augurs well, nevertheless.

Structurally, thematically, and stylistically *The Case is Altered* summarizes and anticipates. Some critics have wished that "in determining the direction of his artistic genius, in pruning its growth, [Jonson] had been a little less severe, less ruthless."[24] For all its Elizabethan elements, this play exhibits Jonson's habitual critical temper and his delight in ideas. *The Case is Altered* differs from its successors in its generous tone. This play ends with a most un-Jonsonian amnesty. Aurelia is married to the man of her choice, Rachel is awarded to Paulo, Jaques is allowed to retain his stolen goods, and all the lost children are returned to their proper families. Maximilian concludes the play in Elizabethan fashion: "Louers to your nuptials, Lordings to your dances" (V.xiii.66). If life were not so short and competition for immortality not so keen, this play would surely not have sunk into its present oblivion.

3. *Every Man in his Humour*

We know considerably more about the circumstances of the first production of *Every Man in his Humour* than of Jonson's other early plays. The 1616 Folio tells us that it was presented by the "then Lord Chamberlaine his Seruants" in the year 1598, and that Shakespeare was among the "principall Comoedians" who acted in it. Ancient tradition reports that Shakespeare persuaded his company to produce it, but one suspects that its possibilities must have been as obvious to the other professionals in the company as to Shakespeare. Kempe, Burbadge, Heminge, and Slye would surely not have overlooked the good acting parts it offered. The play was an immediate success, and it has held the stage intermittently ever since. Perhaps its most famous production was

---

24. Elisabeth Woodbridge, *Studies in Jonson's Comedy*, Yale Studies in English, V (1898), p. 79. See also Swinburne, XII, p. 9; Symonds, p. 16.

32   Ben Jonson's Plays: An Introduction

by Dickens and a group of amateurs in 1847 and 1848, with Dickens
taking the part of Bobadill.[25]
First acted in 1598, *Every Man in his Humour* was first printed in 1601
in quarto. This text was extensively and scrupulously revised before it
appeared in the 1616 Folio. In the revised text the scene was moved
from Italy to England and the language was made colloquial and racy,
"such as men doe vse" (Pro. 21).[26] Swinburne rather paradoxically calls
the finished English version (1616) "certainly his best as it certainly is
not his greatest" play.[27] Most admirers of Jonson could not follow Swinburne so far, but they uniformly admire it. It has its intrinsic interest
quite independent of its historical significance: its topicality, its debt to
the Roman classics, its importance as evidence of Jonson's theory of the
humours, and its relevance to the theatrical quarrels of the day—all
subjects talked of by the critic-scholars. This is the most high-spirited,
the least harsh in judgment, and the most generous in sympathy of the
major plays before *Bartholomew Fair*. In these respects as in others it is
like *The Case is Altered*. Jonson for once seems more concerned with
sporting with human follies than with exposing crimes. In it he invites
us to observe a collection of dolts. The young man in the play collects
fools as the nobility collected dwarfs and jesters: for the sport of seeing
them displayed. A less cruel play than *Volpone*, it is not so rich in its
implications. One could wish for the metaphorical dimension that poetry
could give it, but its rich prose twists and turns with the mind of each
dramatic character.[28] Its greatest merit is its Elizabethan insouciance.

Jonson's "corrections" of the 1598 version show how his dramatic
interests developed during the first decade of the seventeenth century.
The modifications appear in nearly every speech. In the final scene, for
example, Brainworm's explanation of the machinations is drastically cut.
Jonson speeds his action. In the same scene Justice Clement changes his
judgment of Bobadill and Matthew. Instead of sentencing them to jail
and to the stocks, he orders Bobadill to wear motley and Matthew sack-

25. Herford and Simpson provide a stage history of each play, IX, 163–258. The
extended account of *EMI* appears pp. 168–185.
26. The date of the revision is controversial. E. K. Chambers (*The Elizabethan
Stage* [Oxford: Clarendon Press, 1923], III, 359–360) believes it took place about
1605, the date of a Court revival; but Herford and Simpson think much later, about
1612; see I, 332–333; see also *Ben Jonson's Every Man in his Humour*, Percy Simpson,
ed. (Oxford: Clarendon Press, 1919), Introduction, pp. xxxi–xxxii.
27. Swinburne, XII, p. 10.
28. Barish examines the prose, pp. 98–104, 130–141, and speaks, rather infelicitously
in a book otherwise notable for the excellence of its style, of the "associational movement" of much of the prose (p. 99).

cloth, the ashes of poems on his head. Like wayward children, they are sent away without supper. Stephen, another aspiring fool, is ordered to eat in the pantry with Cob and Tib, like a child. As in the rest of the play, Jonson speeds the pace, points up character and theme, and increases the gaiety. He heightens his play with a touch here and there, as a bit of white chalk heightens a pen and ink drawing.

The structural changes from one version to the next are more significant than the verbal. Though both plays have the conventional five acts, the act and scene divisions appear at different places in the two versions, indicating that between 1598 and 1616 Jonson changed his mind about dramatic organization. In the earlier form, because the acts are of about equal length, they have a classic symmetry. The first, third, and fifth acts, and the second and fourth acts, are about equally long. In the 1598 version Act I is introductory, presenting all the characters and establishing basic relationships. In Act II the Knowell story is complicated; Brainworm is shown as a manager of intrigue and Bobadill is identified as a perhaps inadvertent troublemaker. Act III is mostly given over to Kitely's fear of being cuckolded. Act IV sets the stage for the conclusion by sending all the chief characters to Justice Clement's. And in Act V all the strands of the plot are fully knit together; it ends with Clement's meting out of rewards and punishments. This organization meets the handbook requirements: exposition; complication of first plot, complication of second plot; closer and closer involvement of plots with one another; and, in the last act, a settling of accounts. Donatus, a fourth-century grammarian, rhetorician, and commentator on Terence, on whom Jonson seems sometimes to draw, might well have approved, for it neatly separates *protasis* (introduction) from *epitasis* (complication) from *catastrophe* (conclusion).[29] This is all very neat, but in the 1616 version it is upset. Since the 1616 Folio was designed primarily to be read, the divisions would seem to have a particular importance. Why did Jonson change the divisions? By revising, what was Jonson attempting to call to our attention?

Between 1598 and the time of the revision Jonson has moved from architectual to thematic concerns. He sacrifices neatness of structure to fullness of meaning. In the 1616 version, Act I ends after the Knowell and the Bobadill situations have been introduced; we see shortly that these two plot lines are closely connected, but at the moment they appear independent. In Act II Kitely and Downright are introduced; and the

29. Marvin T. Herrick, *Comic Theory in the Sixteenth Century* (Illinois Studies in Language and Literature, XXXIV, Nos. 1-2, 1950). See Chapt. IV, and esp. pp. 106-110.

Knowells, both father and son, are reconsidered. In this act all the characters in the play except Cob and Justice Clement are brought forward one at a time. Thus in Act II we see more clearly the two developing complications: the Kitely plot and the Knowell plot. Act III contains the climaxes of the several plots. Edward Knowell learns from Brainworm that his father is coming after him and is at the Justice's (III.ii); Kitely leaves his young wife (III.iii) only to learn from Cob that the young gallants are headed for his house (III.vi); Cob receives a warrant for Bobadill's arrest (III.vii). Act IV (1616) contains the consequences of these enumerated decisions and discoveries. Act V resolves all difficulties. In the 1598 version a decision and its consequences are not clearly separated; they appear in the same rhetorical division, the act. In the revised 1616 version each act fulfills a rational, even a philosophic, function. Actions and consequences are not now muddled together. They are separated·so that Jonson can emphasize cause and effect.

This concern for cause and effect can be seen clearly by comparing in more detail the construction of the fourth acts of the two versions. Both contain much of the same material, but Act IV (1616) also contains half the action formerly found in Act III. In 1598 the consequences of decisions reached in Act III were left in Act III. In 1616 decisions and results are set in different acts. The two versions of Act IV end differently too. At the end of Act IV (1616) the whole cast gathers at the house of Justice Clement; the results of their gathering appear in Act V. In 1598 the cast appears and is judged in the same act. The preparation is not separated from the conclusion. Jonson sought to show the reasons for actions. He carefully examined each incident when revising in order to determine its place in a causal chain of events. He then placed each event in an act devoted to its category. The formal pattern of his play reflects his rational clarity. He seemed confident that human choice can be explained by analysis, and the vapors did not cloud his eyesight.

Jonson's reconsideration of briefer passages also shows his insistence on reason. Since reason required that the play be a single piece, a unity, with one tone and one central theme, Edward Knowell's speech in the earlier play about the function of poetry (V.v) was excised in the 1616 version. It interests everybody concerned with Elizabethan critical theory, but it had no firm place in a play that does not deal with poetry, except incidentally. It is not characteristically Jonson's and sounds like Chapman.[30] Jonson must have felt as most readers do that both its tone and its content were inappropriate to this play. Delight in incident and character

30. M. C. Bradbrook, *The Growth and Structure of Elizabethan Comedy* (Berkeley and Los Angeles: University of California Press, 1956), p. 144.

RAPIER AND DAGGER

"One valiant man with a sword in his hand will do better than ten Italians, or Italia-nated, with the rapiers." George Silver, *Paradoxes of defence* (1599), sig. F 1 r.

and idea for their own sake, an Elizabethan quality that can be found in *A Tale of a Tub* and *The Case is Altered*, is now disciplined. Not yet so tightly constructed as the later plays, every part now aspires to fulfill its logical part in a determined pattern.

The dissimilarities of the two versions of *Every Man in his Humour* show Jonson's developing dramatic skill and, more important, his moral opinions. The similarities are as important as the dissimilarities, for they develop a single theme: the 1616 version sharpens and clarifies what was implicit in the 1598 version. It deserves close definition. (My references hereafter are to the 1616 Folio version.) In the Prologue, added to the 1616 version, Jonson says that his purpose is to

> ... shew an Image of the times,
> And sport with humane follies, not with crimes.
> Except, we make 'hem such by louing still
> Our popular errors, when we know th' are ill.
>
> (Prol. 23–26)

The first obvious human folly in the play is affectation, but it is affectation of a particular kind. One laughs at the persons in this play because of the discrepancy between aspiration and ability, not between aspiration and accomplishment. These characters are ludicrous because they fail to take stock of their possibilities. They are self-deceived. Stephen, "a countrey gull," affects city manners and ways; Matthew, "a towngull," affects courtly ways; and Bobadill, a "Paulesman," affects the way of the soldier. Each strives to impress his fellows with qualities he can never attain. Their foolishness is the result of their aspiration, not their lack of accomplishment. They posture before the mirror of themselves, pretending they are the men they would like to be. They are not hypocrites; they are sentimentalists. Reason is the antidote to their affliction.

This play is an attack on sentimentality. In it each of the gulls is set against his genuine prototype. Stephen is a country boy trying to learn to quarrel; Downright, his complement, is a "plain Squire" who need not pretend; he does not have to study books of quarreling, hawking, and hunting. He was born to the manner, and he knows it. The contrast is carried out in some detail. Stephen for all his blustering cannot be brought to a quarrel when opportunity presents itself (I.iii;III.ii). Downright, on the contrary, must be restrained (by Kitely, ironically) from avenging his offended honor. The dramatic relationship reaches its peak when Stephen puts on Downright's coat; it is as though Stephen were not only assuming the manner but the very birthright of his betters. Matthew is also accompanied by his complement. Everything that Matthew aspires to be, Edward Knowell already is. Matthew pretends to an ability in poetry to which Young Edward is already committed (I.i.17–18). Young Edward delivers the enconium to poetry in the concluding scene of the play which Justice Clement endorses. We do not see much evidence of Young Knowell's craft and must take his abilities as a scholar on trust, but the circumstantial evidence is quite enough. (Incidentally, Young Knowell's poetic abilities have no function in the play except as a foil for Matthew; this may be a flaw in plotting, for it suggests that poetry has no use in the business of living.)

Matthew's actions parallel Edward's. Matthew courts Bridget in a parody of the courtly manner; Wellbred courts Bridget for Young Knowell without verse or a display of Petrarchan pain. As Matthew overplays the suffering lover, Edward underplays it; and by underplaying he increases the ridiculousness of Matthew's performance. Matthew's relationship to Bobadill is a parody of Young Knowell's relationship to Wellbred. Both go to call on their friends and both allow themselves to be directed by their friends. Young Edward is never obsequious as Matthew is. Though Wellbred is clearly a stronger character than Young Edward Knowell— it is Wellbred who initiates the game of gulling, who schemes and plots —he does not dominate his friend as Bobadill dominates Matthew. The relationship between Knowell and Wellbred is reasonable, that between Bobadill and Matthew is silly. This theme of friendship appears in *The Case is Altered*, it will be remembered, but the dignity of male friendship is an ubiquitous Renaissance theme.[31]

The contrast between Bobadill and Young Wellbred is not so exact and so detailed as that between Downright and Stephen nor that between Matthew and Edward Knowell, but it exists. The essential quality of Wellbred's character is *sprezzatura*, that particular Renaissance delight in life so foreign to the modern despairing seriousness. Wellbred is a young man who knows that he can overcome any reasonable difficulty— even Old Knowell—with grace and gaiety. All his ebullience is natural, so natural in fact that he scarcely knows he possesses it. His is the grace beyond the reach of art, the instinctive gentle behavior, the epicurean delight in the human situation tempered by a sound instinct for the relative worth of things. Wellbred is Lovewit before Lovewit became old and cynical. Bobadill aspires to the graceful manner, this *noblesse oblige*. But he is made of commoner clay. When his military bluff is called, he allows himself to be beaten like a churl, by the broadside of Downright's sword. For confidence, he substitutes the brag, for a rapier he substitutes

31. See Laurens J. Mills, *Two Souls in Bodies Twain, Friendship in Tudor Literature and Stuart Drama* (Bloomington: Principia Press, 1937).

a bedpost; for respect, he substitutes flattery. Through it all he looks for a master. His extravagance has no basis in fact, but soars off into a world of his own imagining. He describes how, with the encouragement of "her Maiestie, and the Lords" (IV.vii.65–66), he would undertake to overcome all enemies, though they were "fortie thousand strong" (IV.vii.81). His exuberance is like Tamburlaine's though not so extraordinary; unlike Tamburlaine's, it is "placed." Wellbred's reasonable gaiety shows it up for nonsense.

In *Every Man in his Humour*, then, each of the principal characters is set beside its opposite number; the essential quality of each is sharpened by contrast. In the subplot, which deals with Kitely's jealousy of his wife, we find similar contrasting situations. Kitely and Dame Kitely are measured against Cob and his wife Tib. Kitely, knowing that he is a December husband with an April wife, fears that he be cuckolded:

> Well (to be plaine) if I but thought, the time
> Had answer'd their affections: all the world
> Should not perswade me, but I were a cuckold.
>
> (II. iii. 22–24)

His unjustified fears motivate all his action. Cob trusts his wife's virtue, though Bobadill lives in his house and receives pocket money from her. Cob is a credulous fool; Kitely a doubter. Both are bested by their wives, and they deserve to be.

These people of the underplot are characters from a Heywood farce. Tib—her very name is borrowed—is the wanton wife of many an interlude. Cob is the conventional, simple cuckold, and Kitely's suspicions are recounted in locker-room anecdotes to this day. The low comedy in this play comes straight from the folk drama, and Jonson continues to exploit the popular narrative in giving us Cob and Tib. The persons from the main plot are also folk types. Wellbred and Young Knowell are cousins to such Prince Charmings as Edward and Lacy in *Friar Bacon and Friar Bungay*. They live now in nursery stories. Jonson is almost as kind to them as Greene and Dekker and Peele; but these young men are not fully drawn. He knows that we will recognize their kind. Bobadill and the gulls also have their popular connections with the folk-morality plays. Bobadill is a kind of *Iniquity*, each of his gulls is a variety of *Lusty Iuuentus*. In *The Devil is an Ass* Jonson explicitly connects these "roaring boys" to the old drama. *Iniquity*, the Vice, speaks:

> I will teach thee [to] cheate, Child, to cog, lye, and swagger,
> And euer and anon, to be drawing forth thy dagger:
> To sweare by Gogs-nownes, like a lusty *Iuuentus*,

In a cloake to thy heele, and a hat like a pent-house,
Thy breeches of three fingers, and thy doublet all belly,
With a Wench that shall feede thee, with cock-stones and gelly.

(I. i. 48–53)

Under the realistic representation of current social extravagance lies the old didactic theater.[32]

Because Jonson is more interested in action than in individual psychology, *Every Man in his Humour* has only two sharply individual characters. They are Brainworm and Bobadill, and even they are re-animations of conventional figures. Brainworm's antecedents are clear enough. The clever companion-servant who manages affairs for his master's success is to be found in Roman comedy, but the type also appears in domestic Tudor comedy right down into Jonson's day. Differing from play to play, the type bears certain consistent characteristics: cleverness, wit, and delight in scheming. Jonson has exploited it in his early plays, as in Basket-Hilts in *A Tale of a Tub*, and he will use it again. Brainworm is not as thoroughly integrated into this play as he might be. He labors mightily to bring forth a mouse of intrigue; the action with a little rearrangement could proceed without him. Some of his counterparts in other plays—Mosca, Face—could not be excised without destruction to the whole composition; others like Truewit in *The Silent Woman* turn more or less irrelevant, if daring, handsprings around the central complication. Dramaturgically Brainworm, for all his wit, is nearly superfluous.

But, as I say, Brainworm is gay and ingenious and given to congratulating himself for a cleverness which consists primarily in fooling everybody with his disguises. Young Edward, Wellbred, and Old Knowell all marvel that they have been deceived. Throughout his career Jonson relies more and more on masquerades to bear the burden of his theme. Disguise is an ubiquitous dramatic device. Shakespeare exploits it, Plautus and Molière use it, and it is a favorite trick of the Restoration. It is one of Shaw's principal stratagems. One can almost set up an axiom: wherever there is classic comedy there is confusion of identities. But where Shakespeare and Shaw are content with a single disguise, Jonson contrives to give his favored characters three or four or five. In *Every Man in his Humour* there are two kinds of disguisings. On the one hand, some characters like Bobadill and Matthew pretend to be *more* than they are. In contrast Brainworm pretends to be *less* than he is: a broken-down soldier, a hireling servant, a police sergeant. Unlike Bobadill and Matthew, he recognizes the ludicrousness of his pretenses. He has a purpose and when it is achieved, he returns to himself. Bobadill has no reasonable end

32. Cf. Baskervill, pp. 107–143.

in view. His counterfeiting, unlike Brainworm's, is conducted for its own sake, because he must live in a flamboyant world. He invents as he goes along, improvising on the theme of himself. Rather like Falstaff after the flight from Gadshill, reality and Bobadill's construction of it are confused. Brainworm, in contrast, understands himself. Brainworm from the beginning has what Bobadill strives to avoid: self-knowledge. The technique of disguise points up a central fact of Jonson's philosophy. We know what we are, our duties and our limitations, only by taking stock of ourselves. The man without self-knowledge, the man who aspires beyond his abilities, is a fool. Knowing himself, a man can trust in the benevolent Lord who calls him to his station. Ambition beyond one's place, which is folly, can be avoided by the exercise of reason.

The irrationality of the characters in this play shows itself in their consistent excess. Each suffers from a surplusage of his chief virtue. Kitely needs to care for his wife's honor, but not to the point of maddening jealousy. Cob needs to allow his wife freedom, but not to license; Knowell may properly protect his son from wantonness, but not from youth. By following his legitimate concern beyond probability, each turns his virtue into vice. *Every Man in his Humour* differs from Jonson's other mature plays in that these dramatis personae are not diseased or depraved. Some are immoderate, like Kitely and Old Knowell; some mistake manner for substance, like Bobadill and Stephen and Matthew. But none is fundamentally unsound like Morose or unnatural like Volpone or malicious like Sejanus. None is past redemption. Should they take stock of themselves, they would discover that each is involved with the relation of reason to faith. They are all excessively trusting; and this is the quality which brings their downfall. Stephen and Matthew trust Bobadill beyond common sense; Bobadill, supremely self-confident, invites their unreasonable fidelity. Kitely lacks a necessary faith in his wife's honesty, and Cob is gullible. Old Knowell does not trust his son. We can only conclude that even faith must be subject to critical examination. Jonson does not peep into human depravity in this play, as he does later. Right and wrong are clearly distinguishable, and circumstances, either social or economical or political, do not complicate his characters' problems. A fool, Jonson says, is one who does not turn his full critical intelligence on his daily life. *Every Man in his Humour* is in the center of the tradition of Christian humanism, that habit of mind that sees reason operating within established limits as the means to a full comprehension of God's law.

CHAPTER III

The Comical Satires

THE THREE COMEDIES that follow Jonson's first great success are inferior because they smell of grease paint both in subject matter and technique. *Every Man Out of his Humour* (1600), *Cynthia's Revels or The Fountain of Self-Love* (1600), and *Poetaster* (1601) seem to have made their mark in their own time, but they are permanently lost to us. Bound closely to Jonson's London, they do not please us even after we have boned up on theatrical history. Their subject matter, only as vital as ancient newspapers, is concerned with Jonson's quarrels and the War of the Theaters, which do not matter to us very much.[1] Indeed one sometimes suspects that the "War" was nearly as much a device to attract customers as it was an intellectual disagreement.

These professional plays have the merits of their limitations. Many of the scenes and characters are finished to a turn and a number of the situations are hilariously farcical. The episode in *Poetaster* in which Horace attempts to escape the boring and tenacious Crispinus (III.i), though not entirely fresh, is funny; it looks forward to the equally funny episode in *Volpone* (III.iv) in which the old fox tries to escape the garrulous Lady Politic Would-Be. In *Poetaster* (III.iv) and in *Cynthia's Revels* (II.iii) a character is given opportunity to mimic a variety of different persons and actions. Good performers could bring down the house with these parts. All three of the plays contain a number of first-class theatrical figures. In *Every Man Out of his Humour* Carlo Buffone and Fastidious Brisk, and in *Poetaster* Tucca, have clearly been created by a man knowledgeable in the theater. Each has a flamboyant quality which invites an actor to display his skill. The flamboyance may or may not have a necessary relevance to the play, but it makes use of the ham in the performer. Tucca, for example, stammers, and this impediment can just barely be justified within the theme of the comedy. It plays, though.

In these comical satires Jonson writes plays on narrowly topical

1. See Chapter I, footnote 10.

41

subjects for his colleagues to act, and he knew that the plays were not altogether viable. In *Every Man Out* a chorus points up the plot significance of various scenes. The action does not carry itself. In *Cynthia's Revels* the plotting is simplified so that we can at least see what is going on, but the meaning is ridiculously hidden in metaphor. Contemporary audiences thought the play silly, too. In *Poetaster*, arguments attempt to convince us when scenes cannot persuade us. In this play Jonson's dramatic shot goes wild, so he tries to hit us with the butt of his intellect-revolver. He reasons where he cannot charm.

Ironically these plays for actors have become hunting grounds for scholars. Scholars have attempted first to explicate the historical allusions in the plays, and a glance at the footnotes in any of the standard editions will show how successful they have been.[2] They have also given attention to the idea of the *humours* to which Jonson makes repeated reference throughout his career. According to ancient physiological theory advanced by Hippocrates and Galen, the health and temperament of a man is influenced by the proportion of four principal fluids in his body: blood, phlegm, choler (yellow bile) and melancholy (black bile). The predominance of one or another determines his disposition as sanguine, phlegmatic, choleric, or melancholy. An extreme imbalance causes disease. Sir Thomas Elyot in his *Castle of Health* (1534, 2nd ed. 1539) provides a relatively complete statement of the theory, but conveniently for readers of Jonson, *Every Man Out of his Humour* defines what he wants us to understand of it:

> . . . in euery humane body
> The choller, melancholy, flegme, and bloud,
> By reason that they flow continually
> In some one part, and are not continent,
> Receiue the name of Humours. Now thus farre
> It may, by *Metaphore*, apply it selfe
> Vnto the generall disposition:
> As when some one peculiar quality
> Doth so possesse a man, that it doth draw
> All his affects, his spirits, and his powers,
> In their confluctions, all to runne one way
> This may be truly said to be a Humour. (Ind. 98–109)

Jonson apparently attributed the success of *Every Man in his Humour* to the doctrine of the humours it purported to contain, and in *Every Man Out* he set out to dramatize it more fully. He was barking up the wrong

2. See for example, H. D. Gray, "The Chamberlain's Men and *The Poetaster*," *MLR*, XLII (1947), 172–179.

tree. *Every Man In* was and is successful because it entertains, not because it refers to a specific theory of physiology. It held its audience because of its gaiety, not because of its intellectual framework. More than three centuries later, Jonson's intellectual assertiveness continues to urge us to talk of its "humours," and the whole matter alienates the reader. In his celebrated essay on comedy (1877) George Meredith scarcely mentions the greatest writer of English comic drama; he makes one allusion to Bobadill, in passing. And Wylie Sypher, who has recently (1956) published his own essay on comedy in a volume with Meredith's and Bergson's, speaks of Jonson only three times, twice dismissing him as a creator of humour types. Jonson's semi-scientific physiological jargon distracts us from the plays. We cannot read Jonson's plays for their prologues.[3]

If Jonson had not labeled his comedies "humourous," nobody would have observed them different from other satires and much other comedy. All satires deal in types of characters and seek to make statements about the world by generalizing from individuals. What Jonson says of the humours may as easily apply to most if not all satiric works. The celebrated portraits in Dryden's *Absalom and Achitophel* are as much humour portraits by Jonson's definition as the sketches of the actors with which Jonson prefaces *Every Man Out*. "One peculiar quality" certainly possesses each of the characters in *The Rape of the Lock*. Swift no less than Jonson is the enemy of imbalance: Gulliver's revulsion against mankind is a violent kind of humour. If Puntarvolo in *Every Man Out* yearns humourously for a "romantic" relationship with his wife, Mirabel in *The Way of the World* yearns just as humourously for a rational relationship with Millamant. And Dickens's celebrated "flat" characters might easily have come from the streets of Jonson's London. Ultimately humour as it appears in the dramas seems to have very little distinctive meaning. Jonson did not define his term until after the success of *Every Man In*; only then did he apparently think it worth defining. And it is characteristic that he should continually return to this theory, even so late as *The Magnetic Lady* (1632). Tenacity is a part of his pride.

Jonson did not have anything technical in mind when he used the term. The idea of humours was to Jonson's day what the idea of complexes is to ours. If someone were to write a comedy today called "Everybody

3. A convenient discussion of the doctrine of the humours in contemporaneous works is to be found in Herford and Simpson, IX, 391–396. See also *Ben Jonson's Every Man in his Humour*, Percy Simpson, ed. (Oxford: Clarendon Press, 1919), Introduction, pp. xxxvi–lxiv. The Meredith, Bergson and Sypher essays appear in a volume entitled *Comedy* (Garden City: Doubleday Anchor Books, 1956).

Has His Complex" and then a second called "How to Cure Your.Complex," we would not assume him to be a student of Freud or Adler. "Complexes" now, "humours" then, were in the air. Clever professional writers turn the fashions of their day to their own purposes. Jonson was concerned with actions and their moral implications, and he was never as interested in the individuality of persons as he was in ideas, ranging ideas about the nature of virtue and vice and the quality of his own times. He was after more than the identification of a few eccentrics and their peculiar personal shortcomings; he was no collector of butterflies. Further, his characters cannot be classified under one or another of his specified headings, not by the best of Procrustean methods. They are beset by ruling passions, but the passions are more complicated than this system explains. As is generally true of Elizabethan literature, the dramatist's understanding of the world was greater than his one-dimensional theories about it.

To insist on the technical meaning of "humour" in connection with the plays is not only to be guilty of rather serious misreadings; it is to make oneself the butt of the satire. All his dramatic life Jonson was the enemy of the technical and the specialized. His concern was with the generality of mankind, and he attacked all the special interest groups that would divide us into factions, either intellectual or moral or economic. His plays consistently ridicule arcane learning used for private purposes, and professional jargon was an anathema to him. The cant of alchemy, of theology, of poetasters, earned his scorn. One needs a liberal education to understand Jonson, not professional training in alchemy or archaic psychology. Jonson expected his readers to be at home in the traditions of Christian humanism. That was quite enough.

Each of his satirical comedies grows out of a general philosophical view however narrow the topic under hand. The subject matter may be dated, but for the most part the ideas are not. In *Every Man Out* Jonson is concerned with the affectation of courtiers; beyond this, he is concerned with the relationship of money to corruption. Money undisciplined by responsibility, he says, rots us. In *Cynthia's Revels*, though again specifically concerned with local affectations, Jonson discusses decorum. The evils of society rise because men presumptuously reach beyond their gifts and station. In *Poetaster* he discusses contemporary poetic excess. He is also concerned with the responsibilities of the artist to his society. In these plays Jonson attempts to wed philosophical meaning to theatrical technique. With their advent the popular theater was to become an intellectual forum. They were supposed to elevate the substance of contemporary comedy. In his first plays, *A Tale of a Tub*, *The Case is*

Altered, and *Every Man in his Humour*, Jonson sought to purify the materials of the indigenous theater. They are not different in kind from the professional plays among which they appeared. The first two of the comical satires stand as far apart from the indigenous drama as any of Jonson's plays. In them Jonson tries to turn London into Augustan Rome. He pontificated from a classical podium, but his borrowed robes do not fit. He is more ridiculous than persuasive. By the time of *Poetaster* he has begun to return to his native haunts; and his subsequent great plays, though influenced by classical models and pseudo-classical experimentation, are back in the native tradition.

For all his stated contempt for the public, in all three of the satirical comedies Jonson tried to bring his most serious conclusions about moral and political and aesthetic questions to a general audience. He sought to entertain so that he could teach. In this respect at least these plays are one with the didactic Tudor theater. Drama, he thought, did not need to be frivolous. Though not solemn, it could concern itself with serious matters; comedy itself might contain some wisdom. His high aspirations we must respect; his accomplishment perhaps not. His tone is altogether too preachy and cock-sure, and the comedy too slight. I would like in the following pages to examine the structure of these three comical satires in order to show how Jonson unites philosophical ideas and dramatic structure. Few people will want to read these dreary plays, but the intellectual attitudes which they represent and the purposes toward which they are directed may be important, both for an understanding of Jonson and, perhaps, of ourselves.

1. *Every Man Out of his Humour*

Readers of *Every Man Out of his Humour* often agree with Herford that this play is "inartistic in composition." At first blush it seems gloriously confused in its "heterogeneous sequence, its motley kaleidoscopic disarray."[4] It contains profane jesters, vainglorious knights, doting citizens, ladies of unsettled virtue, envious malcontents, upstart men-about-town, affected courtiers, threadbare sharks, each following what appears to be his independent way, and it has not one but sometimes two and three choruses to comment on the various actions represented. Yet when it was first given at the newly rebuilt Globe in 1599, it was sufficiently popular to earn presentation at Court, and it was acted now and again in the seventeenth century. Three times published in quarto in

4. Herford and Simpson, I, 379.

1600 and carefully seen through the press by Jonson himself, the printed text "contained more than hath been publickely Spoken or Acted."[5] Presumably Jonson added the "characters" at the beginning of the play, the Grex or chorus, and the elaborate Induction. In spite of their diversities, on close inspection the play can be seen to be more unified than it at first appears.

The central problems facing the critic of *Every Man Out* are those facing him in any play: Why are these particular incidents and not others represented? What is the principle around which these seemingly disparate elements are arranged? Various kinds of answers can be found. Professor Campbell gives a historical explanation. This play, he thinks, is Jonson's attempt to circumvent the ecclesiastical authorities, who in 1599 forbade the publication of satires. Jonson determined to incorporate "as many of the distinguishing characteristics of the suppressed literary art [satire] as he could."[6] This tells us of Jonson's possible motive for writing a "comicall satyre," but it does not explain *this* satire. "Satire" refers to the treatment of a subject; it is not itself a subject. We have still to find what at bottom Jonson was attacking, and we can get at the hard, cold vices he wanted to expose by examining the organization of the play.

This play contains, unhappily, a number of extraneous elements, but they are decorative pilasters accenting structural members. Cordatus, the chief spokesman in the chorus, is the "Author's friend; a man only acquainted with the scope and drift of his Plot" (Characters 111–112). He constantly tells us what the playwright has striven for in the various scenes, and he often admits their limitations. Mitis, his companion, criticizes the point and structure of the play. He notices when a scene has been too long (II.iii), he asks for identification of new persons (II.vi), he complains when the subject matter is not comic (III.viii), and he questions seeming inconsistencies of behavior (IV.viii). Cordatus attempts to answer his criticisms. Every time a new situation is introduced, Cordatus and Mitis remark it; and they summarize for us (II.vi). Jonson attempts to give dramatic interest to these choric comments by introducing a degree of conflict within them, and they contain a certain amount of jolly byplay. But though Jonson through Cordatus announces that the apparent difficulties have been deliberately built into the play, we do not believe him. A well-made play needs no gloss.

5. See W. W. Greg, "The First Edition of Ben Jonson's *Every Man Out of His Humour*," *The Library*, I n.s. (1920–1921), 153–160.

6. Oscar James Campbell, *Comicall Satyre and Shakespeare's "Troilus and Cressida"* (San Marino: Henry E. Huntington Library and Art Gallery Publications, 1938), p. 54.

In addition to Cordatus and Mitis, Jonson introduces a second chorus. Macilente is more involved in the various actions than Cordatus and Mitis; he speaks directly to the other players and participates in their plot. Through much of the play, however, he stands to one side, his relationship to them not made clear. In most scenes he seems to have no plot reason for his presence. Macilente must be recognized as a second, complicating chorus. One may not object to a double chorus as a kind. Every playgoer is accustomed to scenes within scenes. But here are scenes within scenes within scenes, and this is too much. The dramatic organization—in which the observer is observed—in later plays becomes standard, but in *Every Man Out* the various groups get in one another's way. Perhaps a judicious director could station the various groups about his stage and separate the actions, but it would be difficult. In later plays Jonson does not shift his action and our interest from one to another group within a single scene; later he introduces the actions separately and treats them individually. *Every Man Out* is Jonson's first, unsuccessful essay in the glorious juggling of disparate elements which produced *Bartholomew Fair*. He knew he was not successful. The introductory character sketches, though brilliant, are evidence he recognized that readers could not keep his people and their activities straight. These character sketches are tantamount to an acknowledgment that the play lacks focus and the actions, emphasis.

But admitting all this, the play though a failure is still not "inartistic in composition," as Herford says. Jonson is attempting a new, panoramic kind of comedy. He says it is "somewhat like *Vetus Comoedia*" (Ind. 232); it is like him to give his innovation an antique name (see Chapter I, p. 6). In the composite motto quoted from Horace on the title page, Jonson asserts that this is a comical satire, and Cordatus in the Induction underscores its strangeness. Certainly *Every Man Out of his Humour* has little in common with *Every Man in his Humour*. The earlier play is one of intrigue. This is a satiric pageant. It is, however, more than a parade of fools. Critics and scholars have generally regarded it as an excuse for Jonson's indulgence of his talent "for crude and also cruel caricature . . . which probably wrung the withers of now forgotten jades,"[7] but it and the comical satires to follow are remarkable for other reasons.

Every Man Out is an intellectual's play, and its very considerable reward is intellectual. Jonson raises economic questions. Concerned as he is with the community, he strives for a portrait of the age. This comedy is, you might say, an Elizabethan *Street Scene*. Professor Campbell and others have pointed out that Renaissance writers conceived of social troubles as

7. John Addington Symonds, *Ben Jonson* (London, 1888), p. 34.

the result of individual immorality.[8] They did not generally blame the system for what we would think of as social difficulties; the social sciences had not yet been invented. When farmers suffered from deflation, somebody someplace was manipulating the market for private advantage, Jonson's contemporaries thought, perhaps without total error. In this play, like his friend Chapman, he was examining the flaw within the order, not within men.[9] Anatomizing the "times deformity," he does not stop with manners, though the "correction of manners" is the function of comedy according to Cordatus, who quotes from Cicero (III.v.208–209). Puntarvolo, Sordido, and Deliro would all have had to be excluded if Jonson were concerned only with manners, narrowly conceived. In *Every Man Out* Jonson looks beyond individual conduct to search out wider causes of difficulty.

If we search the play for its thesis, we can soon see that its seeming "disarray" is only superficial. The characters in the play can be divided into three groups, each pursuing a similar purpose and all unconcerned with similar values. The groups define the limits of the society. In the first act Carlo Buffone directs Sogliardo in how to be a courtier. He says, "But Sogliardo, if you affect to be a gentlemen indeede, you must obserue all the rare qualities, humours, and complements of a gentleman" (I.ii.20–23). Sogliardo is to become a member of court, not by virtue of his birth or accomplishment, but by decorous dress and deportment. Fungoso no less than Sogliardo is to be another of "these mushrompe gentlemen" (I.ii.162)—the word *Fungoso* means mushroom. Fungoso spends all his money, even pawning his lawbooks at last, to buy clothing of the latest cut, and he "followes the fashion a farre off, like a spie" (Characters 72–73). Instead of being a courtier, Sogliardo would act like a courtier, and Fungoso is content to look like one. Fastidious Brisk is the prototype of the affected and false courtier, for he both looks—is dressed like—and acts—has the manners of—what he is not. The concern for clothing and manner is symbolic. With them fashion replaces principle.

Puntarvolo and Deliro also strive for the manner and neglect its content. In them we see a degeneration of chivalric courtesy. When Puntarvolo courts his wife as though she were his mistress shut away in a tower fortress (II.ii), he uses chivalric language without chivalric substance. This burlesques the romances then popular. *Amadís of Gaul*, the most famous of them, was translated by Anthony Munday in 1590; Jonson glanced at Munday satirically in *The Case is Altered*, one will remember,

8. Campbell, pp. 15, 16n.

9. See K. M. Burton, "The Political Tragedies of Chapman and Ben Jonson," *Essays in Criticism*, II (1952), 397–412.

ELIZABETHAN COSTUME

From the *Roxburghe Ballads.*

"They have great and monstrous ruffs made either of cambric, holland, lawn or else of some other the finest cloth that can be got for money, whereof some be a quarter of a yard deep, yea, some more, very few less. Wot you what? The devil, as in the fulness of his malice, first invented these great ruffs; the one is a certain device made of wires, created for the purpose, whipped over either with gold thread, silver or silk, and this he calleth a supportass or underpropper. . . . The Gally-hosen are made very large and wide, reaching down to their knees only, with three or four guards a-piece laid down along either hose. And the Venetian-hosen, they reach beneath the knee to the gartering place of the leg. It is a small matter to bestow twenty nobles, ten pound, twenty pound, yea, a hundred pound, of one pair of breeches." Philip Stubbes, *The anatomie of abuses* (1583), sigs. D 6 v.—E 3 r.

and he repeatedly disparaged the romances in his later plays. In *The New Inn* he calls them "publique Nothings; Abortiues of the fabulous, darke cloyster" (I.vi.126–127). When we are reminded, close on the heels of the talk of romantic chivalry, that Puntarvolo "deales upon returnes" (Characters, 21;II.iii.243ff.), we see clearly that for him substance and manner are totally divorced. If he were genuinely chivalrous, he would be concerned with honor; when he speculates, he is in a world of quick profits where honor is irrelevant. Puntarvolo is a sentimentalist. He measures all activities by how he is affected by them. He courts his wife not out of respect for her but for his own pleasure, and when he insures his dog he makes the dog disproportionately valuable. A member of the landed gentry, he is an aristocrat gone into decay.

Deliro apes Puntarvolo. He borrows the forms of courtliness but not their spirit. He becomes uxorious. St. Paul prescribes that the husband shall rule his household, and Macilente and Jonson agree (II.iv); Deliro takes the courtly traditions too literally. He indulges his emotions when he ought to discipline them. When he turns himself and his wealth into his wife's keeping (II.iv), we see that he, like Puntarvolo, is a sentimentalist. Shift, "A Thred-bare Sharke" (Characters, 84) is the third of this "romantic" trio. He too misunderstands the nature of honor. He claims a military esteem which he has not earned. No less than Puntarvolo and Deliro, he retains, or attempts to retain, the forms without the substance. These six characters and Carlo Buffone as their chief usher—the Brainworm of the piece—have two qualities in common. The first and more obvious is their false courtliness. According to Castiglione, one will recall, genuine courtiers strive to "bende all oure force and thoughtes of soule to this most holye light, that showeth us the waye which leadeth to heaven; and after it, puttynge of the affections we were clad withall at our cominge downe, let us clime up the stayers . . . ." One can obtain excellence by striving, but striving of a particular kind: "betwene thys excellent grace, and that fonde foolyshnesse there is yet a meane, and they that are not by nature so perfectly furnished, with studye and diligence maye polishe and correct a great part of the defaultes of nature."[10] It is this "study and diligence" which these courtiers falsify, for they seek out the latest fashion rather than the "waye which leadeth to heaven." Macilente and Jonson say:

> Why, all their *Graces* are not to doe grace
> To vertue, or desert: but to ride both

10. Baldassare Castiglione, *The Book of the Courtier*, done into English by Sir Thomas Hoby, 1561. I quote from the Tudor Translations, XXIII (London, 1900), 361; 45–46.

With their guilt spurres quite breathlesse, from
themselues. (IV.iv.84–86)

Jonson is satirizing manners; but, more basically, he is attacking the
assumption that manner may be separated from content and ends from
means.

The second quality which these characters share is their universal
concern for finance. In every scene costs, returns, profits, losses are
discussed. Money is a prominent and recurring motif. Everybody in the
play is troubled, deformed as it were, by his relation to money. Puntarvolo
—etymologically the name seems to mean "little gambler"—insures his
cat and dog against accident. Deliro thinks that he can be a gentleman
because he now has money—from trade, significantly. Sogliardo tries to
buy a place in court, and Fungoso attempts to buy position with money
from the sale of his lawbooks. Shift will sell his rapier as he will sell
himself. He fails to see that in such buying and selling, honor is lost. The
envious Macilente also yearns for that wealth which brings position. He
has his "eyes continually fixt vpon another mans prosperitie, that is, his
chiefe happinesse, and to grieue at that" (I.iii.165–167). The women in
the play are as false as the men, and we gradually suspect their "honesty."
Money corrupts them all.

All the dramatis personae are involved with both money and courtliness. Only Sordido is not concerned with position. He does not aspire
to courtly elegance or to the appearance of chivalry. He is a miser. He
hoards his grain though the poor starve for lack of bread; and he sells to
enrich himself though he impoverish others (I.iii). He forgets that men
raise grain, not that farmers may be rich, but that all may eat. The most
original and the most ludicrous creation of the play, Sordido underscores
the basic thesis of the whole play. The "times deformity" is not simply
the separation of means and ends, though it is certainly that. The play is
an attack on capitalism. In this society money has usurped the place of all
other values, including human values. Money is the open sesame of this
world. Money is the tempter and the agent. Money is the cause of decay.
And a society based on money, we see, invites its own destruction.[11]

It is not difficult to see why money corrupts. It has no intrinsic value,
as land has; and no obligations are inherent in its possession. Land must
be tended, and tending teaches duty. Land cannot be stored selfishly, and
it encourages humility. Jonson would agree with Lord Burghley, who
advised his son: "The gentlemen that sell an acre of land sell an ounce of

11. Cf. L. C. Knights, *Drama and Society in the Age of Jonson* (London: Chatto and
Windus, 1937, 1951), esp. Chapts. VI and VII, pp. 179–227. My general debt to
Professor Knights is great, as all readers of his book will see.

credit [i.e., reputation]; for gentility is nothing else but ancient riches; for that if the foundations sink, the building must needs follow."[12] Another Elizabethan, Gresham, observed that bad money drives out good; Jonson would suggest that no money is good, because it makes men bad. It absolves them of social responsibility. It teaches men to forget their obligations. The *nouveau riche* see the manner of the gently born, not their duties, and as such Sogliardo and the others do not know what to do with their wealth. Their new wealth imposes no duty, and they follow fashion. For them, fashion replaces taste and etiquette, valor. The courtesy books of the Renaissance universally insist on the importance of birth. This insistence is not merely a matter of snobbery. Castiglione and the others thought that one learns judgment and ultimately wisdom from habitual responsibility, the kind of responsibility that land brings. As an intellectual Jonson is as conservative as Richard Hooker and Edmund Burke, and long before Weber and Tawney he noted the rise of the moneyed classes and diagnosed a growing ailment.

Jonson shows us the connection between speculation and human suffering, in the person of Sordido. He shows us the connection between money and degenerate taste in Sogliardo, Fungoso, and Fastidious Brisk; between money and sentimentality in Deliro and Puntarvolo; between money and the loss of honor in Shift. Jonson writes other plays about courtly affectation. In this one he analyzes its economic causes. He criticizes not simply the moral lives of men in his time. He criticizes the nature of society itself. In anatomizing the aspirations of his day, he looks beyond individual morality. *Every Man Out of his Humour* is a less considerable drama than *Every Man in his Humour*, but intellectually it is quite remarkable.

2. *Cynthia's Revels or The Fountain of Self-Love*

Recent critics have not found *Cynthia's Revels* entertaining, but they have been able to discover in it a unity that earlier commentators did not discern. Swinburne called it "formless ... incoherent ... defective in structure," and Baskervill said it is "composed of a large number of diverse elements."[13] Though it may very well be the dullest of all of

12. Quoted at length in *Advice to His Son*, by Henry Percy, Ninth Earl of Northumberland, G. B. Harrison, ed. (London: E. Benn, Ltd., 1930), "Introduction," p. 39.

13. "A Study of Ben Jonson," *The Complete Works of Algernon Charles Swinburne*, Edmund Gosse and Thomas James Wise, eds. (London: W. Heinemann Ltd., 1926), XII, 15. Charles Read Baskervill, *English Elements in Jonson's Early Comedy* (Bulletin of the University of Texas, Humanistic Series, No. 12, Studies in English, No. 1, 1911), p. 217.

Jonson's plays, it is certainly not "formless." As Jonas Barish says, it is "less a vaudeville than its predecessors."[14] On close examination the characters and actions turn out to be united thematically. For all that, this is probably Jonson's most boring play.

In *Cynthia's Revels or The Fountain of Self-Love* Jonson took some of the materials and dramatic techniques he had used in *Every Man Out of his Humour* and turned them to what he hoped was effective purpose. The differences in the two plays can be accounted for in part by the different audiences for which they were prepared. *Cynthia's Revels* was acted in 1600 by the Children of Queen Elizabeth's Chapel, and it was dedicated in the 1616 Folio "To the Speciall Fovntaine of Manners: The Court." *Cynthia's Revels*, played as it was by children, depended for success on grace, lyricism, and pageantry; and its theme was partially dictated by its selected audience. Jonson here tries his hand at Lyly's kind of entertainment, but he is less pleasing because he is so heavily didactic. *Every Man Out*, on the other hand, acted a year earlier in 1599 at the Globe by the Lord Chamberlain His Servants, was addressed to the Inns of Court. It was made for a more popular audience and is of wider scope; it is concerned with questions of general concern and depended on robustness of character and ingenuity of situation. *Every Man Out* was a success, but Dekker reported that *Cynthia's Revels* was "misse-likt."[15] Even the Court apparently preferred Jonson's robustness to his courtliness. The limitations of its subject might be overlooked now, but the ugliness of its tone cannot. He makes Olympian judgments, even of the Queen herself, without Olympian wisdom, and as a result he seems more presumptuous than the courtiers he attacks. The play is not only dull. It is repugnant.[16]

The cast of characters in *Cynthia's Revels* is scarcely different, in plan, from that of the earlier play. Asper in *Every Man Out* becomes Crites here; Fastidious Brisk becomes Hedon; Fungoso becomes Asotus; Saviolina becomes Philautia. Amorphus of *Cynthia's Revels* reminds us of Puntarvolo, and Anaides of Carlo Buffone. Jonson, trying a second chess game, repeats his gambit. The action of *Cynthia's Revels* is simpler than that of *Every Man Out*, because these dramatis personae are engaged in less activity than their counterparts. No character here changes his

14. Jonas A. Barish, *Ben Jonson and the Language of Prose Comedy* (Cambridge: Harvard University Press, 1960), p. 113. See also John J. Enck, *Jonson and the Comic Truth* (Madison: University of Wisconsin Press, 1957), pp. 66–69.

15. Quoted in "Stage History of the Plays," Herford and Simpson, IX, 189.

16. See Ralph W. Berringer, "Jonson's *Cynthia's Revels* and the War of the Theater," *PQ*, XXII (1943), 1–22, for a discussion of theatrical history.

costume several times like Fungoso in an attempt to approximate courtly elegance, and Anaides is less vigorous and less noisy than Carlo Buffone. In *Every Man Out* four or five groups simultaneously observe and comment on one another; in the later play the various characters are engaged in a single action, or what is offered as action. They do not pass independent judgment on one another, and thus they avoid some of the confusion of the earlier play.

Compared to *Every Man Out*, *Cynthia's Revels* is easy to follow. Cordatus and Mitis, standing to one side of the stage in *Every Man Out*, are extraneous to the plot. They are choric commentators on the action. Mercury and Cupid in *Cynthia's Revels* are also choric figures, but they participate in the action as pages to the courtiers. Throughout this play Jonson tries to dramatize his choric comment. Cupid acts in the concluding masque under a symbolic name as the courtiers do, and Crites is also involved in the stage action. The opinions of both are often Jonson's. Dramaturgically Crites is to this play what Macilente is to *Every Man Out*, but Crites is on stage scarcely half as long as Macilente, and his nature is less complicated. Crites is a prototype of the perfect man; by the end of the play he is seen as an agent of the gods. Macilente is the envious man occasionally expressing Jonson's views. As a stage figure he is more confusing than Crites. Some scholars have attempted to identify him with Jonson, but this is uneasy. The identification is "a legend strangely accepted by his admirers, though it was in truth invented by his enemies."[17] Jonson was independent—he signs the dedicatory epistle of this play "thy servant, but not slave"—but to identify him with Crites is to oversimplify his nature and to falsify his play. Crites is arrogant. Jonson, though proud, was not. He could never have become the literary arbiter of his time nor enjoyed the friendship of the political and literary "great" if he had been so "perfect" in his own opinion. Crites and all of the figures in *Cynthia's Revels* are types and symbols, not individuals. The play is about types of behavior and kinds of actions, not about persons at all. It is not a lampoon, because, like its predecessor, it was designed to stimulate thought. *Cynthia's Revels* is more craftsmanlike than the earlier satirical comedy because it is more unified, but it is a good deal less interesting. Very tidy, it is short on that *Poeticall Rapture* which alone gives life to art.[18] Even *Every Man Out* has a passion lacking in *Cynthia's Revels*.

17. John Palmer, *Ben Jonson* (New York: Viking Press, 1934), p. 51. See also William D. Briggs, "*Cynthia's Revels* and Seneca," *Flügel Memorial Volume* (Stanford: Stanford University Press, 1916), p. 68.
18. See *Discoveries* 2409 ff. (Herford and Simpson, VIII, 637).

The play is neat thematically as well as architecturally. After an Induction which is filled with horseplay scarcely above the level of Dekker's *Satiromastix* and a dozen other bawdy comedies—the Induction may even be distasteful when we remember that it was performed by boys—the action begins with two short scenes in which Cupid, Mercury, and Eccho discuss Narcissus, Niobe, and Actaeon. These scenes are not extraneous to the major action, as they might appear; and they are not solely decorative. Professor Talbert suggests persuasively that Narcissus, Niobe, and Actaeon are emblematic and represent presumption born of self-love. They are, as it were, individual variations on a main theme.[19] Eccho in telling Mercury how Narcissus came to his disastrous end defines the motif for us:

> Tis now the knowne disease
> That beautie hath, to beare too deepe a sense
> Of her owne selfe-conceiued excellence.
> O, hadst thou [Narcissus] knowne the worth of
> heau'ns rich gift,
> Thou wouldst haue turn'd it to a truer vse . . .
>
> (I.ii.42–46)

All the characters in *Cynthia's Revels* suffer because they do not turn their considerable merits to "truer use" than private indulgence. In good humanist fashion, Jonson maintains that the value of an action depends on its purpose. These men and women are guilty of self-love when they take their beauty as an end rather than as an instrument. "Beautie stands a woman in no stead vnlesse it procure her touching," Wellbred tells Bridget in *Every Man in his Humour* (IV.viii.110–111). "Our beauties are not ours" (I.ii.71), Eccho sings in one of the finest lyrics in English. In contrast Narcissus thinks of himself as "nature's pride"; Niobe boasts that she is superior to Latona, mother of Apollo and Artemis; Actaeon presumes to look on Diana in her bath; Eccho profanes her gifts by incessant babbling. Mercury reproves her:

> Stint thy babling tongue;
> Fond Eccho, thou prophan'st the grace is done thee:
> So idle worldlings (meerely made of voice)
> Censure the powers aboue them. Come, away,
> Ioue calls thee hence, and his will brookes no stay.
>
> (I.ii.92–96)

19. Ernest William Talbert, "The Classical Mythology and the Structure of *Cynthia's Revels*," *PQ*, XXII (1943), 193–210.

These semi-allegorical characters define the moral of the play. Professor Talbert states it: "Men should not be too curious about matters which do not concern them, particularly about the secrets of communities, princes, great men, and above all, gods."[20] Men should humbly observe decorum.

After this mythological prologue, the play turns to a consideration of the Court. In Act II representative courtiers are statically characterized by Mercury and Cupid. In *Every Man Out* similar characterizations were prefatory to the play; and in subsequent plays character sketches are worked into the drama so neatly that Dryden among others could praise Jonson for preparing us for each new figure in advance of his appearance.[21] But these portraits in *Cynthia's Revels* are more narrative than dramatic. The middle acts rather arbitrarily satirize the courtier who assumes the manner without achieving the substance, and they are clearly connected with the general theme of presumption as defined by Professor Talbert. *Every Man Out* also attacks courtly affectation, but in it we see how affectation is related to money. *Cynthia's Revels* is narrower. It preaches modesty and humility and makes little attempt to link these virtues to a world of wider experience.

In the long and dreadfully tedious fifth act, the affectations previously described are more closely examined. If the two masques are read allegorically, we can see that their action parallels the action of Act I. In the first masque we see that *Cynthia's Revels* "deals not with the four cardinal virtues—prudence, justice, temperance, and fortitude—fundamental to human character, but rather with those qualities necessary to 'complement' [them] (V.ix.9), that is, the amenities of the courteous life," Professor Gilbert has said.[22] When the courtly virtues are not "turn'd to a truer vse"—when they remain essentially self-love—they become vices. Unrestrained by reason, allowable self-love (self-respect) becomes vanity, and pleasant conversation becomes frivolity. Light wittiness, on the other hand, when directed by reason, becomes "well conceited Wittinesse" and Folly becomes "Plaineness itself" (V.vii.55). In the second masque (V.ix) we learn that undisciplined generosity becomes prodigality, good audacity unrestrained becomes impudence; variety of mind, voluptuousness; courtly grace, deformed affectation. One distinguishes between virtues and their complementary vices by

20. Talbert, p. 204.

21. "An Essay of Dramatic Poesy," *Essays of John Dryden*, W. P. Ker, ed. (Oxford: Clarendon Press, 1899, 1926), I, 87–88. Quoted in Herford and Simpson, XI, 518.

22. Allan H. Gilbert, "The Function of the Masques in *Cynthia's Revels*," *PQ*, XXII (1943), 228. This whole essay (pp. 211–230) is helpful.

exercise of the mind. Crites is a perfect man, for he "doth neyther couet, nor feare; hee hath too much reason to do eyther: and that commends all things to him" (II.iii.143–145). The perfect man is the reasonable man. Dramaturgically this play is a clarification of techniques Jonson has used before, and intellectually it is part of Jonson's consistent and settled views. As early as *The Case is Altered* (1597?), he had been pleading the cause of reason. In the dedicatory epistle of this play he writes: "It is not pould'ring, perfuming, and euery day smelling of the taylor, that couerteth to a beautiful obiect: but a mind, shining through any sute, which needes no false light either of riches, or honors to help it" (Ded. 13–17). He applies the lesson of the sermon "Against Excess of Apparrel" from the celebrated *Book of Homilies* to the Court: "Who can paint her face, and curle her hayre, and change it into an unnatural colour, but therein doeth worke reproofe to her maker, who made her? As though shee could make her selfe more comely than GOD hath appointed the measure of her beauty. What doe these women [and men], but goe about to reforme that which GOD hath made? not knowing that all things naturall are the worke of GOD, and things disguised and unnaturall be the workes of the Diuell . . ."[23] Jonson knew that the mind distinguishes virtue from error, and that the courtiers acted irrationally. The road to virtue, he thought, was marked by legible, reasonable signs. In *Every Man Out* he attempted generalizations about economics and society. In this play his subject is smaller. It deals with the rational moral responsibilities of courtiers. In his day the duties of courtiers may not have been less important than the relation of men to society generally. The play fails, however, for other, dramatic reasons. It is more expository than dramatic, more assertive than demonstrative, more local than philosophical. For all its thematic unity, *Cynthia's Revels* has earned its oblivion.

3. Poetaster

Poetaster (1601) has given the critics a good deal of trouble. Though Herford and Simpson refer to its disorderly organization, John Palmer thinks it has two themes which are "held together by skilful plotting and unity of interest," and Campbell attempts to show that it is unified about a single theme, that of Ovid's "dangerous eroticism."[24] Certainly

23. *Certaine Sermons Or Homilies appointed to be read in Churches* . . . (London, 1623), p. 106. The sermon from which this passage is taken appears in *The Second Tome of Homilies*, originally published in 1563.

24. Herford and Simpson, I, 415–441. Palmer, p. 56. Campbell, p. 113, the whole chapter (pp. 109–134) is relevant. See also Eugene Waith, "The Poet's Morals in Jonson's *Poetaster*," *MLQ*, XII (1951), 13–19; this is particularly helpful.

Poetaster was hurried. Jonson himself admits as much in the Induction (14–18). But its organization is not so much "disorderly" as unfinished. Campbell's reading of the play, which is the most detailed, unfortunately leaves Act V unaccounted for; he calls it a "kind of appendage." Though he does not say as much, he also fails to consider almost all of Act III. Further, the theme of the play, as he defines it, leaves many incidents and details unaccounted for. Professor Campbell's analysis fails to convince many readers that Herford is altogether wrong in calling this a "loose mixture of different techniques." Palmer may be right in suggesting that the play contains two related themes, but to most readers they do not seem to possess a completely "unified interest," except perhaps embryonically. Compromise may be tiresome, but the truth seems to be a kind of middle position among the varied opinions. Though the play surely has a core of central meaning which has never been fully stated, *Poetaster* has a number of diverse elements which never get swept up into its main action.

The haste with which the play was written explains in part its lack of total unity. After some provocation, Jonson in *Every Man Out of his Humour* (1599) ridiculed Marston's dramatic language. Marston took offense, and there followed a series of plays in which he and Jonson attacked each other. The series culminated in *Poetaster*. It was hurried onto the stage when Jonson heard that Dekker and Marston, stung by references to them in *Cynthia's Revels*, were planning a satire. His play attacking the attackers was finished in fifteen weeks, he tells us (in the Induction, 14), and Dekker's *Satiromastix* followed rather than led the assault. In *Poetaster* Crispinus is clearly a representation of Marston, Demetrius Fannius is Dekker, and Horace is audaciously (or arrogantly) Jonson himself. Attempts to identify other characters as theatrical figures, including Shakespeare, have proved risky. The play is interesting in spite of its topical references, for it transcends the circumstances of its writing.[25]

Poetaster is an Elizabethan play written for an Elizabethan theater by a practicing playwright and former play doctor. It contains a promise, unachieved, of unity. In *Poetaster* Jonson constructs a play on which we might call Shakespearean form. Its two main plots complement each other, and a third supplements the first. Shakespeare's *Henry IV*, which was the rage of London in this period (1600–1601), and *Satiromastix*, Dekker's answer to *Poetaster*, are both plays of multiple plot and are rather like it.

25. See Roscoe A. Small, *The Stage-Quarrel between Ben Jonson and the so-called Poetasters* (Breslau, 1899). Campbell and Herford and Simpson also discuss the historical significance of the play.

The first theme deals with Ovid and his kind of false love. The story of Chloe's ambitions is related to it and introduces a variation; her story is really a second (rather minor) plot. The third plot deals with Crispinus and his false poetry. In *Poetaster* we are shown two kinds of perversion, and these perversions give the play a thematic coherence. The Ovid-Chloe stories are concerned with private emotions (romantic love) and their public consequences. The Crispinus story is concerned with public poetry and the poet's private integrity. Both show what happens to public and private life when men and women are not disciplined by a sense of general responsibility. The structure shows Jonson drawing on the indigenous tradition of playwriting that he earlier deserted. *The Case is Altered* (1597?) is antiphonal also, in that it too has a plot and an under-plot related at the level of idea. The first two comical satires are different and relatively monolithic. Now with this third comical satire, Jonson returns to what he had learned as an apprentice which presumably came easiest to hand. *Every Man Out of his Humour* is a panoramic considera-tion of problems common to his day; *Cynthia's Revels* is a topical allegory; *Poetaster* is a personal satire with philosophical overtones. It is much the most interesting of the three.

The first act of *Poetaster* introduces us to the two major themes of the play. In Act I, scenes i and ii, Ovid defends the public dignity of poetry: poetry brings eternal fame to those celebrated in it (I.i.43–84), and poetry, especially dramatic satire, purges the state of false values. We see later how these high aims are perverted by false poets and bad actors. The second theme, false love, is introduced in Act I, scene iii. Here we see young Ovid's excessive love for Julia:

> Hencefoorth, I promise faith,
> And all my serious houres to spend with you:
> With you, whose musicke striketh on my heart,
> And with bewitching tones steales forth my spirit,
> In Ivlias name; faire Ivlia: Ivlias loue
> Shall be a law, and that sweet law I'le studie,
> The law, and art of sacred Ivlias loue:
> All other obiects will but abiects prooue. (I.iii.51–58)

Erotic love, unlike divine love, is not law, but must itself be controlled by law. This speech and the whole scene recall Edward II's Elizabethan sensuality and pride, and for a moment we are back in Marlowe's world of self-assertion. The character of Ovid in this first act is complicated. In this mouth we find the defense of poetry which we are to endorse, but we also find a defense of love which we should reject. Indeed, half the play is given to showing how dangerous this uncontrolled passion is. From the first, Ovid is an attractive young man, rather like Wellbred and Young Knowell in *Every Man in his Humour*. He is unlike them in his double-dealing and in his defense of the unacceptable. This first act may lack emphasis, but it introduces the themes of *Poetaster*.

Act II is less complex. It is taken up exclusively with the theme of love. Chloe, a citizen's wife, aspires to life in the court. Impatient with her husband Albius, she listens to flatterers who instruct her in the love games carried on there. In Act II the courtiers' romantic behavior seems silly. In Act IV we meet Chloe and her friends again, and now we see that the courtiers are libertines. We see that the court entertainment serves as an escape from marital fidelity: it is a cover for wantonness. When Caesar appears in Act IV, scene vi, the nature of the court and Ovid's "misbegotten love" of Julia are linked and condemned together. The theme of false love is concluded in the celebrated love scene between Ovid and Julia (IV.ix).

Acts II and IV are thus taken up almost exclusively with considerations of false love. Acts III and V deal with false poetry. After a series of very funny scenes in which Horace, the true poet, is annoyed by Crispinus, the false poet, the concluding scene of Act III points a moral. When Jonson edited the Folio he must have felt that the idea with which he had been dealing needed strengthening, for this scene (III.v), though not in the 1602 quarto, was significantly placed in the folio of 1616 following the scenes between Horace and Crispinus. Horace (Jonson) explains the duties of the satirist: it is his high responsibility to present a clear and polished mirror to the times in order to show the moral limitations of society about him. He must not fear to act (III.v.103–106). The false poet (Crispinus) and the ranting actor (Histrio) in failing to hold up a true mirror betray the high ethical aims of their art. Bad actors and bad poets pervert noble purpose. In this act Crispinus is measured against the massive integrity of Horace, and the Kydian rant of the *pyrgi* contrasts with the restraint of the Jonsonian language elsewhere in the play. In Act V the theme of false poetry is more fully developed than in Act III; it is also less funny. After the divinely judicious Caesar praises poesie (V.i), Jonson brings his ideal poet on stage in the person of Vergil (V.ii), and the false poets are exposed. The grand pattern of the play is now clear. Jonson attempts to set the theme of false love against the theme of false poetry in alternating acts. Act I is a general introduction of both.

This balanced double structure is not characteristically Jonsonian, but it is characteristically Elizabethan. It is not the only Elizabethan quality of the play. The Julia-Ovid love scenes, which Lamb admired and reprinted in his *Specimens*,[26] not only recall *Romeo and Juliet*, but their exuberance of language generally recalls the Elizabethan manner. In Act IV, scene ix, Julia appears "aboue, as at her chamber window" and calls down to her lover; she indulges in the verbal gymnastics which were now in 1601 going out of fashion:

> Here? and not here? O, how that word doth play
> With both our fortunes, differing, like our selues,
> Both one; and yet diuided, as oppos'd?
> I high, thou low? ô, this our plight of place
> Doubly presents the two lets of our love,
> Locall, and ceremoniall height, and lownesse:
> Both waies, I am too high, and thou too low. (IV.ix.2–8)

The lovers cannot force themselves to separate; their partings and re-unions are reminiscent of *Rómeo and Juliet*. Such love scenes were common during the decade after the first appearance of Shakespeare's love tragedy. Marston had written such scenes in *Antonio and Mellida* (1599), which were so elaborate that one cannot wonder that Jonson attacked them. His love scenes are a correction of Marston's. In the first act of *Antonio and Mellida*, Antonio on the lower stage, seeing Mellida approaching from the upper stage, cries:

> Come downe, she comes like: O, no Simile
> Is pretious, choyce, or elegant enough
> To illustrate her descent: leape heart, she comes,
> She comes: smile heaven, and softest Southern winde
> Kisse her cheeke gently with perfumed breath.
> She comes: Creations purities, admir'd,
> Ador'd, amazing raritie, she comes. (I, pp. 17–18)[27]

And so on. Marston is unconsciously ludicrous. A moment later when Mellida's companion wants us to know her name, she says:

> It pleas'd the Font to dip me *Rossaline*: (I, p. 18)

Translated, she means: "I was christened Rossaline." Antonio in describing a sea battle says:

> ... when loe, the sea grewe mad,
> His bowels rumbling with winde passion ... (I, p. 19)

26. "Specimens of English Dramatic Poets," *The Works of Charles and Mary Lamb*, E. V. Lucas, ed. (London: Methuen and Co., 1903–1905), IV, 245–249.

27. *The Plays of John Marston*, H. Harvey Wood, ed. (Edinburgh and London; Oliver and Boyd, 1934–1939), I. All my quotations from Marston are from this edition. Since Wood does not number the lines, in addition to act and scene ascription I append page references.

The funniest line in Marston's play is in the next act. Matzagente directs Antonio, who is now disguised as an Amazon, to stand up. He says:

> Ladie, erect your gratious summetry: (II, p. 26)

Even the audience which first saw the Children of Pauls perform Marston's play must have found this mannered. The style is fair game for any satirist. Jonson in *Poetaster* "corrects" Marston by writing love scenes in an Elizabethan style stripped of its worst extravagances. The Ovid-Julia scenes are not burlesques of the Antonio-Mellida scenes; they are rather exercises which show up Marston's affectation by their relative simplicity.

The Elizabethan nature of *Poetaster* was not lost on Dekker when later in the year 1601 he completed *Satiromastix*. With its multiple allusions to Jonson's play, it was an answer which had originally been planned as an attack. Its multiple plot corresponds to Jonson's multiple plot; like *Poetaster* the first deals with romantic love, the second with the corruptions of poetry, and the third with social climbers. The linking is not so "unhappy" as the handbooks say.[28] It was certainly not in the least accidental. The Ovid-Julia situation is concerned with the relation of personal love to public responsibility; so is the Caelestine-Terill story of *Satiromastix*. In the Dekker play, the evil king, William Rufus, forces the young bridegroom to allow him to test his bride's virtue on their wedding day. The young bridegroom must thus choose between his duty to his monarch and his love for his new wife. This is the subject of a Jacobean tragicomedy by Ford or Beaumont and Fletcher. It is similar to the romantic situation in *Poetaster*. In that play young Ovid must choose between his love for Julia and civil obedience. In Dekker the young people are sympathetic, the king a villain; in Jonson, Caesar is honorable, the young people willful. Dekker is not introducing a romantic love story as a simple play filler as is sometimes said; he is responding to Jonson's play by writing a play structurally parallel to it. In his soft and journalistic way Dekker defends the easy cause where Jonson asserts the difficult. What popular audience does not prefer young love to old authority, passion to responsibility? Who would not like to sympathize with separated lovers and disparage constituted authority?

The second theme of *Satiromastix*, the decay of poetry, parallels the Horace-Crispinus action of the earlier play so closely that Dekker even borrows Jonson's names; but his attack on Jonson is cautious. He does not deny Jonson's basic assumptions that art has a public responsibility

---

28. Thomas Marc Parrott and Robert Hamilton Ball, *A Short View of Elizabethan Drama* (New York: Charles Scribner's Sons, 1943), p. 109. Parrott and Ball share Small's opinion, pp. 119–120.

and that satire should correct the evils of society. But he complains that Jonson has attacked the wrong persons, that he has an ugly disposition, that he is a faithless friend and a moral coward, and that he brags of influence in high place. The charges are not entirely trumped up. Jonson was overbearing. And yet one recognizes that Dekker respects and even fears the man he attacks. Dekker of course writes whatever will sell to the largest market. He is a journalist, following the fashion not so far off, repeating the current clichés, unaware of them as clichés. His understanding of character and issues is commerical. Nothing shows Jonson's artistic quality more clearly than a glance at Dekker.

The third plot of *Satiromastix* is entertaining if superficial, and it too parallels a plot in the Jonson play. Mistress Miniver, a middle-class widow of social pretensions whose name has its significance, is courted by several gentlemen. She aspires to a "ladyship" (II.i; III.i). Chloe, wife of Albius, in *Poetaster* similarly yearns for a place in the court and is similarly flattered by courtiers. In both plays Tucca—Dekker borrows the name from Jonson—seems most attractive to the ambitious lady. Though the situations in the two plays are parallel, the attitudes of Jonson and Dekker are strikingly different. In Dekker's play Mistress Miniver is courted for her money in the manner of many stage widows. Dekker drags out his old bag of tricks; it happens that he knows very good tricks, but they remain tricks nevertheless. We need think only of Widow Pliant in *The Alchemist* to recognize her ubiquitous type. Chloe, the citizen's wife whom Jonson introduces, is hardly original either; one remembers the wives of the citizens in Chaucer's *Canterbury Tales* who dressed elaborately and put on airs (Prologue, 376–378). But Jonson understands that the woman is pursued for illicit and wanton purposes, and we see that the court dance to which Chloe goes is an excuse for libertine action. Chloe acts in wider moral context than Mistress Miniver. In *Poetaster* Jonson shows us that social aspiration leads to immorality. Such ambitions are not just silly. Dekker in turning Chloe into Mistress Miniver attempts to soften the bite. Dekker is saying, in effect, that Jonson is excited about nothing. According to Dekker, Chloe is no worse than many others, and for that matter not different. In his good-humored way Dekker accepts the world as he finds it and misses what Jonson is driving at. Perhaps he does not want to understand.

There is a consistency of theme in *Poetaster*. Unfortunately the various themes and the dramatic actions which ought to embody them are not irretrievably connected. In the most successful scenes (III.i,ii,iii) Horace is annoyed by Crispinus, but the relationship between these two is not peculiar to poets; Horace might be a soldier, or any successful man, and

Crispinus might be any ambitious sycophant. The scenes do not elucidate the theme of poetry as they ought. Jonson's appending of Act III, scene v, a most undramatic expository dialogue, is tantamount to acknowledgment of the weakness. The difficulty comes, at heart, because the play contains no single dramatic conflict embodying the two principal ideas of the play. Our attentions are scattered among a wealth of incident. The only character who takes an active part in all plots is Crispinus. He urges Chloe to come to court, he annoys Horace, and at last he is purged of his affected diction, but his presence does not unify the play, and in none of the actions is he a protagonist. It is significant that he can only react to situations, that he cannot create them: this is the nature of imitators and poetasters.

Poetaster is, I think, too rich. Though it sets out to be a drama of idea, the ideas are never absolutely clear because the story which should embody them is muddled. We are embarrassed by a wealth of incident. There is a second kind of embarrassing wealth in this play, a rather surprising kind. Its characters are too complex. In *Poetaster* we find ourselves asking, What kind of man is this Ovid anyhow? We ought to be thinking about the nature of love in which he is caught up, not about his personality. The play ought to lead to moral and intellectual speculations, not to psychological inquiry. If the other characters in *Poetaster* are less complicated than Ovid, many are more complicated than their counterparts in other Jonson comedies. Chloe seems more complex than Fallace in *Every Man Out of his Humour*, Albius more complex than Deliro, Tucca than Carlo Buffone, Ovid senior than Knowell senior in *Every Man in his Humour*. They are complicated, not by the accidental introduction of contradictory elements, but in fundamental conception. *Poetaster* is a failure because of what we normally think of as excellences. There is an accidental wealth in the plotting and in characterization. All kinds of suggestive hints of characterization and situation are dropped which are never picked up. One would be glad to see more of Luscus, a promising Plautine servant like Brainworm, but nothing is made of him; and Julia's relationship to her father, like Ovid's relationship to his father, invites question.

Still, in spite of the undigested detail, the false leads, the overcomplex characters, *Poetaster* is a worthy play. Jonson is able to suggest a significance in his situations which may or may not have been caviare to the general. When Caesar finds Ovid, Julia, and members of the court impersonating the gods in a masque-like pageant, he becomes angry; but he objects, not because the masque allows wantonness, but because the entertainment makes light of the gods. It undermines the metaphysical-theological basis of law. Piety is necessary, Caesar says, for the continuing moral health of society (IV.vi). (It is interesting that Ovid, whose sly and cynical *Metamorphoses* was a handbook of the Renaissance, should have been singled out as chief offender.) If poets and courtiers treat the gods flippantly, the people who imitate them will become irreverent of the values which the gods embody. Persons in the public eye ought to encourage piety. The kind of love which unites Julia and Ovid is impious because it puts passion ahead of filial respect. Jonson in this play complains that the poets and the courtiers in searching for personal pleasures pull down the order of society. No Puritan, he distinguishes between frivolity and gaiety. *Cynthia's Revels*, the play written immediately before *Poetaster*, deals with self-love; in it we see the consequences of exclusive concern with oneself. *Poetaster* deals with the same problem in larger context, for here we see its theological and political implications.

Poetaster is a great improvement in tone over *Every Man Out of his Humour* and *Cynthia's Revels*. The earlier satires are smug and belligerently self-defensive. Jonson shows no humility, and the resulting superciliousness is almost more than the modern stomach can take. His spokesman in *Poetaster*, Horace, shows a weak side which is attractively human. In the Prologue (25–26) we see the old arrogance, but in the concluding dialogue Jonson's humanity shows. Having been finished quickly, the play must be appreciably closer to a first draft than the others. Examining it, one is forced to several conclusions about Jonson's natural talent and his aspirations. *Poetaster* is weak in organization, but it is strong in characterization. It is uneven, but its themes are shrewd, if not profound. Much of its incident is unrelated to the general action, but the tone is pleasing. The satire sometimes misses. fire, but it is funny. Apparently Jonson could have out-Dekkered Dekker and challenged Marston at his own game if he had tried. To achieve his characteristic elegance, Jonson sacrificed those qualities that we find most attractive in other Elizabethans. Perfection was more to be valued than richness, he thought. Had he not been motivated by an ideal of rigorous symmetry, Jonson might have seemed less heartless. On the evidence of *Poetaster* one can see the Elizabethan plays of psychological complexity and human complication behind the perfect facades of *The Alchemist*, *Volpone*, *The Silent Woman*. Jonson paid a high price for his elegance.

4. *Eastward Ho*

Jonson had some part in *Eastward Ho* (1604), but it is difficult to determine just how great it was.[29] Three editions of the comedy appeared in

29. See Percy Simpson, "The Problem of Authorship of Eastward Ho," *PMLA* LXIX (1944), 715–725.

quarto with his name linked with Marston's and Chapman's on the title page. The play offended the government, and Chapman and Marston were thrown into prison, where Jonson voluntarily joined them. He told Drummond years later that he had had no part in the portions of the play which offended,[30] and in a letter to the Earl of Salisbury he makes the same claim. But, he says, if he be made guilty, he "must embrace the Asinine vertue, Patience."[31] From this distance it is difficult to spot the passages that might have caused offense. The play seems innocuous enough, and extremely entertaining. Apparently commissioned by a manager who needed a play in a hurry, "the stream flowed freely, and the writers had no time to check and make it turbid."[32] It deserves at least a brief note in a consideration of Jonson's dramatic work because it indicates somewhat the direction of Jonson's development and sympathies just before his greatest comedies. Like *Poetaster* it hints at what the unbraced Jonson was like.

Some readers have noted the "prodigal son" theme in this play.[33] The theme was standard subject matter for Tudor morality plays, and Jonson was to use it himself in *The Silent Woman*. Readers note the concluding lines of the action:

> Now London, looke about,
> And in this morrall, see thy Glasse runne out:
> Behold the carefull Father, thrifty Sonne,
> The solemne deedes, which each of us haue done;
> The Vsurer punisht, and from Fall so steepe
> The Prodigall child reclaimd, and the lost Sheepe.
>
> (V.v.205–210)

The play is indebted to the native, moral drama in more ways simply than this theme of the prodigal son. *Eastward Ho* is allied to those old Tudor plays generally. Nearly all the characters here may be read, indeed must be read, as allegorical representations of human characteristics, even while they are realistic London types. Their names indicate their emblematic significance. The old usurer is called Security, and Sindefy is called Sinne. Scapethrift and Spendall are adventurers bound for Virginia. All of the dramatis personae may be identified as either "good" or "bad," and the central figure, Quicksilver, is drawn in good morality fashion away from Touchstone, his master, toward Security, the usurer. This pattern of action is a Contention of Virtues and Vices.

30. *Conversations*, 273–276 (Herford and Simpson, I, 140).
31. Herford and Simpson, I, 195.
32. Simpson, 725.
33. Baskervill, 29.

The various actors are conventionally paired off. The ambitious Gertrude is contrasted to the patient Mildred, Sir Petronel Flash—a cousin of Fastidious Brisk, no doubt—is compared to Golding, an apprentice. In the middle scenes Quicksilver, working at a swindling game with Security, engages in high-spirited slapstick which recalls Diccon of *Gammer Gurton's Needle* and the Hodge type of character in a dozen Elizabethan comedies. As Professor Parrott has said, here is "a sharp differentiation between vice and virtue—the latter, to be sure, presented in a somewhat bourgeois form—an open conflict, and the final triumph of the good."[34]

One cannot be sure how much of the play Jonson was responsible for, as I say; but he apparently accepted some responsibility for it in 1605. After the Elizabethan *Poetaster* one cannot be surprised to find Jonson associated with an indigenous morality like *Eastward Ho*. The themes of the two plays have a great deal in common, and Mildred sums them both up when she says, "*Where ambition of place goes before fitnesse of birth, contempt and disgrace follow.*" (I.ii.34–35). Both *Eastward Ho* and *Poetaster* are conservative, morally, socially, and dramatically. If they attempt a realistic picture of London and the Court, it is for a didactic purpose. The affinities of the play with the ancient Tudor moralities lead one to suspect that the great comedies upon which Jonson was about to launch may have their morality elements too. Before he worked them over, enriching their language, complicating their dramatic implications, and simplifying their characters, they may have looked something like *Eastward Ho*.

34. Chapman, Jonson, and Marston, *Eastward Hoe*, Julia Hamlet Harris, ed., Yale Studies in English, LXXIII (1922), ix–xxiv; *The Comedies of George Chapman*, Thomas Marc Parrott, ed. (London: G. Routledge and Sons, 1914), p. 840.

CHAPTER IV

Sejanus His Fall and Volpone or The Fox

In *Poetaster* (1601) Jonson sought to dignify contemporary "contemned strifes" by direct allusion to the classics. But the satire nonetheless remained narrowly allied to local circumstance: one does not change one's nature by masquerading as Horace, Vergil, or Ovid. For two years after *Poetaster*, Jonson produced no plays; and only in 1603 did his promised tragedy appear. *Sejanus His Fall* seemed even more assiduously "classical" than the satirical comedies from which he had just turned. Laid in ancient Rome, embroidered when published with multiple marginal references to ancient historians, this tragedy at first blush appeared to be the apotheosis of native classicism. Yet for all its Augustan rhetoric *Sejanus* is as deeply English as it is manifestly Latin. It is a medieval tragedy only festooned with Senecan drapery. *Volpone*, the comedy which followed *Sejanus* within a year, exploits popular materials too. In the dedicatory letter of *Volpone*—"To the most noble and most eqvall sisters, the two famovs vniversities"—Jonson shows his respect for ancient comic law. His comedy is nonetheless an elaboration of a folktale. After *Volpone*, Jonson continued to use English materials. Only in *Catiline His Conspiracy* (1611) does he hide his English nature under his Latin tags.

1. *Sejanus His Fall*

According to its title page in the 1616 Folio, *Sejanus His Fall* was first played in 1603 by Shakespeare's company. Because of the plague which closed the public theaters in March, 1603, it must have been produced at Court before it was given at the Globe. Hissed off the stage at its first public presentation, its fiasco was subject to extended literary discussion. Jonson had staked much on the success of this play—he had announced its coming as early as *Poetaster* (1601)—and its failure caused him more than the usual chagrin. He subsequently published it in quarto (1605) with commendatory verses to show that though he had not pleased the crowd, he had pleased those rarer wits for whom quality mattered. A succès d'estime, however, was not enough for Jonson; and in a prefatory address he frankly acknowledges his concern for "popular delight." *Sejanus His Fall* was not produced again in Jonson's lifetime; apparently the Restoration saw it but then it was not seen again until staged by William Poel in 1928. Critics have agreed that the tragedy has literary merit, but of a rhetorical rather than a dramatic kind. Jonson says that in composing it he had been much concerned with "truth of Argument, dignity of Persons, gravity and height of Elocution, fulnesse and frequencie of Sentences"—qualities not necessarily theatrical. One doubts that it will ever receive acclaim outside the study.

Most of the attention accorded *Sejanus*—and it has received surprisingly little, all things considered—has been confined to its classical echoes. The scholars have tracked every word to its classical source, and most have concluded with Hazlitt that this is a great collection of second-hand beauties.[1] Jonson himself is responsible for the direction of the criticism. When he published his play, by citing Tacitus and Dio and Suetonius in footnotes he seemed to be asking his readers to admire his historicity whatever they might think of his drama. Largely for this reason, the play has been little examined independent of its sources. Even the latest and best critic of *Sejanus*, following Jonson's false lead, has concluded that the play cannot be properly understood without a detailed knowledge of the Latin historians. Echoing Una Ellis-Fermor, Joseph Allen Bryant, Jr. observes that "though written to edify the masses, [Jonson's tragedies] are written so far above their knowledge that anyone but Jonson would have expected of the masses that only the specially learned can comprehend them at first reading."[2] When one remembers Jonson's apprenticeship in the popular theater and his acknowledged concern for popular success, one is a little dubious of the validity of this judgment. Though learned, Jonson was a practical man; and he said himself of his Latin sources: Since "the *Quotations* might sauour affected, I doe let you know, that I abhor nothing more; and haue onely done it to shew my integrity in the *Story*." He continues in his prefatory address "To the Readers": "Whereas, they are in *Latine* and the worke in English, it was presupposd, none but the Learned would take the paynes to conferre them" (26-29;

---

1. "Lectures on the Dramatic Literature of the Age of Elizabeth," *The Complete Works of William Hazlitt*, P. P. Howe, ed. (London: J. M. Dent and Sons, 1931), VI, 263.
2. Joseph Allen Bryant, Jr., "The Significance of Ben Jonson's First Requirement for Tragedy," *SP*, XLIX (1952), 212. Cf. Una Ellis-Fermor, *The Jacobean Drama* (London: Methuen and Co., 1936, 1953), pp. 109-113.

34–36). *Sejanus* may be more interesting to persons who can see it as one dramatized episode in a long and familiar history, but a knowledge of history does not seem more necessary here than in other plays with a similar setting. Still, Bryant's basic judgment, that the play is not self-contained, has considerable merit. Without doubt it is less unified in tone and method than *Every Man in his Humour* and Shakespeare's *Julius Caesar*. But what distresses us finally are not its complicated historical associations; *Sejanus* troubles us because it is dramaturgically eclectic, an incomplete linking of Senecan and native tragedy. Specifically Senecan, it contains all the conventional Senecan elements: violent action and bloody death, internecine strife and reports of tragic horror. Its style ("height of Elocution . . . frequencie of Sentences") is purified Senecan rant. The speeches are rhetorical, the scenes expository. Much of its action takes place off-stage. In a drama contemporaneous with Shakespeare one might have expected a more detailed dramatic handling of Livia's plot to kill her husband; and at another point in his career, Jonson might have shown us Sejanus separating Agrippina from her sons. Instead, these superbly dramatic situations are hastily passed over. Remarkably the final climactic scene, in which Sejanus is removed from his high office, is accomplished through a rhetorical messenger. That the scene is effectively dramatic (at least in the study) is startling indeed.

But even when the action takes place before our eyes, it is not of the popular theater. Rather than an interaction of developing figures, Jonson gives us the reaction of one person to a presented situation. In the middle of the play Silius kills himself on stage: learning of the charges brought against him, he reacts consistently, following his conception of honor to its natural conclusions. The scene is monodrama. Agrippina and the others are equally consistent. Their scenes give them a chance to express themselves verbally, to narrate their emotions and convictions, but they give no opportunities for dramatic development. The quasi-choric figures of Arruntius and Lepidus underscore the expository nature of the play. They comment on the action as it is presented even as they seem untouched by surrounding dangers. The scenes represent the triumph of logic over theater.

Since the major part of the drama takes place at one remove from our direct participation, we can see that this play ought to be judged by standards different from those applied to many contemporaneous tragedies, including most of Shakespeare's. Its plot is an excuse for a moral essay. In this respect *Sejanus* is like the tragedies of Chapman, who incidentally may have had a hand in an earlier form of the play.[3] As with

3. See "To the Readers," ll. 43–48.

some of the comedies—*Poetaster* for example—when we finish *Sejanus* we question ourselves about the ideas it raises, not its historical verisimilitude or even its characters. *Sejanus* agitates the speculative, philosophic mind.

It is here that this rather un-Elizabethan play participates in the medieval heritage of Elizabethan tragedy. To see what Jonson is driving at, we must look for elements which are only incidentally Roman. This "Roman" play is in theme not so much "classical" as it is "Gothic." Herford observed that "what [Jonson] felt to be tragic in the story of Sejanus was in part that which the whole medieval world understood by tragedy, and the authors of the *Mirror for Magistrates* still exemplified in their tragic tales,—the sudden passage from prosperity to adversity."[4] Curiously, no one has followed up this suggestion or examined the debt of *Sejanus* to the traditions of native tragedy. Scrupulously scholarly in detail, in general outline, and in purpose, the play was and is Elizabethan.

Though ordinarily referred to as *Sejanus*, the play's title more properly is *Sejanus His Fall*, and that is its theme. In his dedicatory letter to Lord Aubigny, Jonson himself called it *The Fal of Seianus*. Its subject is not the man who was Tiberius's favorite, but the arrogance which doomed him. *Sejanus His Fall* could almost serve as an exemplum in one of the collections of stories dealing with the rise and fall of eminent men which had been standard for generations. Shortly after Boccaccio had written the *Decameron*, in a new moral and humanistic fervor he produced *De Casibus Virorum Illustrium* (ca. 1360). A series of prose stories culled from history and tradition telling how eminent men and women suffered falls from prosperity into misfortune, they were pyramidic in structure. The first part of each told of the glorious rise of an eminent person; the second part described his descent from high place. He may or may not have earned his position of power, and he may or may not deserve his fall. The course of his rise and decline was ruled by Fortune, a goddess whose activities are not amenable to logical analysis. The protagonist rose and fell as Fortune's Wheel turned; as one man was carried upward, another was carried down. The stories taught a medieval contempt for the world: the wise man would not trust his own destiny, they said, for all men are subject to an irrational chance which he may neither avoid by taking thought nor understand by protracted study. Fortune acted independently of human will and knowledge, but it acted inexorably and inescapably. *De Casibus Virorum Illustrium* gave a form to the vague medieval conception of tragedy which Dante had defined: "Tragedy is calm and noble to start with, but in its ending or outcome stinking and terrifying (*foetida*

4. Herford and Simpson, II, 24.

et horribilis) . . . as appears by Seneca in his Tragedies. Comedy on the other hand begins with the harshness of some affair (*asperitatem alicuius rei*) but its matter ends happily (*prospere*) as appears by Terence and his Comedies."⁵ Jonson uses tragedy in this sense in the body of his play (IV.379).

Boccaccio's stories seized the imagination of men all over Europe and were shortly translated into every European language. Chaucer imitated the form, writing a series of stories in the *De Casibus* manner which he put in the Monk's mouth in the *Canterbury Tales*. Lydgate made a kind of loose translation-adaptation of Boccaccio called *The Fall of Princes* (1430–1440), which retained its popularity well into the sixteenth century; and the celebrated *Mirror for Magistrates* (first published in 1559) revived an interest which had never really died. The *Mirror* and its progeny continued to be read and imitated, but by Jonson's time the genre had been modified. New tales in its manner now took on psychological complexity and causal sophistication. Dame Fortuna began to escape the full blame for human misfortune, for it was suggested in some stories that each man constructs his fortune and is thus at least partially responsible for his own tragic end. But for the most part the moral that these tales teach is simple. They insist, as Sir Philip Sidney says, on "the vncertainety of this world, and vpon how weake foundations guilden roofes are builded."⁶

Sejanus His Fall teaches the virtue of humility before the will of God and the transience of the world's rewards in the manner of the earlier tales, but it is not simple. It belongs among the later developments of the *De Casibus*. If Sejanus had been content to remain Tiberius's minion and had not aspired to marry into Caesar's family and become a Caesar himself, perhaps his nemesis would not have been so prompt. His descent is marked from the moment he proposes the marriage to Tiberius. In a sense *Sejanus* is the tragedy of a man who overreaches himself and thus shares in the responsibility for his disaster. As the play advances we recognize that Sejanus's ambition and defeat are not the only themes of this play. The tragedy has broader implications. We are shown that neither virtue nor vice brings wordly success, and we are asked to think about the moral order which allows evil men to rise before it pulls them down. Some of the virtuous members of Germanicus's party are falsely accused

---

5. Quoted in Nevill Coghill, "The Basis of Shakespearian Comedy: A Study in Medieval Affinities," *E&S*, III (1950), 5.

6. Quoted in Willard Farnham, *The Medieval Heritage of Elizabethan Tragedy* (Berkeley: University of California Press, 1936), p. 341. I am of course much indebted to this celebrated study.

and suffer, like Sabinus and Cordus; others like Arruntius and Lepidus escape. Through it all the horrendous Tiberius continues to rule. When the evil Sejanus falls from his high place, he is replaced by the evil Macro. Rewards and merits are shockingly ill matched because the affairs of men under the sun are ruled by irrational Fortune. The Wheel of Fortune turns, bringing new men to the top, carrying established men down.

Lepidus, the voice of wisdom, significantly summarizes this central point near the end of the play:

> How fortune plies her sports, where shee begins
> To practise 'hem! pursues, continues, addes!
> Confounds, with varying her empassion'd moodes!
>
> (V.888–890)

Allusions to Fortune and to Fortune's Wheel run through the play like a scarlet thread, tying it together. They become more prominent as the tragedy draws to its close. When we first meet Sejanus we see him as a kind of Roman Tamburlaine. Tamburlaine, Marlowe tells us, had the Fates bound fast with iron chains; so also does Jonson's fiend-hero:

> Sejanus, whose high name doth strike the starres,
> And rings about the concaue, great Sejanus,
> Whose glories, stile, and titles are himselfe,
> The often iterating of Sejanus: (II. 98–101)

Greater than all the gods, this Sejanus addresses his soul in Marlovian terms:

> On then, my soule, and start not in thy course;
> Though heau'n drop sulphure, and hell belch out fire,
> Laugh at the idle terrors: Tell proud Ioue,
> Betweene his power, and thine, there is no oddes.
> 'Twas onely feare, first, in the world made gods.
>
> (II.158–162)

Sejanus thinks himself superior to the forces of law in nature. His arrogance reaches its climax when he offers homage to the goddess Fortune in Act V. The scene begins with Sejanus's exultation: "I did not liue, till now . . . 'tis aire I tread:/And, at each step, I feele my' aduanced head/ Knocke out a starre in heau'n!" (V.3,7–9). He continues: "Is there not something more, then to be Caesar?" (V.13). Is it not passing brave to be a king, and ride in triumph through Persepolis? Sejanus is confident that the laws of the world can be comprehended by human reason and, discovered, worked to his advantage. He is profoundly impious. To suggest that the universe is not totally comprehensible by reason is, he says, to yield to superstition; to think that offerings on the altars of the gods—assuming that there be gods—placate their anger and earn their favor, is stupidity. Sejanus's single goddess is Fortune; and when she turns her face from him, she only shows "her selfe the lesser deitie,/And but my seruant" (V.208–209). Sejanus is one of the Renaissance hero-villains; and he learns what the medieval preachers taught: though we may sleep each night with conquest on our brows, behold we will yet fall. Shortly Sejanus is cast down. That new fellow, Macro, becomes "A greater prodigie in *Rome*, then he/That now is falne" (V.752–753). "His fall/May be our rise," Macro has said (III.747–748). Arruntius, Jonson's spokesman, sums up the moral of the play:

> Forebeare, you things,
> That stand vpon the pinnacles of state,
> To boast your slippery height; when you doe fall,
> You pash your selues in pieces, nere to rise:
> And he that lends you pitty, is not wise. (V.893–897)

It is the better part of wisdom not to claim too much for yourself; Fortune is capricious. And it is blasphemous to claim credit oneself for one's high place:

> It is odious wisedome, to blaspheme,
> Much more to slighten, or denie their [the gods'] powers.
> For, whom the morning saw so great, and high,
> Thus low, and little, 'fore the 'euen doth lie. (V.900–903)

The moral is clear and appropriate: the rewards of the world are uncertain and the ways of God inscrutable. What is bright in the morning may not outlast the day, nor is the humble necessarily the least enduring. For Jonson as for the Elizabethans generally Fortune was but one of the obscure ways in which God expressed his will in the world. Humility becomes us all. This "moral" is foreign to Jonson's Latin sources. Tacitus and Suetonius make only the slightest allusions to it. Tacitus does not intend to teach us humility. Though a moralist, he writes for other reasons: "few men distinguish right and wrong, the expedient and the disastrous, by native intelligence," he says; "the majority are schooled by the experience of others."[7] Tacitus would instruct his readers in ethics. Jonson's aspirations are finally religious. For him there is a cosmic order against which one's actions must be squared. Ethics for him is a branch of metaphysics, or theology; for Tacitus it is a branch of law, or

---

7. Tacitus, *The Annals*, trans. John Jackson (Loeb Classical Library, Cambridge: Harvard University Press, 1937), IV, xxxiii, 57.

prudence. Jonson inserts the medieval idea of Fortune in his Latin play, and he may or he may not have recognized how foreign it was to his classic originals. Ultimately *Sejanus* is more Christian than Latin and more at home in the Christian than in the classical tradition.[8]

Even those parts of the play which appear to be most Roman can be seen, with a little thought, to be also Elizabethan. The most explicitly classical section of the play is Lepidus's advice to Arruntius. When the troubled Roman asks the old man what are his arts of living in a country ruled by madmen and villains, Lepidus replies:

> Arts, Arrvntivs?
> None, but the plaine, and passiue fortitude,
> To suffer, and be silent; neuer stretch
> These armes, against the torrent; liue at home,
> With my owne thoughts, and innocence about me,
> Nor tempting the wolves iawes: these are my artes.
>
> (IV.293–298)

This passage is echoed from Juvenal's sketch of Vibius Crispus, in *Satire* IV (86–93), and similar ideas can be found in Seneca and the Stoic philosophers. But though the advice constitutes the most Roman element of *Sejanus*, it is Elizabethan as well. It might easily have come from the mouth of a Christian observer of the Renaissance political scene. The Stoic element in Christianity is admittedly great; we find Stoic advice to withdraw and endure in St. Paul, and Stoic-Christian philosophy was regularly preached from the Elizabethan pulpits. Admonitions to forebearance resembling Lepidus's are frequent in the *Book of Homilies* (first collection 1562; collected edition 1623), which was generally known. The sermons from this book were read and reread on order of the Crown. "Parsons, Vicars, Curates, and all other hauing spirituall cure, euery Sunday and Holyday in the yeere" were instructed "to reade and declare to their Parishioners plainely and distinctly one of the sayd *Homilies* . . ."[9] The sermons were repeated year after year. In them the people were told: "Finally, that if seruants ought to obey their masters, not onely being gentle, but such as be froward: as well and much more ought subiects to be obedient, not only to their good and courteous, but also to their sharpe and rigorous Princes. It commeth therefore neither of chance and fortune (as they terme it) nor of the ambition of mortal men and women

---

8. Cf. D. J. Enright, "Crime and Punishment in Ben Jonson," *Scrutiny*, IX (1940), 231–248. See also Helen Gardner, "Milton's 'Satan' and the Theme of Damnation in Elizabethan Tragedy," *English Studies*, I (1948), 46–66.

9. *Certaine Sermons Or Homilies appointed to be read in Churches* . . . (London, 1623), "The Preface, as it was published in the *yeere* 1562," a2ᵛ.

climing vp of their owne accord to dominion, that there bee Kings, Queenes, Princes, and other gouernours ouer men being their subiects: but all Kings, Queenes, and other gouernours are specially appoynted by the ordinance of GOD."[10]

One cannot be surprised to find that the rebel in this world is regarded as the worst of sinners: "But whereas indeede a rebell is worse then the worst prince, and rebellion worse then the worst gouernement of the worst prince that hitherto hath beene: both rebels are vnmeete ministers, and rebellion an vnfit and vnwholesome medicine to reforme any small lackes in a prince, or to cure any little griefes in gouernment, such lewd remedies being far worse then any other maladies and disorders that can bee in the body of a common wealth" (p. 279). Lepidus, though an ancient Roman, was at home in England; and the playgoers of Jonson's time, who were also churchgoers, would have seen nothing anachronistic in his doctrine. Resignation to God's appointed lieutenant was a chief virtue then—and whenever tyrants exist. Though Jonson's monarchs were not tyrants, Jonson got into trouble with the authorities because of this play. The Earl of Northampton summoned him before the Privy Council to explain what he took to be treasonable matter in *Sejanus*.[11] When one considers the conservative philosophy of political resignation contained in the play, one can only wonder at Northampton.

The Stoic-Christian philosophy of *Sejanus His Fall* is dramatized by setting in opposition two groups of characters. Professor Bryant has said that good and evil confront one another on stage "squarely, openly and knowingly" only in the climactic scene of the play (III.i), which matches the virtuous Germanicans against the villanous Tiberius. Silius's death speech in this scene perfectly summarizes the Stoic-Christian view that life is to be endured rather than loved.[12] But *Sejanus His Fall* is not so black and white as this view suggests. As the play proceeds, we see that

10. "An Homilie against disobedience and wilfull rebellion. The first part," *Certain Sermons Or Homilies*, pp. 277–278.

11. Cf. *Conversations with Drummond*, 326–327, (Herford and Simpson, I, 141). See also Herford and Simpson II, 4–5, and IV, 329. Jonson was a Papist at this time, but he had grown up in the Church of England: his father was said to have been a "grave minister of the gospel" (I, 2). He returned to the Anglican Church about 1610. His concern in theology, he said, was with "the Fathers, and those wiser Guides/ Whom Faction had not drawne to studie sides" (*Underwoods*, xliii, 103–104 Herford and Simpson, VIII, 207). See also *Discoveries*, 1046–1062 (Herford and Simpson, VIII, 595–596).

12. Joseph Allen Bryant, Jr., "The Nature of the Conflict in Jonson's *Sejanus*," *Vanderbilt Studies in the Humanities*, R. C. Beatty, J. P. Hyatt, Monroe K. Spears, eds. (Nashville, Vanderbilt University Press, 1951), p. 215.

THE TRAGIC SCENE

A drawing by Inigo Jones (date unknown). Reproduced by courtesy of His Grace the Duke of Devonshire.

the party of Germanicus is not totally virtuous, nor is Tiberius totally vicious. *Sejanus* is not a melodrama. Though their rebellion is not armed or complete, the Germanicans are partially in the wrong, for they resist constituted authority. Emperor Tiberius is God's agent on earth, set in his place by God's divine command. That he is evil is itself a judgment of God; it is not an excuse for resistance. According to the *Book of Homilies*, "the neerer and neerer that an earthly Prince doth come [to the heavenly kingdom] in his regiment, the greater blessing of GODS mercy is he vnto that countrey and people ouer whom he reigneth: and the further and further that an earthly prince doth swarue from the example of the heauenly government, the greater plague is he of GODS wrath, and punishment by GODS iustice, vnto that countrey and people, ouer whom GOD for their sinnes hath placed such a Prince and gouernour" (p. 278).

The chief fault of the party of Germanicus is its lack of faith in Providence. In resisting the emperor, the Germanicans do not trust God. Because their eyes cannot perceive benevolence rising from a corrupted state, they doubt that it exists. The unmodified Stoic virtues which are preached by Silius and which lead to suicide ultimately must be rejected. In its lack of faith we can see that the party of Germanicus is not totally virtuous. Neither is Tiberius the personification of unqualified vice. Personally beyond redemption, as a Prince he represents authority. If Tiberius did not remain in authority, the crowd's violent treatment of Sejanus and his family, described in the last shocking speeches of the play, would be extended into civil war. Though he encourages Sejanus and Macro for a time, he can also restrain them and their wholesale ambition, that "vnlawfull and restlesse desire in men, to bee of higher estate then GOD hath giuen or appointed vnto them."[13] By the end of the play Arruntius and to a lesser extent the other members of his party are freed of Ignorance. "By ignorance, I meane no vnskilfulnesse in artes or sciences, but the lacke of knowledge of GODS blessed will declared in his holy word, which teacheth both extreamely to abhorre all rebellion, as beeing the roote of all mischiefe, and specially to delight in obedience, as the beginning and foundation of all goodnesse, as hath beene also before specified" (p. 307).

If Tiberius is seen as the means of God's vengeance, *Sejanus His Fall* becomes intellectually more interesting than if he is viewed as a simple tyrant. When we recognize that this evil man is the instrument of stability, we know also that virtuous men may under certain circumstances be the

13. "The fifth part of the Homily against disobedience and wilfull rebellion," *Certaine Sermons Or Homilies*, p. 307.

agents of error just as evil men under certain circumstances may be the agents of good. Judgment of good and evil is complicated by the limitations of human understanding. This is not the first time a fiendish man has been the carrier of God's justice; indeed Satan is always God's instrument, for God is omnipotent. The difference between Satan's and angels' actions, between the actions of good men and of bad, cannot be measured by results. The virtue of a deed must be measured by motive. Virtuous men and the angels do the Lord's work willingly and knowingly; vicious men and the fallen angels do it with sullenness and unwittingly. While *Sejanus His Fall* preaches the classic virtues of fortitude and patience, as Bryant points out, it also preaches the Christian virtues of faith and humility. Jonson makes this indigenous moral theme very explicit in a note which he added to The Argument printed in the 1605 quarto; he omitted it from the folio version of the play. He wrote: "This [*Fall of Sejanus*] do we aduance as a marke of Terror to all *Traytors, & Treasons*; to shewe how iust the *Heauens* are in powring and thundring downe a weighty vengeance on their vnnatural intents, euen to the worst *Princes*: Much more to those, for guard of whose Piety and Vertue, the *Angels* are in continuall watch, and *God* himself miraculously working." (Argument, 38fn.) Sejanus is an Elizabethan clad in a borrowed toga.

2. *Volpone or The Fox*

Volpone or The Fox was "acted in the yeere 1605," according to the folio of 1616. In writing it Jonson was attempting to serve two masters. First he wrote to meet the classical requirements of comedy; and he cites the precedence of the ancients. Not only is the Dedicatory Epistle addressed to "The most noble and most eqvall sisters, the two famous vniversities," the homes of classical scholarship; but in the Prologue he claims

> The lawes of time, place, persons he obserueth,
> From no needfull rule he swerueth. (31-32)

He also set himself to meet the requirements of the popular theater, for he intended to entertain the crowd. His attitude toward the general public seems to have become more candid than in the days of the "satyricall comedies"; and in his next, great plays—*The Silent Woman, The Alchemist, Bartholomew Fair*—he sets out even more openly to please his audience.

As is true of all his plays, the native elements here are strong, fundamental, and interesting, though they may not be obvious. Jonson constantly underscores his debt to the Romans. Indeed the unbiased student might think he protests too much. Curiously, these native and popular elements in *Volpone* have gone pretty much unexamined, and in the following pages I would like to discuss some of them.

One need only glance at the footnotes to any edition of the play to see in what vineyard the scholars have labored. Dr. Rea, for example, can claim on the scholarly evidence he assembles that this play is little more than a pastiche of quotations and a mosaic of borrowings from the classics;[14] and Herford, in the very act of defending Jonson's English originality, neglects to identify the native tradition within which he writes.[15] Herford and Simpson are exclusively concerned with Jonson's debt to the Latin classics. The most recent critics, like Enck, Partridge, and Barish, while ignoring Jonson's classical debt, have for the most part also left the native elements in *Volpone* largely undiscussed.[16] They are concerned with form independent of native affinities. When one examines these affinities they turn out to have considerable significance for an understanding of the drama. Before I can discuss them, however, I must consider briefly the "needfull rules," in order to show their limited critical value in a study of this play.

i

The most famous classical requirements for drama, and ones which Jonson specifically claims for *Volpone*, are of course the unities (Prologue, 31). It is perhaps characteristic that a discrepancy exists between what Jonson claims for his play and what he offers in it. He observes the unity of time (one day) and, hedging a bit, the unity of place (one city rather than one street or house); but he does mighty violence to the third and most important, the unity of action, which he calls the unity of "persons." The play contains two separate groups of persons; that is, it contains two actions—the major plot dealing with Volpone and the legacy seekers, and an independent underplot dealing with Sir Politic and Lady Would-

14. Ben Jonson, *Volpone, or The Fox*, John D. Rea, ed. Yale Studies in English, LIX (1919), xiii and *passim*. The play has been edited for the *Yale Ben Jonson* by Alvin B. Kernan (New Haven: Yale University Press, 1962). But also see P. H. Davison, "*Volpone* and the Old Comedy," *MLQ* XXIV (1963), 151–157, in which the play is seen "close in tone and certain aspects of its techniques to Old Comedy, the comedy of Aristophanes" (p. 157).

15. Herford and Simpson, II, 49–65.

16. John J. Enck, *Jonson and the Comic Truth* (Madison: University of Wisconsin Press, 1957), pp. 110–131. Edward B. Partridge, *The Broken Compass: A Study of the Major Comedies of Ben Jonson* (New York: Columbia University Press, 1958), pp. 70–113. Jonas A. Barish, *Ben Jonson and the Language of Prose Comedy* (Cambridge: Harvard University Press, 1960), *passim*.

Be. The subject of the underplot may be subtly related to the major theme (which I take to be the unnaturalness of avarice) but its existence destroys any classical symmetry.[17] The underplot is in the manner of Elizabethan rather than Roman comedy, and in introducing it Jonson yields to Elizabethan habits of multiple construction. The unity of persons or action is further abused by the presence of Volpone's clowns, Nano, Androgyno, and Castrone, who provide interludes of music and dancing. They are unorganic extrusions tacked onto a classic simplicity. As in Shakespeare, the divertimenti heighten the theme of the comedy, but in an unclassical way.

Dryden, who insisted on Jonson's indebtedness to the ancients,— praised the classical quality of Jonson's comedy; but even he complained that the comedy was insufficiently classical. He wrote (1668) that the "unity of design . . . was not exactly observ'd in it."[18] He observed two actions in it. The first, dealing with the Fox's voluptuary qualities, ends naturally in the fourth act; the second, dealing with his covetousness, ends in the fifth. Though Dryden praised the brilliance of the final catastrophe, he remarked that it did not "naturally proceed from the former" act. This double interest in covetousness and the voluptuary, like the double plot—Volpone's machinations as contrasted to Sir Politic's—is common in the popular theater. The faulty logic of the conclusion which Dryden noted is of an Elizabethan kind. One must conclude, I think, that *Volpone* is not organized like a classical comedy, whatever its author implies. It is indigenous.

Perhaps in claiming a classical mantle for *Volpone* Jonson meant that his play was classical in another sense. The plot might be said to be developed according to the requirements of Donatus who gathered up much conventional rhetorical opinion and had a vogue in the Renaissance.[19] *Volpone* can easily be divided into the *prologus, protasis, epitasis,* and *catastrophe* which he prescribes; Jonson himself uses these Greek terms in *The New Inn* (1629) and *The Magnetic Lady* (1632). But after even brief consideration we see that Donatus's understanding of dramatic structure is not overwhelming. Jonson, or any man interested in dramatic organization, could surely have conceived of a unity which consisted of an introduction, a complication, and a resolution. Jonson may have known

17. See Partridge, especially pp. 98 ff.

18. The relevant passages are conveniently gathered in Herford and Simpson, XI, 513–529. The passage to which I refer is to be found on page 514. *Essays of John Dryden*, W. P. Ker, ed. (Oxford: Clarendon Press, 1899, 1926), I, 73.

19. Marvin T. Herrick, *Comic Theory in the Sixteenth Century* (Illinois Studies in Language and Literature, XXXIV, Nos. 1–2, 1950). See especially pp. 109–110.

Donatus's treatise, but he did not need to know it. If Donatus is typical, and I think he is, one can only conclude that Jonson's debt to classical sequence was no more important than his debt to the classical unities.

Jonson's indebtedness to the classics for his subject matter presents a problem somewhat different from that dealing with his relationship to the "rules" and to rhetoric. It has been said that the central situation in *Volpone* is derived from the classics. The legacy hunting which is so prominent in *Volpone* has been tracked back to Horace and Lucian, and one finds passages in Jonson which echo passages in their work. He was of course thoroughly familiar with their satires; but what Jonson had read was assimilated before he used it, and in this play his learning does not come to our attention as learning. If his scholarly friends recognized certain parallels between *Volpone* and the old poets, so much the better for them. They got a private dividend. But Jonson was writing for a popular audience, and in the theater only scholars would be aware of his borrowings. His indebtedness to the classics, though profound, is not specific and limited. He had declared earlier, in his address to the readers of *Sejanus* (26–30), that he disliked the incorporation of recognizable quotations in a text. He took from the ancients a sense of form and an idea of order rather than any particular form or any particular order. He was influenced by the idea of decorum rather than any particular rules. With this qualification one can say that structurally *Volpone* is more akin to the English than to the Roman drama. It is true that in his introduction to *Volpone* he paraded his learning, but this introduction was an advertisement with which he sought to dignify his labors. One must not mistake the blurb for the book. Like G. B. Shaw's marvelous prefaces, ultimately it renders the play a disservice, for it leads us away from the plays into a waste land of extraneous speculations.

Even the most casual reader realizes that *Volpone or The Fox* grew out of popular beast fables. The names of "The Persons in the Play" are insistent. Each bears a name which translates into an English word: Voltore means vulture; Corbaccio means crow; Corvino, raven; Mosca, fly; Volpone himself, fox. One might expect from the name Peregrine that its bearer is a traveler, and Politic Would-Be's name gives a clue to his chief characteristic. Androgyno is a hermaphrodite, Nano a dwarf, and Castrone a eunuch. Yet only one student, so far as I know, has identified the folklore to which this play is endebted, and he has made nothing of his discoveries.[20] It is time to ask, What beast fables are relevant to this play? How can we be sure that the Elizabethans knew them? And, most

20. D. A. Scheve, "Jonson's *Volpone* and Traditional Fox Lore," *RES*, I (n.s.) (1950), 242–244.

important, How does a knowledge of them influence our understanding of the play?

ii

The handbooks say that the characters of *Volpone* are "labelled with names from the old Beast Epic," but they do not note that these old stories supply more than the names.[21] At center *Volpone* is a folk tale embellished, and it makes explicit allusions to a particular story that held children from play and old men from the chimney corner. Jonson expects his audience to know this story. The central dramatic situation of the play is lifted from the legend of "The Fox Who Feigned Death." In the first act of the play, Volpone says:

> Now, now, my clients
> Beginne their visitation! vulture, kite,
> Rauen, and gor-crow, all my birds of prey,
> That thinke me turning carcasse, now they come:
> I am not for 'hem yet. (I.ii.87–91)

And a moment later he says:

> Good! and not a foxe
> Stretch'd on the earth, with fine delusiue sleights,
> Mocking a gaping crow? (I.ii.94–96)

Mosca describes his master as he lies on his deathbed:

> His speech is broken, and his eyes are set,
> His face is drawne longer, than 't was wont— ...
>   ... his mouth
> Is euer gaping, and his eye-lids hang. ...
> A freezing numnesse stiffens all his ioynts,
> And makes the colour of his flesh like lead ...
> And from his brain ...
> Flowes a cold sweat, and with a continuall rhewme,
> Forth the resolued corners of his eyes.
>   (I.iv.38–39;41–44;46;48–49)

Volpone returns to this fox lore late in the play. He says:

> I shall haue, instantly, my vulture, crow,
> Rauen, come flying hither (on the newes)
> To peck the carrion, my shee-wolfe, and all,
> Greedy, and full of expectation— (V.ii.64–67)

There can be no doubt, I think, that Jonson's popular audience would

21. See, for example, Thomas Marc Parrott and Robert Hamilton Ball, *A Short View of Elizabethan Drama* (New York, Charles Scribner's Sons, 1943), p. 139. Enck, pp. 116–117, takes more extended note of the animal names but he does not discuss their specific legendary qualities.

have recognized these repeated references to the central situation of this play as a dramatization of "The Fox Who Feigned Death." According to the story, when the cunning fox becomes hungry, he engages in an elaborate masquerade. He covers himself with red mud, to suggest that he has been wounded and that death approaches. Then he stretches himself out where birds of carrion might see him. He awaits their coming with mouth agape, eyes fixed, breath held. The birds of prey arrive and exult over him. They prepare to devour him and even perch on his prostrate body. Some say that the raven attacks the eye first. When they approach the fox's mouth, suddenly he comes to life in all his vigor and grabs at least one of them. The devourers are thus devoured. Clearly this is the story of *Volpone*. The Venetian fox stretches out, dressed as though in the agonies of death. His mouth is agape, his eyes filled with rheum. Voltore, Corvino, and Corbaccio—vulture, raven, and crow—approach. As they come closer and closer they are increasingly in danger. At last the fox leaps lustily out of his bed.

The story of the legendary fox was part of everybody's stock of general information in Jonson's time. We find it in all the medieval natural histories; and medieval natural history and Renaissance natural history —until the middle of the seventeenth century—were virtually synonymous. The medieval bestiaries listed birds and beasts, some actual, some only mythical, with their appearance, habits, and qualities. While many— to quote from one (1582)—were "only of such birdes and foules, which be specificallye spoken of in the text of the Bible, or in the glose,"[22] others included all manner of bird and beast. The accounts were generally "moralized" (as Ovid and Virgil were moralized right down to the end of the sixteenth century) so that the various beasts and their various habits became emblematic. These bestiaries were "learned"; their authors drew on the church fathers and the Greek and Roman classics, and they were in fact compilations of all learning concerning birds and beasts. They repeat one another. The basic text was the *Physiologus* of Alexandria, a book which must have come into being between the second and fourth centuries A.D. Our earliest Latin version is from the eighth century. Soon after its original composition it was translated into a dozen languages, gathering beasts as it moved from country to country.[23]

The bestiaries were not only "learned" but "popular." Aelian,

22. *Batman vpon Bartholomew* (London, 1582), XII, Intro., 175.

23. See Florence McCulloch, *Mediaeval Latin and French Bestiaries*, Studies in the Romance Language and Literature, 33 (Chapel Hill: University of North Carolina Press, 1960). *The Book of Beasts, being a Translation from a Latin Bestiary of the Twelfth Century*, T. H. White, ed. (London, Jonathan Cape, 1954). This beautiful and readable book has a full bibliography and many illustrations.

Razullo.   Cucurucu.

Cap. Mala Gamba.   Cap. Bellauita.

Actors in the masks, costumes, and postures of the *commedia dell' arte*. Etchings by Jacques Callot, the *Balli* (ca. 1625).

Isidore, Pliny, and the other authorities constantly cited in it had gathered their information from folk sources; and the books, for all their learned references, were little more than records of folk opinion. One modern student of the bestiaries, E. P. Evans, suggests that "perhaps no book, except the Bible, has ever been so widely diffused among so many people and for so many centuries as the Physiologus."[24] It is worth noting that England was especially hospitable to the bestiary descendants of the Physiologus, and that they retained a certain dignity there right down to the time of Sir Thomas Browne, who, as one might expect, drew on them for his *Pseudodoxia Epidemica.*[25] That the beast tales belong in an oral tradition acceptable to the people is clear from the style in which such tales are related. They are not "composed"—constructed with beginning, middle, and end—and their sentences are not rhetorical. Informal, their diction is conversational, their sentences uncomplicated, and their detail homely and specific. The teller interrupts himself, sometimes even giving his opinion of the action he is describing. As one reads them, one hears the voice of the ancient narrator.

By Jonson's time a dozen works which retained some of the qualities of the *Physiologus* and much of its information were generally available, but they were no longer true bestiaries. Of the two Jonson is known to have had in his private library,[26] one is a collection of extracts from Aelian, Porphyry, Heliodorus, and Oppian, by one Peter (or Pierre) Gilles (1490–1555), entitled *De Vie et Natura Animalium* (Lyons, 1533). (It is falsely attributed to Arrianus by Herford and Simpson.) Gilles was a distinguished scholar and traveler who wrote some sixteen books on the nature of animals (including *Elephanti Descriptio*, in octavo, published after his death in Hamburg in 1614) and on topography, especially that of Constantinople and surrounding areas. In the book which Jonson possessed, Gilles attempted to return to some of the classical sources of natural history, but he did not go back far enough; he records the same old qualities concerning the same old animals which the compilers of bestiaries had been recording for a millennium. Aelian and Porphyry, whom he drew on, like the monkish authors of the bestiaries had gone to Pliny and Aristotle. Gilles's work is not strictly a bestiary, but it contains information often found in them. Jonson could have got facts from it which were repeated of an evening about the hearths of Elizabethan England.

24. Quoted by White, p. 232.
25. See for example V, XXII, 1 & 2 *The Workes of Thomas Browne*, Charles E. Sayle, ed. (Edinburgh: John Grant, 1912), II, 264–265.
26. Herford and Simpson list the books in Jonson's library, I, 250–271.

A second work in Jonson's library is more interesting and more significant. It is Conrad Gesner's *Historia Animalium* in four volumes, published in Zurich in 1555. Gesner (1516–1565) was one of those formidable universal scholars. Though born of poor and uneducated parents, at twenty-one he became professor of Greek at the newly founded academy of Lausanne. Within four years he had moved to Zurich, where he practiced medicine (he took a doctorate of medicine at Montpellier in 1541) and lectured in physics. Best known as a botanist in his own day, he has been called the German Pliny. He published only two volumes in botany during his lifetime. Modern zoology is said to start with him. His *Historia Animalium* is a compendium of all that was then known about birds and animals; a fifth volume, published in 1587, dealt with snakes. In 1545 he brought out his *Bibliotheca universalis*, in which he catalogued all the writers who had ever lived, listed the titles of all their writings published or unpublished, and gave a brief account of each. In another work on comparative philology, *Mithridates: de differentiis linguarum, tum viterum, tum quae hodie apud diversas nationes in toto orbe terrarum in usu sunt* (1555), he describes 130 languages known to him and translates the Lord's Prayer into twenty-three different tongues. In his spare time Gesner climbed mountains, both to collect natural specimens and to enjoy the scenery. With all this, he died before he was fifty not of exhaustion, but of the plague! Gesner's scientific work was known to Jonson in Latin, as it must have been known to many Englishmen, but extracts from it found their way into the vernacular as well. Edward Topsell (d. 1638?) in 1607 published a charming, illustrated work titled—in part— *The historie of foure-footid beastes. Describing the true and lively figure of every Beast, with a discourse of their severall Names, Conditions, Kindes, Vertues (both natural and Medicinall), Countries of their breed, their love and hate to Mankinde, and the wonderful worke of God in their Creation, Preservation, and Destruction . . . collected out of all the Volumes of Conradus Gesner, and all other Writers to this present day.*[27]

Other natural histories in both Latin and English had appeared earlier than Topsell. William Turner, a friend of Gesner's, published a work on botany in 1538, and in 1544 a volume on birds in which he drew on Pliny and Aristotle. Edward Wotton wrote *De Differentiis Animalium* in elegant Latin (published 1552), and John Maplet's *A Greene Forest, or a natural historie* appeared in 1567. Probably the most important source of general information of this kind in the sixteenth century was a reissue of Bartholomaeus Anglicus's encyclopedia *Liber de Proprietatibus Rerum*,

27. Selections from Topsell are contained in *The Elizabethan Zoo*, M. St. C. Byrne, ed. (London: F. Etchells and H. Macdonald, 1926).

which was originally compiled about 1260. An English translation by John of Trevisa was printed by Wynkyn de Worde in 1494, and in 1582 it reappeared with additions and corrections as *Bateman vppon Bartholome*. Stephen Bateman (or Batman) was domestic chaplain to Bishop Parker. Like Turner, Wotton, Maplet, and even Gesner, Bateman repeats the traditional lore. Through this great volume if by no other means, Aristotle, Pliny, and the *Physiologus* got into the stream of general knowledge. The story of "The Fox Who Feigned Death" can be found in it.

A variant of the basic tale is found among the numerous editions of the Reynard stories which appeared during the Renaissance. Chapter twenty-four of Caxton's version of *The hystorye of reinard the Foxe* (first printed edition in 1481) is entitled "How corbant the roeke complayned on the foxe for the deth of his Wyf." (Rook, or roeke, is another name for crow— *corvus frugilegus*.) The rook tells how Sharpebek, his wife, and he going out "for to playe vpon the hethe," found "reynart the foxe don on the ground lyke a dede keytyf, his eyen stareth and his tonge heuge out of his mouth." After they felt his belly to see if he had any life still, Sharpebek laid her ear close to the fox's mouth "for to wyte yf he drewe his breeth." This was her mistake, "for the false felle foxe awayted wel his tyme & when he sawe her so nyghe hym he caught her by the heed and boote it of!" (sig. Di, 1494 edition).[28] Appropriately enough it is Corvino (crow) whose wife is snapped up by Volpone in the play. There is of course a considerable difference between Corbant's account of how his wife was stolen and Jonson's account of how Corvino offered his Celia, but in both the masquerading fox seizes the crow's credulous spouse. The knowledgeable Elizabethan must have got an extra anticipatory laugh from the scenes in which the wife and the fox are together.

One finds references to this story in all sorts of places, likely and unlikely. Francis Meres in *Palladis Tamia* (1598) speaks of crows in a way that shows he expects his readers to know their habits (folio 62v.). Other commonplace books contained similar allusions. In his book on heraldry, *The Accedens of armory* (1568), Gerard Legh refers with apparent total assurance to the stories of the fox: "I coulde speake good thinges of this wylye beaste, but I referre those to the olde weomen of the countrey, who more delyte in his case then in the beast hymselfe" (folio 82v.). For people who could not read—becoming fewer in Jonson's time—animal fables were disseminated through pictorial representations. The churches and cathedrals were covered with carvings which drew on the bestiaries. The tale of "The Fox Who Feigned Death" is among them, and though

---

28. A convenient reprint is *The History of Reynard the Fox*, Donald B. Sands, ed. (Cambridge: Harvard University Press, 1960), p. 109.

many carvings have now been destroyed or mutilated, enough remain to suggest that they once were very common. Indeed this story was so frequently utilized that a complete list of the surviving representations of it has not yet been made.[29] "The Fox Who Feigned Death" turns up periodically even now, more than three centuries later, and modern ecologists report that it has a certain basis in fact: foxes actually do feign death upon occasion, though they never eat birds of prey.

iii

One may legitimately ask how the knowledge of this beast fable affects our understanding of *Volpone* and our delight in it. Broadly speaking it enriches our reactions to the play, as general familiarity with the Scriptures and apocryphal stories of the Bible enriches our understanding of the mythological paintings of the Italian Renaissance, or as the knowledge of the history of the New England Puritans enriches our reading of Hawthorne. Piero della Francesca, Hawthorne, and Jonson all expect us to bring some general information to their creations even while they strive to make their work in some degree autonomous and universal. Because we know something of the beast fable, our experience with *Volpone* becomes multiple rather than single. In each action of the play, we see not simply the interplay of specific characters, but we see the latest re-enactment of an archetypal action to be found in all times and all places, from days of legend until now. The action is moved outside time into a legendary world; or, rather, the action moves in the world of created Venice and, simultaneously, in the legendary world. The play thus encompasses more of life, for more is associated with it.

But our knowledge of the beast fable contributes not only generally but explicitly to our pleasure. When we see the play as a retelling of an animal story, the action becomes less human, less immediate. It is pushed into the realm of the imagination, and actions that might be painful in a simple, one-dimensional comedy are here made remote. Some critics have said that the behaviour of Corvino and Corbaccio is so outrageous that they and the situations they promote are not funny.[30] We cannot laugh, some say, when the innocent Celia is offered as a commodity to a seducer, even so fascinating and ingenious a seducer as Volpone. One

---

29. See Mary Désirée Anderson, *Animal Carvings in British Churches* (Cambridge: The University Press, 1938), pp. 35-36, 77.

30. See, among others, John Addington Symonds, *Ben Jonson* (London, 1888), pp. 86-87. Elisabeth Woodbridge, *Studies in Jonson's Comedy*, Yale Studies in English, V (1898), 7. George Gregory Smith, *Ben Jonson* (London: Macmillan and Co., 1919), p. 108.

might say that Celia is so simple, so silly in her reliance on a benevolent Deity, that she forfeits much of our sympathy, and that to a degree, at least, we feel she deserves something of what she gets. On the stage, foolishness can be made a sin.

The truth is that Jonson has left the characterization of Celia incomplete. We simply cannot learn enough about her to be able to decide whether she is a simpering fool or a much abused lady. The play contains an unfinished sketch where there ought to be a full-scale figure. (In *The Alchemist*, written some five years later than *Volpone*, each figure is fully drawn though each does not require our full attention.) Celia can be made out to be a Griselda, and it may be significant that her name means *heaven*. But Jonson has left her incomplete; he is rarely much interested in young women. Overall unity requires that Celia be acted as irritating and cloying. If Celia is a Desdemona, *Volpone* cannot be a comedy, nor Volpone less than an ogre. Logic demands a silly woman. Jonson does much better in characterizing Bonario, the other "virtuous" character in the play. Bonario is self-righteous and silly and without the backbone that he pretends. He is mildly ridiculous. An actor can develop this part. The female part does not lend itself to development.

But quite aside from the dramatic success or failure of the two "virtuous" characters, one might protest that the actions of Celia's husband and Bonario's father are not in themselves comic. Even if we could persuade ourselves that Bonario and Celia deserve what Corvino and Corbaccio have in store for them, it can be said that the actions of husband and of father are entirely repugnant. This cruelty of Corbaccio and Corvino, we ask uncomfortably—is this fit subject for comedy?[31] Any director must come to Jonson's aid and minimize the play's inherent malevolence in order to accent its fun. That all satire has a malevolent edge, no one need deny; but in more skillful comedies (including some of Jonson's) it is not brought forward so baldly.

It is at this point that the beast fable comes to the rescue. We are reminded throughout the play of the peculiar world in which the play exists. In the last lines of the play one of the avocatori says sententiously:

> Mischiefes feed
> Like beasts, till they be fat, and then they bleed.
>
> (V.xiii.150–151)

The beast fable removes the play from our daily experience. Since these dramatis personae are not human beings but animals masquerading as

---

31. *Representative English Comedies*, Charles Mills Gayley, ed. (New York: Macmillan Co., 1913), II, p. xlvi.

VENETIAN STREET SCENE

Detail from a 1697 reprint of a woodcut by Jost Amman, German, 1539–1591. Whittelsey Fund, 1949, The Metropolitan Museum of Art. Reproduced by courtesy of The Metropolitan Museum of Art.

human beings, we can be amused by their antics, as we are amused by monkeys dressed in human clothing: when the monkey-dressed-as-a-nurse drops the monkey-dressed-as-a-baby we are able to watch them with a certain dispassion. Because the play is a retelling of an animal story, we *observe* more than we participate. This invitation to objective, critical attention is the pleasure that Jonson offers. The beast fable is the means to this end.

In providing aesthetic distance, the beast fable sometimes hides the ugly while at other times it guides our judgment. It helps us, for example, in our final understanding of the protagonist of the play. Critics, both admirers and disparagers, have said that the character of Volpone nearly oversteps the limits of the comic.[32] His fall leaves us more disturbed at his unhappy lot than exhilarated at the return of some modicum of justice to Venice. Jonson himself seems uneasy about the final impression of *Volpone*, and in his prefatory letter "to the most noble and most eqvall sisters" he justifies, or attempts to justify, the catastrophe.

The conclusion is not at all tragic, and Volpone is not a tragic figure for an instant; he never inspires our pity and, sinister though he is, what terror he inspires is hardly Aristotelian, and it is very remote anyhow. We feel respect for him and we marvel at his high inventive imagination. Moreover, Volpone is ultimately not defeated, nor does he yield to circumstances. In the final scene, assaying the costs—imprisonment—and the returns—revenge—he determines the price is not too high, and he pulls down his accuser. Like a Renaissance prince he is extravagant to the end. When finally he is condemned "to lie in prison, crampt with irons,/Till thou bee'st sicke, and lame indeed" (V.xii.123–124), he answers with a joke. His last words in the play are a multiple pun. He says, "This is call'd mortifying of a Foxe" (V.xii.125). At base *to mortify* means to deaden, to kill, ultimately, to humiliate. Volpone means that his oppressors are destroying his vital qualities. But more. *To mortify* as used in religion means to subject the appetites by austere living; Volpone says that willy-nilly he is about to receive severe religious instruction. Since he is a sensualist, such mortification of the flesh is appropriate. But he means still more. In cookery, *to mortify* meat, especially game, is to make it tender by hanging and abusing it. Foxes are not normally eaten; one feels sure that it will take a good deal of "mortifying" to make this old fox edible. Far from having his spirit broken, Volpone retains a wonderful *joie de vivre*. In the Book of Reynard, the Fox more than once escapes tighter predicaments than this, and when we leave the play we do not

32. Una Ellis-Fermor, *The Jacobean Drama* (London: Methuen and Co., 1936, 1953), p. 114, and Enck, p. 112.

envy his keeper. No prison is tight enough, no chain cramped enough, to hold this shrewd fellow. He will shortly regain his trappings; his magnificence he has never lost.

Volpone, like Reynard, cannot be caught. Volpone is bigger than the play in which he finds himself. If we cannot imagine *Hamlet* without the Prince, we cannot conceive of *Volpone* without the Fox. In his little dissertation on decorum in the introduction to *The Alchemist*, Jonson condemns those popular playwrights of his day "who alwaies seeke to doe more then enough" ("To The Reader," 21–22). He inadvertently judges *Volpone*. The knowledge of the legendary cleverness of the fox makes *Volpone* the more remarkable, but it also makes it the more indecorous. The more we ponder the play and its folk-tale origin, the larger if not the more tragic its protagonist grows. It would be churlish of us to regret the delights of *Volpone*, but it would be injudicious to fail to note that this play does not meet Jonson's standards of decorum. Paradoxically, the play's greatest weakness is its greatest strength.

iv

We find when we read *Volpone* that very shortly we are led to a concern for kinds of actions, for types of people and qualities of existence, more than for individual acts, persons, and conflicts. Jonson writes a morality play in the guise of a beast fable based on one elaborate conceit: As Volpone is like The Fox Who Feigns Death, so avaricious men are like beasts of prey.

In medieval times the fox was frequently represented as the devil,[33] and in Protestant Tudor times he commonly appeared as the Roman church. Such books as *The hunting and fyndyng out of the Romishe Fox* (Basill, 1543) (attributed to W. Turner) attempted to exploit the latent allegorical possibilities of the fox stories. Aesop's fox is of course the most famous of the fox legends. Jonson refers explicitly to Aesop a number of times in *Volpone*. In passing he alludes to the story of the fox and the grapes (I.v.121) and later to the story of the fox and the cheese (V.viii.13). Volpone's general demeanor always reminds us of the demeanor of Aesop's fox. In both, the fox has marvelous gaiety: it is this quality which makes him so perenially attractive. Aesop's fables were widely current by 1605. Caxton had translated them as early as 1484, and some eight editions of his English version had appeared before 1600. About six editions of Aesop were published in Latin by 1600, and by 1624 (if not earlier) Aesop was prepared for use in the grammar schools.[34]

33. See, for example, *The Bestiary of Philippe de Thaun*, ll. 872–896. This bestiary belongs to the first half of the twelfth century.

34. *Esops fables*, tr. for the grammar schoole. by J. Brindley (1624). This book had been entered September 7, 1617.

MASQUING IN A CARNIVAL IN VENICE

Etching from Giacomo Franco's *Habiti d' Huomeni et Donne Venetiane*, about 1610.
Dick Fund, 1947, The Metropolitan Museum of Art. Reproduced by courtesy of the
The Metropolitan Museum of Art.

Though he was doubtless aware of the specific allegorical uses to which the fox stories had been put, Jonson's play is not allegorical. It escapes allegory because its actions are not consistently symbolic, however symbolic its characters may be. One might say that here symbolic characters are engaged in typical (rather than symbolic) action. Nor does *Volpone* have specific political reference like other fox stories. In fact Jonson explicitly forbids "decyphering" it in this way.[35] The play contains allusions to folklore independent of the central story, and they are suggestive. Each of the figures in the chief plot, Celia and Bonario excepted, bears an animal name. The name with its miscellaneous associations helps to describe him, but it does not limit our understanding of his possibilities. It prompts our imagination.

The title character, the fox, seems to be representative of sensuality, of a broadly conceived gluttony. Not an ordinary kind of miser, he knows "the vse of riches," Mosca says (I.i.62), and he anticipates the sensual pleasure Celia can give him. His interest in the gulls is less in their money than in his sensations in outwitting them. Power for him is an ultimate delight:

> What should I doe
> But cocker vp my *genius*, and liue free
> To all delights, my fortune calls me to? (I.i.70–72)

He does not hate and he does not envy, for these emotions are self-defeating; there is no delight in envy, only pain. He disciplines his appetites in order that their gratification may yield fullest reward.

Discriminate in quality, Volpone's appetites are indiscriminate in kind. His lust for Celia, for example, is matched with an even greater lust for Mosca. He embraces the servant at every opportunity and finds his very presence a kind of erotic stimulus. Mosca does not at first respond, though midway through the play he says, "Successe hath made me wanton" (III.i.5). This homosexual attachment sharpens the final catastrophe of the play. When Mosca out-maneuvers him, Volpone finds himself doubly betrayed. Not only has his trusted servant turned against his master, but the man to whom he is unnaturally attracted repulses him. However, Volpone differs from Jonson's other great glutton-sensualist, Sir Epicure Mammon, in being strong and self-possessed. His reliance on Mosca is not complete, as Mammon's is on the alchemist. Mosca only embroiders on what is essentially the old fox's scheme. Unlike Mammon, Volpone is not a sentimentalist and does not delude himself. Far from being the simple glutton, he is the humanist stripped of

35. "To the most noble and most eqvall sisters," 66ff.

all religious aspiration, all moral restraint, all supernatural direction. In him we see the Renaissance man awake to his pleasurable world of sensation, asleep to all others. He sees himself as the summation of all creation, and to him all creation lies open.

    T. S. Eliot has noted similarities between Jonson and Marlowe. In characterization, he says, both narrowly skirt a kind of parody.[36] More recently Professor Enck (pp. 151–171) has compared *The Alchemist* to Marlowe's *Faustus*. It seems to me that *Volpone* is also significantly related to *Faustus*. Both plays reach back to the moralities. Both have certain dramaturgical elements in common which derive from the homiletic drama. In both, the protagonist is a representation of Cynical Everyman yielding to worldly temptation. Both Faustus and Volpone search out temporal rewards. Both are New Men for whom the world awaits pillaging: The world was made for man, they say; man is therefore more excellent. Faustus leaves off thinking of "these vain trifles of men's souls" (iii.65), and Volpone, a generation more sophisticated, never even considers them. From his very first words we see that he substitutes gold for God, the temporal for spiritual things. Though Marlowe treats his humanist tragically and Jonson satirically, they dramatize similar problems.

    What these two plays have in common basically is this: they are both religious plays dealing with the poverty of humanism. In both we are shown that a life measured only in human terms is self-defeating, that life pursued for the satisfaction of human desires is ludicrous. Having sold his soul to the Devil, Faustus can do nothing but pull the Pope's beard and lust after the phantom of Helen. In exchange for his soul, he is entertained. Volpone is not different. Substituting animal for extra-material satisfactions, he lusts after Celia, tricks his Venetian contemporaries, and sports gloriously with the law. Volpone is diabolical and dangerous, rich and well fed. But at last he no less than Faustus is short-changed. In both characters a life lived in human terms, measured by human standards for exclusively human rewards, is seen to be shallow and irrational. Though Volpone, the fox, is not specifically *the devil*, nor even *the Roman church*, he is nevertheless emblematic: the fox in this play is ultimately a symbol of the humanist undirected by religion.

    Both Faustus and Volpone are accompanied by what must be recognized as creatures of the lower regions, "servants of great Lucifer." Mephistopheles is from Hell, nor is he out of it. Mosca is also a creature of Lucifer: Volpone calls him "My diuine Mosca!" (I.v.84) and once "My better

36. T. S. Eliot, "Ben Jonson," *The Sacred Wood* (New York: Alfred A. Knopf, 1921), p. 110.

Angell" (II.iv.21), ironic epithets appropriate to the inverted world of satire. In his glorious dissertation on parasites, Mosca is ironic about himself:

> O! Your Parasite
> Is a most precious thing, dropt from aboue,
> Not bred 'mong'st clods, and clot-poules, here on earth.
>
> (III.i.7–9)

And he concludes his mock confessions:

> This is the creature, had the art borne with him;
> Toiles not to learne it, but doth practise it
> Out of most excellent nature; and such sparkes,
> Are the true Parasites, others but their *Zani's*.
>
> (III.i.30–33)

As the arch parasite, he lays claims to superhuman origins and powers.

Mosca is the fly, and in Jonson's day flies and demons were commonly associated. The connection is explained by Thomas Moffet or Mouffet (1553–1604), a learned early entomologist, in his *Theatre of Insects* (written before 1590, published in Latin 1634, in English 1658): "the *Hebrewes* to set out the Prince of Devils, called him Bahalzebub, i.e. a Fly: which useth the same diligence, and never leaves off doing of hurt. Which is the reason that Witches and Wizards will have their Familiar to be alwaies in likenesse of a Fly, using the body of a bad creature to far worse purposes" (p. 932). Native folklore joined classical learning, lexicographers say, to associate flies and devils,[37] and elsewhere Jonson connected them—in *The Alchemist* (V.iv.35–39), for instance. Clearly we are expected to identify Mosca as Volpone's evil spirit.

Volpone and Mosca, as I say, are not alone: all the figures bearing beast-names are either symbolic or emblematic. Volpone says to Corvino:

> Me thinkes,
> Yet you, that are so traded i' the world,
> A witty merchant, the fine bird, Corvino,
> That haue such morall *emblemes* on your name,
> Should not haue sung your shame; and dropt your cheese
> To let the Foxe laugh at your emptinesse. (V.viii.9–14)

He underscores the symbolic nature not simply of Corvino but of all his beast-characters. Corvino, one must remember, is a crow and a crow was

---

37. Hope Emily Allen, "Influence of Superstition on Vocabulary: Two Related Examples (Prepared from the Files of the *Early Modern English Dictionary*). *Fly and Bug*," *PMLA*, L (1935), 1033–1046.

the symbol of Christian constancy.[38] It was thought that crows were particularly dutiful toward their children, feeding them long after the normal period of parental responsibility. They were rewarded, the bestiaries and folklore agreed, by a marked filial devotion; the parents were cared for by their children in their old age. In Jonson's hands, this symbol of constancy offers his wife to the fox in order to further his own aspirations: a bitter inversion. Voltore, the vulture, "smelt a carcasse, sir, when he but heard/My master was about his testament" (I.iv.61–62). Vultures, it was said, had such a remarkable sense of smell that they could detect carrion five hundred miles off. They were also said to live to great age, longer than foxes.[39] The raven, the model-beast for Corbaccio, was traditionally the emblem of the Jews, for the raven was notoriously "carnal minded." The female raven was thought to feed her young only when identifiably hers, when the blackness of the feathers showed black; until this time they were fed by providential dew.[40] Corbaccio's harsh treatment of his son Bonario is an ironic comment on this fable; Bonario's trust in the benevolence of Providence is no doubt related to the Scriptural assurance that young ravens receive manna from the Heavens until the parent awakens to his responsibility. Jonson clearly plays a variation on the miscellaneous themes which he found in the bestiaries, sometimes inverting the stories, as with the crow; sometimes presenting them unmodified, as with the raven; sometimes simply alluding to them, as with the vulture. One rather regrets that he could not have included other current and entertaining facts about these birds. The female vulture, for example, was said to conceive without assistance from the male by flying into the wind, and the raven was thought to have sixty-four changes of voice—which perhaps suggested Corbaccio's aged croaking, though of course Jonson needed no source for this.

The relevance of the folk tale to *Volpone* needs to be before us as a reminder that we are dealing with ideas, not simply with the interplay of characters in a one-dimensional action. A skillful director could no doubt point up certain similarities between the actors and the birds they

38. See White, 142–143; *Batman vpon Bartholomew*, XII, 9, 182; Francis Meres, *Palladis Tamia* (1598 ed.), folio 62v.; E. P. Evans, *Animal Symbolism in Ecclesiastical Architecture* (London, 1896), p. 147.

39. White, pp. 108–110; *Batman vpon Bartholomew*, XII, 35, 183; John Maplet, *A greene Forest, or a naturall Historie* . . . (London, 1567), pp. 107–108; Sir Thomas Browne, *Pseudodoxia Epidemica*, V, xx (Sayle ed., II, 259); *Turner on Birds*, A. H. Evans, ed. (Cambridge, 1903), pp. 177–179.

40. *The Bestiary of Guillaume le Clerc*, trans. George Claridge Druce (privately printed, Ashford, Kent, 1936), 615–626; Gerard Legh, *The Accedens of armory* (London, 1568), pp. 60–61; White, pp. 141–142; *Batman vpon Bartholomew*, XII, 10, 182; *Turner on Birds*, p. 65; Evans, *Animal Symbolism*, pp. 76, 149.

resemble by costuming and stage business. It has been suggested that Lady Politic Would-Be is a kind of human parrot.[41] If this were exploited, the lady's first entrance could be made particularly brilliant. The bestiary descriptions of parrots often begin with accounts of the bird's neck-band.[42] Maplet writes (1567), for example: "The Parret hath all hir whole bodie greene, sauing that onely about hir necke she hath a Coller or Chaine naturally wrought like a Sinpole or Wermelon" (p. 98). Lady Pol's opening words on making her first entrance are: "This band/Shewes not my neck inough" (III.iv.2–3). A Lady Pol dressed out in green with a vermilion collar could be made to recall the bird. Through the next twelve lines the bird-woman seems to preen herself, turning her head from side to side with little jerking motions that are reflected in the choppiness of her speech.

In the next passage, from about line 19—"Do's 't so forsooth? and where was your deare sight/When it did so, forsooth? what now? bird-ey'd?"—she turns on her women and scolds them, jerking her head forward as though pecking with her great beak; the play gives evidence of the beak in IV.ii.72. Her speech ends with a shaking out of her clothing, rather as a bird shakes its feathers after making a toilet. In short, the analogy between the bird and the woman which is implied in the lines can be profitably pursued on the stage.

One feels confident that Burbage and Condel and Lowin and Heminge, who first acted the play, dressed to emphasize the animal characteristics of the characters. Voltore might well have worn a great black cloak with a long sword forcing its hem to rise like tail feathers, yellow stockings like a vulture's bare legs, and some kind of white headpiece recalling the cormorant's naked head and neck. Volpone himself no doubt wore a russet cloak and a peaked hat low over his forehead suggesting the snout of a fox. The *commedia dell'arte* (to which there are allusions in the play) was full of such costumes. This animal costuming would be consistent with the general tone of the play, for only *The Alchemist* is more given to changes of clothing than *Volpone*. Here as in the masques Jonson makes an appeal to the eye of his audience, and if we fail to visualize the scenes and the movements on stage, we miss half the fun and two-thirds of Jonson's dramatic genius. But by whatever means the beast analogy might be emphasized, the fact is that Jonson, by constant allusion to the folklore of beasts, writes a symbolic play which invites us to considerations of general ideas.

41. See Helena Watts Baum, *The Satiric and the Didactic in Ben Jonson's Comedy* (Chapel Hill: University of North Carolina Press, 1947), p. 174. Rea ed., p. xxxiii.
42. White, pp. 112–114.

Occasionally the significance of particular details is puzzling because we cannot perceive what they signify. The episode with the tortoise-shell (V.iv) is one of these. Sir Politic Would-Be is an Englishman whose consuming passion is statecraft. He engages in all kinds of "policy"—or pretends to; his talk is full of plots and counterplots. In matters of state he pretends to be as sly, as clever, as wily as Volpone is in private affairs. He is the ludicrous mirror-image of the old fox, failing in his duplicity where Volpone succeeds. His reward for his pretensions is the news that the *mercatori* are after him. They will "rack" him, he is told, in order to discover what he has learned from his "politique" spying. To escape, he creeps into a "tortoys-shell." The hilarious scene that follows recalls the Tudor farce—how Heywood's rascals hid in baskets to escape threatening husbands, and Falstaff's unhappy experience in a laundry hamper of a Merry Wife of Windsor.

It is not too difficult to explain why Jonson has substituted a tortoise-shell for the more conventional basket. The tortoise had become, by Jonson's time, the symbol of Polity. According to Wilson's *Three Lords and Three Ladies of London* (1590), the tortoise was an appropriate emblem for Polity because its shell, one character says, "is so hard that a loaden cart may go over and not break it, and so [the tortoise] is safe within, and wheresoever she goes she bears it on her back, needing neither other succour or shelter, but her shell. The word underneath her is *Providens securus*, the provident is safe, like the tortoise armed with his own defence, and defended with his own armour; in shape somewhat round, signifying compass, wherein always the provident foresee to help themselves within their own compass, my boy."[43] Sir Politic is called "most politique tortoyse," and his last words in the scene are:

> And I, to shunne, this place, [go away] and clime for euer;
> Creeping, with house, on backe: and thinks it well,
> To shrinke my poore head, in my politique shell. (V.iv.87–89)

In putting Sir Politic Would-Be into a tortoise-shell, Jonson dramatizes the emblem.

When we see that many of the characters and incidents in the play are symbolic, we can see that the much maligned "entertainment" provided by Volpone's fools (I.ii) is not extraneous to the drama as has been suggested.[44]

---

43. *A Select Collection of Old English Plays*, Robert Dodsley, ed., 4th ed., revised by W. C. Hazlitt (London, 1874), VI, 383.

44. Enid Welsford, *The Fool, His Social and Literary History* (London: Faber and Faber, 1935), p. 244.

DWARFS DRESSED FOR THEATRICAL ENTERTAINMENT
Etching by Jacques Callot, *Varie Figure Gobbi* (1616).

It is rather a preliminary summary, pointing up the meaning of the full action. Nano says:

> . . . *why doe men say to a creature of my shape,*
> *So soone as they see him, it's a pritty little ape?*
> *And, why a pritty ape? but for pleasing imitation,*
> *Of greater mens action, in a ridiculous fashion.*
>
> (III.iii.11–14)

When Mosca tells Corvino that "The Dwarfe, the Foole, the Eunuch are all his;/H' is the true father of his family" (I.v.47–48), he speaks symbolically rather than factually. Earlier Volpone has said, "I haue no wife, no parent, child, allie . . ." (I.i.73). Volpone and the jesters are of a kind, whatever their physical relationship. Stage fools in Jonson, as in Middleton, Webster, and Shakespeare, are no ordinary characters. They bear peculiar significance, and from their mouths comes wild wisdom. They strike through appearances. Lear's Fool differs in quality, not in kind, from his contemporaries'.

Outside the drama, in the palaces and great houses of the high Renaissance, the fool, the court jester, was specially privileged because, it was thought, he was hedged with divinity. Queen Elizabeth had a dwarf whom she called Monarch: he was too great a lord to need lands. Some of the privileged Italian court jesters, like Antonio da Trento, nicknamed Nanio, were celebrated all over Europe for their privilege and their astuteness.[45] The most notable fool-jesters were in the Spanish court and were painted by Velasquez. In the celebrated picture of the Spanish Infante Balthasar Carlos and his jester, the dwarf holds his rattle like a scepter and his apple like the symbol of authority. He clearly plays the king, in the very presence of the true crown prince. Such audacity could only have been allowed in one who was specially privileged. In the days and places of absolute authority, the poor misshapen creatures reminded even kings of their mortality. The aura of divine favor clung to them, for they were the agents of God's wisdom.

The misshapen jester cannot escape from knowledge of the human condition—suffering, anguish, loneliness—which the normal, healthy man spends his time trying to evade, yet half-consciously acknowledging by caring for these tragic fools. In ministering to them perhaps we minister to ourselves. But Volpone's fools happily do not remind us of death and judgment. In ironic contrast to the wise fools, they assure him that to become a "*creature of delight*" (I.ii.49) is to achieve the highest aspiration

45. E. Tietze-Conrat, *Dwarfs and Jesters in Art* (London: Phaidon Publishers, 1957), p. 13. Welsford, p. 136.

of the reasonable man. No less than Volpone himself, they deny the permanent value of all but pleasure, the satisfaction of everything but appetite. Only when one can be "*Like one of the reformed, a Foole, as you see,/Counting all old doctrine heresie*" (I.ii.31–32), can one be called "blessed" (I.ii.57). One must reject "the old doctrine" if one is to be

> *Free from care, or sorrow-taking,*
> *Selues, and others merry-making.* (I.ii.68–69)

The entertainment of the dwarf, the hermaphrodite, and the eunuch summarizes the theme of the play. Volpone's creatures are unnatural. Though physically they are monsters, their bodies are no more misshapen than their spirits.

v

Volpone is about nature. Our central objection to Volpone is that his activities are unnatural, not simply selfish. In the middle of the play, Bonario, that good if rather obtuse young man, is told by Mosca of his father's plan to disinherit him in favour of Volpone. His reaction is telling: "I know not how to lend [your news] any thought,/My father should be so *vnnaturall*" (III.ii.53–54)—my italics. Mosca reports to Corbaccio that Bonario has called his father "*vnnaturall*" (III.ix.6), and later the Avocatori too speak of the "vnnaturall" father who disinherits his son. They also call Corbaccio's treatment of his wife "vnnaturall" (IV.v.1–10). The first lines of the first judgment scene are enacted against a background of "natural law." In the courtroom four senile judges (avocatori), sharp-featured but dull-witted, mutter confusedly among themselves as Volpone is tried in absentia before them:

Avoc. 4 The gentlewoman has beene euer held
  Of vn-reproued name.
Avoc. 3   So, the yong man.
Avoc. 4 The more vnnaturall part that of his father.
Avoc. 2 More of the husband.
Avoc. 1   I not know to give
  His act a name, it is so monstrous! (IV.v.3–7)

The word *unnatural* as used in this play at first seems to mean what "unnatural" means to modern man: activity contrary to what we might normally expect. It seems thus to be descriptive. When Mosca says, "All the wise world is little else, in nature,/But Parasites, or Sub-parasites" (III.i.12–13), the nature he refers to is of this kind. But Jonson means much more than "out of the observed ordinary." The word *nature* is used in this play as Hooker and the Christian humanists used it. Since Jonson's nature is a divinely ordered universe, a natural act is one in harmony with the cosmic design; an unnatural act, one which violates the design. This is what St. Augustine meant when he wrote, "Every vice as it is a vice, is contrary to nature," and St. Thomas Aquinas quoted him approvingly.[46] This was in fact the orthodox Christian view. At bottom the play is about the unnaturalness of sinful behavior, or, better, the sinfulness of unnatural behavior.

In its first lines, Jonson announces that this play deals with natural virtue. At the beginning of the first scene, Volpone displays his corrupted soul. This kind of unnatural inversion of values can be seen in all his actions thereafter. They are, as it were, variations on the initial statement of theme. His lust after Celia, the central motif of the first half of the play, is as unnatural as his worship of gold. In being unnatural, he is bestial. "If wee had the witte to conceiue the basenesse of sinne, or from what abiect Parentage it is sprung, we would hate it as a Toade, and flye from it as an Adder. Not without reason have manie learned Wryters called it Bestiall, for it is all derived & borrowed from Beastes," Thomas Nashe wrote in *Christs Teares over Jerusalem* (1593). Nashe continues: "So that as wee apparraile our selues in Beastes skinnes, in selfe same sort we clothe our soules in theyr sinnes. . . . Let vs not glory that wee are men, who haue put on the shapes of Beastes."[47]

Jonson's theme in *Volpone or The Fox* is the unnaturalness of sin; he dramatizes his theme by reference to the beast fable which constantly reminds us that unnatural, sinful, men are bestial; that by striving to measure all our actions by human standards, we ironically cease to be human. The beast fable points ultimately to the idea which the dramatic action clothes. *Volpone* is not simply a satire of avarice in Jacobean England. It is not a play of topical interest; it is a play for everybody concerned with the eternal verities.

46. See *De Libero Arbitrio*, III, xii, 38 (*Patrologiae Cursus Completus* [Paris, 1815], XXXII, 1290). Aquinas alludes to this passage in the *Summa Theologica*, II, Q. 71; Art. 3, Obj. 3 (*Basic Writings of Saint Thomas Aquinas*, Anton C. Pegis, ed. [New York, Random House, 1945], II, 563.

47. *The Works of Thomas Nashe*, Ronald B. McKerrow, ed. (London: Sedgwick and Jackson, 1910; rev. F. P. Wilson, ed. Oxford: Basil Blackwell, 1958), II, 112, 113.

CHAPTER V

The Silent Woman, The Alchemist, and Catiline his Conspiracy

AFTER WRITING *Volpone* Jonson used native materials even more than before. *Sejanus His Fall* is a dramatization in the manner of the medieval tales *de casibus vivorum illustrium*; *Volpone* is a variant on the beast fable. Both preach a moral commonplace: the natural order provided by a benevolent Providence cannot be violated with impunity. Both assert traditional values in ancient forms. *The Silent Woman* and *The Alchemist* similarly allude to well-known stories in order to assert established values. They differ in being told from what can be taken for a religious point of view. In varying degrees their fables and ethics have religious connotations.

One should not be totally startled at any religious form and feeling in these plays, though on the evidence of the "comicall satyres" and later plays, Jonson would seem to be the least pietistic of playwrights. He seems to have had a religious streak which he normally repressed. In 1619 he told Drummond of certain emotional experiences which appear inconsistent with his settled rationality. When his son died of plague, before he had had word of it by letter he saw a vision of the boy. The mark of a bloody cross was on his forehead; and, he recalled, "amazed he prayed unto God." Drummond reported that on other occasions "he heth consumed a whole night jn lying looking to his great toe, about which he hath seen tartars & turks Romans and Carthaginions feight in his jmaginagion."[1] He had had his "mystical" experience, for all his hard-headed common sense.

Such extra-rational experience he found inappropriate for straight translation into the drama, but several of his plays have religious dimensions nevertheless. *The Alchemist* more than any grows from night-time vision and gives a hint of his awe before the starry vaults at night. It is ironical that *The Alchemist* should be related to Christian experience, for

---

1. *Conversations*, 226 (Herford and Simpson, I, 139).

it is the most strictly "classical" of the plays. It is fully contrived. *The Silent Woman*, being contrived and rational and clever, does not encourage us to a sense of awe. It seems wholly the product of ratiocination, and this may be the reason Dryden thought so highly of it. The play has a direct relationship to Christian humanism, but it is not intuitive. *Catiline his Conspiracy*, like *The Silent Woman*, deals with ethics rather than piety and lacks the fervor of *The Alchemist*. In all three plays Jonson has placed the eternal, essentially Christian verities in a local habitation and has given them a local name. His classicism has become assimilated into an English nature which has grown from traditional sources.

1. *Epicoene, or The Silent Woman*

According to Jonson's dating in the 1616 Folio, *Epicoene, or The Silent Woman* was acted four years after *Volpone*, in 1609. Scarcely less Elizabethan than Jonson's earlier plays, it exploits native dramatic traditions even more than *Volpone*. In it Jonson runs through his usual dramatic tricks once more. *The Silent Woman* is not so profound as *Volpone*, so elegant as *The Alchemist*, or so panoramic as *Bartholomew Fair*, but it is good fun in the manner of *Every Man in his Humour*. It lacks the heavy, even arrogant, didacticism of the comical satires and the rhetoric of the tragedies. More interesting than these satires and generally better than the plays Dryden hastily labeled his dotages, it is nothing like so remarkable as the four greatest comedies; in withholding a central fact—that the Silent Woman is really a man masquerading—to make the denouement brilliant, Jonson has not played fair. The play was not an initial success, but subsequently it has been admired. Dryden dignified it with his careful analysis in the "Essay on Dramatic Poesy."[2] In calling Jonson "the Virgil, the pattern of elaborate writing" who "has given us the most correct plays," Dryden tells us much about himself. The characters of this play are similar to those with which Restoration comedy dealt— young men about town, foolish uncles, pretentious ladies, affected parvenus. The neatness of its comic movements has its Restoration elegance. Jonson, like the Restoration writers, specialized in oiled dramatic machinery.

In his essay Dryden calls our attention to Jonson's classical indebtedness and notes that in *The Silent Woman* Jonson scrupulously observes "the unity of time": the time of the action and the time required for its presentation on stage are the same. Further, the action is continuous, the

2. *Essays of John Dryden*, W. P. Ker, ed. (Oxford: Clarendon Press, 1899, 1926), I, 83–89. Portions of Dryden's criticism of Jonson may be found in Herford and Simpson, XI, 513–529.

stage being empty only on one or two occasions. The scene of the play is London. "The latitude of place is almost as little as you can imagine," Dryden says. When one recalls the bare Elizabethan-Jacobean stage for which the play was written, this simplicity of setting is of less consequence than appeared to Dryden in his Restoration theater or, for that matter, to modern scholars with the proscenium arch in their minds. Jonson's concern for unity of place must have been more academic than practical; it is rather the so-called "unity of action" that requires scrutiny. Although Dryden says, "The action of the play is entirely one; the end or aim of which is the settling of Morose's estate on Dauphine," there are in fact three actions. These plots are contiguous but they are almost independent of one another.

The main plot deals with Dauphine's efforts to get his uncle's wealth settled on him; he is the legitimate heir. The uncle's name, Morose, gives a key to his character and contrasts his conduct to his nephew's cheerful machinations. Dauphine alone has knowledge of his full campaign against the uncle; his friends, with whom we are much involved, have only limited intelligence of it. Though Dauphine pursues his ends vigorously, he is not the protagonist of every scene. Indeed, two quite independent actions take up about one-third of the play. The first of the underplots centers on a group of bluestockings, the Collegiate Women. They are introduced as pretentious and then exposed as licentious. Their abusive chatter drives Morose to seek peace in the rafters of his garret— "sitting ouer a crosse-beame o' the roofe, like him o' the sadlers horse in *Fleetstreet*, vp-right: and he will sleepe there," Dauphine reports (IV.i. 24–26). Their actions are not integral to Dauphine's schemes. The second underplot concerns the gulling of Sir Amorous La Foole and Sir John Daw. Dauphine uses them as opportunity suggests, but like the ladies they are only supplementary to his purposes. In both underplots, Dauphine's ally, Truewit, is his majordomo. It is worth noting that Truewit has no major part in the principal action of the play—the securing of the legacy—and his activities constitute a kind of obbligato to Dauphine's. All three plots reach a simultaneous denouement, but one or both underplots could be removed without destroying the central action. The play would be ruined, but it would still have a beginning, a complication, and a resolution. All things considered, *The Silent Woman* is hardly more unified than *Volpone* and much less so than *The Alchemist*. With its plot and underplots, it has an Elizabethan structure like Jonson's earlier plays.[3]

If the play does not have unity of plot, it has unity of theme; and it is

3. Cf. Freda L. Townsend, *Apologie for Bartholomew Fayre* (New York: Modern Language Association of America, 1947), p. 65.

ELIZABETHAN STREET MUSICIANS
From the *Roxburghe Ballads*.

this which is most characteristic of Jonson. The theme which brings the disparate elements together has turned up before, in *Volpone* for example. In *The Silent Woman* Jonson again shows us what happens to a number of persons who deviate from reasonable temperance.[4] Morose, the figure around whom the action turns, is "unnatural" in this sense. In his opening speech, Morose tells us that "all discourses, but mine owne, afflict mee, they seeme harsh, impertinent, and irksome" (II.i.4–5), and on every occasion he himself makes long and noisy speeches.

The quiet for which he seeks is private and excessive: "I'll haue none of this coacted, vnnaturall dumbnesse . . .," his bride tells him (III.iv. 54–55); and a moment later Truewit supports her: "she speakes but reason: and me thinkes is more continent then you" (III.v.42–43). Morose gives way to such an excess of emotion in times of crisis that it amounts almost to hysteria. In attempting to shut himself away from the human community, he reveals his misanthropy and tries to live by a private code rather than a general law. Pridefully he attempts to force the world to accommodate itself to him. He is unnatural in another way. He wants to disinherit his heir and strives to "thrust him out of my bloud like a stranger" (II.v.100–101); this metaphor of "thrusting the nephew from the blood" appears twice, once in Morose's mouth, once in Dauphine's (I.ii.18–19). Everybody who hears of the disinheritance is shocked by what they take to be an unnatural decision. Not only in yearning for artificial quiet but in seeking to repudiate his own flesh and blood, Morose offends against God's holy ordinances. Dauphine's determination to correct his uncle is thus no impertinence but duty.

Morose is another in Jonson's gallery of extravagant, brilliant, un-natural characters. He and Volpone are cut of the same tapestry, but from opposite sides of the fabric. Both arrogantly attempt to mold life to their own specifications, regarding society as their raw material. They seek complementary ends. Volpone wants more from life than it is prepared to give. Avaricious for more than money, he wants all the world's sensual wealth. Morose refuses the world's generosity and turns his back on its splendor, its gaiety, and its charm. While Volpone would bring all the world to his apartments, Morose wants only his narrow cell. As dramatic conceptions Volpone is larger than life; Morose is smaller. Volpone is expansive and radiant; Morose is niggardly. Volpone delights us, for he embodies the eternal principle of affirmation. Morose sets our teeth on edge, for to him all life, all activity but his own, is vanity. One can think of Volpone in the company of Drake and the Elizabethan marauders;

4. John J. Enck, *Jonson and the Comic Truth* (Madison: University of Wisconsin Press, 1957), p. 145: "The unifying theme of the play involves marriage."

he looks backward to Tamburlaine and to *sprezzatura*. Morose looks forward, to capitalistic prudence and Puritanism. One thinks of him in the company of Malvolio. In him we glimpse the pragmatic future. One can exhaust his psychological complexity, for he is one-sided; but his intellectual implications stretch out before us.

Morose is not the only irrational figure in *The Silent Woman*. The two underplots deal with unnaturalness perhaps even more explicitly than the Morose plot. The Collegiate Ladies violate the natural order of things and are both funny and startling. "Why, all their actions are gouerned by crude opinion, without reason or cause; they know not why they doe any thing" (IV.vi.64–66), Truewit says. Jonson has attacked such learned ladies before, in the "comicall satyres," and he will return to them later in *The Magnetic Lady*. In all his plays he satirized the feminine use of cosmetics, then a subject of much talk.[5] These "adulteries of art" are but one rather symbolic aspect of their pride. When Epicoene joins the company of women, she asks: "And haue you those excellent receits, madame, to keepe your selues from bearing of children?" and is told: "O yes, ... How should we maintayne our youth and beautie, else? Many births of a woman make her old, as many crops make the earth barren" (IV. iii. 57–61). In rebelling against their maternal responsibility the Collegiate Women reject their nature. Like Morose they would make the world over to their mean and selfish specifications. Through these figures, Jonson attacks once more the unnatural feminine desire for what the Wife of Bath called "masterie." What first appeared to be only their vanity comes to be seen as sin.

The story of Captain and Mrs. Otter dramatizes this disturbance of the natural order of the sexes. In the Otter household, the Captain is weak and the wife an abusive dictator. Their relationship is implicit—or was to an Elizabethan audience—in the name that Jonson gave them. Since the otter lives on both land and sea, it is appropriate for the captain, a land-bound seaman, to be called after this amphibious creature.[6] But the otter

5. King James is supposed to have said, "I wonder not so much that *Women* paint themselves, as that when they are painted men can Loue them." James I, *Flores Regii or Proverbes and Aphorisms Divine & Morall* (London, 1627), p. 25.

6. Izaak Walton says in *The Compleat Angler* (1653) that whether the otter be a beast or a fish "has been debated among many great Clerks, and they seem to differ about it; but most agree, that his tail is fish" (Part I. ii). The Second Day, Chapter II, 42. I quote from a facsimile of the first edition (London: A. and C. Black, Ltd., 1928) made from the copy in The Trenville Collection at the British Museum. This passage in the Everyman edition is on page 46 (London: J. M. Dent and Sons; New York: E. P. Dutton and Co., 1916). Edward Topsell, relying on Conrad Gesner, knew better. He says in the 1607 edition of his natural history (*The historie of foure-footid beastes* . . .

had other relevant ambiguities. Edward Topsell confused it and the ichneumon—a kind of mongoose—in the 1658 edition of his bestiary. "*Aelianus* affirmeth," he wrote, "that both sexes of the otter bear young, having seed in themselves, whereby they conceive. For those that are overcome in combates one with another, are branded with a warlike mark of Villanage, or subjection to their Conquerours; and on the contrary side they which are conquered and overcome in fight, do not only make vassals of them whom they overcome, but in token thereof for further punishment, fill them with their seed by carnal copulation, so putting off from themselves to them, the dolours and torments of bearing young."[7] Mrs. Otter and Thomas Otter were given this name not only because they are fish out of water, or beasts in the sea, but because they violate the natural hierarchies.[8]

The names of the Collegiate Ladies point up their artificial, unnatural, even sinful qualities. They are clearly related to the representations of Vanity commonly found in the Tudor morality plays. The first of them, Lady Haughty, is the spokesman for those who, like Mistress Otter, take more authority to themselves than is properly theirs; they recognize no restraints beyond their own wills. Like Morose they are evil rather than mistaken. The second of these ladies is called Lady Centaure. As Partridge observes, Lady Centaure has distinct hermaphroditic associations.[9] He points out that in Elizabethan times the centaur, being neither beast nor man but having qualities of both, was regarded as an unnatural, hybrid creation. The significance of the name of the third lady, Mistress Mavis, is explained by John Daw. When Morose protests the verbosity of his Silent Wife, Daw diagnoses an illness in him: "The disease in Greeke is called MAVIA, in *Latine, Insania, Furor, vel Ecstasis melancholica,* that is, *Egressio,* when a man *ex melancholico, euadit fanaticus*" (IV. iv. 68–70). We are told, in short, that like the courtiers in *Cynthia's Revels,* the ladies suffer from

---

collected out of all the volumes of Conradus Gesner [London, 1607]), p. 574: "Although it live in waters, yet it doth not sucke water, but aire; that is, it doth not breath like fishes though the benefit of water, and therefore it maketh his den neer the water, wherein also they are wont to bring forth their young ones." The 1658 edition of Topsell is less straightforward. In this later edition one finds more and stranger information, quoted from ancient, standard authority.

7. Edward Topsell, (London, 1658), pp. 349, 350. See also Percy Ansell Robin, *Animal Lore in English Literature* (London: J. Murray, 1932), pp. 103, 185.

8. See Edward B. Partridge, *The Broken Compass: A Study of the Major Comedies of Ben Jonson* (New York: Columbia University Press, 1958), pp. 161–177. Partridge discusses the hermaphroditic elements in *The Silent Woman* but he makes no reference to the animal lore. He concludes that this is a comedy "about nature, normality, and decorum" (p. 176).

9. Partridge, p. 163.

THE DEVIL APPLYING COSMETICS
From the *Roxburghe Ballads*.

the disease of self-love. They violate the natural law for their private pleasures.

Sir Amorous La Foole and Sir John Daw, courtiers devoted to the Ladies, are as uncertain of their masculinity as the Collegiate Ladies are of their femininity. The central joke of the episodes concerning them comes when they run away after their dignity has been assaulted. Though aspiring to the latest fashions in the dress of men, they are not men. Jonson apparently received his inspiration for this scene from Shakespeare. In *Twelfth Night* Viola runs from a quarrel rather as La Foole and Daw run; but Viola, though timid, is not unnatural: women need not face down cold steel. Further, Shakespeare's characters, including Viola, are too complex to be simply labeled. La Foole and Daw, like the Collegiate Ladies, have close affinities with stock morality figures, and like them their names are indicative of their quality. As Jonas Barish has observed, they "belong to an older generation of Jonsonian types" who "command no language beyond the one that registers their folly; they are ... incapable of inflection or change until silenced at the end."[10] They resemble New-gyse and Now-a-days of *Mankind* (1475), Ignorance in *Wyt and Science* (1530?) and Simplicitie in *The Three Ladies of London* (1584). Pretentious courtiers and licentious ladies can be found in classical comedy, because no generation and no people have a corner on foolishness; but Jonson's fools speak with an English accent and talk of native concerns.

Various kinds of irrational behavior are dramatized by Morose, the Collegiate Ladies, and the buffoon-courtiers. By way of contrast, rational, natural behavior is represented in Sir Dauphine Eugenie. Even the Collegiate Ladies recognize his health. His interesting name means *well-born heir*, and he conducts himself in accord with it. His manner has the authority that one may expect of the well born, and he has an aristocratic

---

10. Jonas A. Barish, *Ben Jonson and the Language of Prose Comedy* (Cambridge: Harvard University Press, 1960), p. 169. Barish's discussion of Truewit deserves some comment. Everyone will agree that "Truewit is unmotivated by the itch for gain or by moral fervor," and that he "remains master of his [world], because he never ceases to keep one foot planted solidly in the real world" (p. 156). Not everyone thinks, however, that he "resembles a disembodied intelligence flickering over the action and lighting up its dark corners" (p. 157). Nor will everyone agree that Truewit "sees the vanities of life as plainly as Morose, [but] differs from Morose in that instead of recoiling furiously from them, he accepts them as a game that men are doomed to play" (p. 177). Barish makes Truewit more of an intellectual than Jonson's text will bear. The young man is resourceful, but no speech of his gives evidence of the critical intelligence attributed to him. He "stalks folly purely for the pleasure of the chase, staking nothing but his wit" (p. 177). He does not speculate about life's vanities.

indolence. Lady Haughty says that "sir Dauphines carelesnesse becomes him" (IV. vi. 36–37). Though he has cause to be annoyed with Clerimont when his friend tells Truewit of his secret plot against Morose, he controls himself. Anger is beneath his dignity. He shows even greater restraint when he has brought his willful uncle to terms, and promises that "I will not be so vn-reasonable" as to abuse his advantage (V. iv. 176). Not averse to scheming when scheming is necessary, he rarely indulges in chicanery for its own sake. He enjoys a practical joke inaugurated by somebody else, for he is no prig. At home in the court—Morose makes some point of title (II.v)—he remains uncontaminated by courtly affectation. Dauphine's friend, Clerimont, lacks judgment and perseverance, and is rather colorless. And Truewit, the third gay young man, is an opportunist and a troublemaker. Dauphine alone has integrity. His character is pivotal, and the depravity of the fools is made obvious by his sanity.

Truewit has attracted critical attention ever since Dryden, and perhaps because of him. Though Dauphine allows Truewit to work on his behalf, their relationship is not that of equals. As his social superior he does not confide in Truewit or treat him with full respect. Negligently indulgent of his foibles and irresponsibilities, he rescues him when, hurrying into action without taking thought, Truewit tries to gull the courtiers and the Ladies. The *wit* in Truewit is like the *wit* in Lovewit: it means cleverness, not wisdom, and indicates that its bearer is a prankster. Truewit's historical affinities are with certain Vice figures in the Tudor drama, like Mischief in *Mankind*. Mischief—he is surely brother to Tyl Eulenspiegel —is a type of character ubiquitous throughout the century, who indulges in practical joking out of a desire for present laughter. A figure in farce primarily, he is not to be taken with any degree of seriousness. Rather he is an object of fun. When Truewit sets out to abuse Morose before considering the consequences of his conduct, he acts like the.tribe of Mischief and shows his ancestry. Subsequently in the seventeenth century, Truewit's literary progeny rise on the social scale to become the young wits of Restoration comedy. Dryden might have been surprised at the humble origins of his gentlemen.[11]

In organization *The Silent Woman* is a good deal like *Every Man in his Humour*, differing from it chiefly in being simpler. In both plays young men set out to "correct" an older man's failings. Dauphine is older and more mature than Young Knowell, and Clerimont is less reliable and less attractive than Wellbred. Dauphine and Clerimont are serious about their undertaking as Young Edward and his friend never need to be; but

11. Ker, ed. I, 86; Herford and Simpson, XI, 517.

Dauphine and his friends are wittier than their counterparts—this is Dryden's chief reason for admiring them. Their urbanity, however, is not carefree. Should Dauphine be disinherited, his future at best will be unlovely (see II.v.88–131), and so he laughs in the face of serious vicissitude. The associates of the young men differ from the earlier collection, too. Old Knowell is a healthy innocent compared to Morose, Brainworm a shrewder and less witty Truewit, and Bridget a colorless pawn compared to Epicoene. Matthew and Cob and Bobadill all have their rather childlike charms, and sometimes they earn our affection; but La Foole and Daw, the Collegiate Ladies, and the Otters are not so innocent. In them human possibilities are suggested which one would like to be able to deny. They border the nefarious.

For all its laughter, this is farce raised to a philosophical level. It is a grimly serious play which exposes moral disease. With uncompromising secondhand materials, Jonson comments on the ugliness of human beings and our propensities to evil. *The Silent Woman* continues the ideas and dramatic methods which Jonson has been using since early in his career. With its multiple plots related primarily by theme, it is structurally Elizabethan and in gaiety it recalls Jonson's earlier, unreformed comedy. His sympathy for the young men, his general tolerance of high spirits, and his delight in prankishness for its own sake recall the older kinds of romantic drama. Only when we take thought do we see that this play, like *Volpone*, opens the door into darkened, interior chambers of the mind.

The Silent Woman has affinities with the Bible as well as with the morality plays. This is a variation on the story of the Prodigal Son, freshly told. Jonson's play and the parable both deal with gay young men estranged from their elders: they tell of young men returning from escapades which have devoured their livings to be received into the family bosom. The tale of the Prodigal is constantly recurring in Tudor drama; a recent, conservative historian of English religious drama has said again that these numerous plays "form an important element in the sixteenth-century biblical drama in England."[12] *The Silent Woman* may be compared to the contemporaneous *A Trick To Catch the Old One* (1604–1606?) by Middleton, a less complicated prodigal play. The central situation is the same in both. A young man about town, anxious to retrieve his position with a rich uncle, maneuvers him into providing a present living and a future legacy by artful use of marriage contracts. Witgood, the Dauphine of Middleton's play, is repeatedly identified as a Prodigal, and many times the uncle is accused of "unnatural" behavior because he has abused his heir. Jonson

12. Hardin Craig, *English Religious Drama of the Middle Ages* (Oxford: Clarendon Press, 1955), p. 366.

and Middleton start with the same material: unnatural uncles, disinherited and free-wheeling heirs, marriage arrangements through which they are restored to their own. The plotting of *A Trick To Catch the Old One* is as skillful as that of *The Silent Woman*; indeed it is more skillful than Jonson's, in spite of Middleton's neglect of the unities of time and place. All except one of the strands of Middleton's play are joined to a single dramatic situation; the two extraneous scenes, both involving Dampit, a drunken usurer, were no doubt added to provide a part for some actor. In contrast, the underplots of *The Silent Woman* are, as we have seen, thematically but not dramatically linked to the basic action. If we mean by "classic," neat and orderly arrangement of parts around a single idea, we must conclude that Middleton is as "classical" as the erudite Jonson. Indeed Middleton has united theme and action better even than Jonson.

Many of the differences between these Jacobean plays and the basic Biblical story recall Terence: the Prodigal Son of the morality plays is the Prodigal Nephew of the Roman plays, and Dauphine's intrigues are rather similar to Roman intrigues. The character of Truewit may owe something to the clever Roman slave, Syrus of *Heautontimorumenos*, for example, and the trick revelation of Epicoene may be Jonson's sophisticated version of the ubiquitous Roman device of mistaken identity. But the moralities had assimilated the Latin plays long before Jonson's generation. Tudor schoolmasters had adapted Terence to their didactic purposes, as is well known; in their hands the standard Terence plot had become reminiscent of the Scriptural Prodigal. *The Silent Woman* and *A Trick To Catch the Old One* are examples of this "Christianized Terence."[13]

The Middleton play is much less thoroughly Christianized than the

13. Madeleine Doran, *Endeavors of Art: A Study of form in Elizabethan Drama* (Madison: University of Wisconsin Press, 1954), pp. 160–166.

General note: When Stefan Zweig adapted *The Silent Woman* for opera in 1924, he completely removed this central Prodigal theme and the subplots. Dauphine, now called Henry, sinks into a secondary position, and Epicoene, now a woman and Henry's wife, comes to the center of the action. Morose is made quite sympathetic, and touching. He suffers from a physical rather than a moral malady: his ship, blowing up under him, broke his eardrums. As a result he is in discomfort with the slightest noise. This discomfort is aggravated by loneliness. Zweig sentimentalizes Morose, for he turns him from a self-righteous martinet into a pathetic solitary. In Zweig's version he is more a victim of his nephew's caprice than of his own pride, and we may shed a tear over him if we like. As characters in opera go, he is interesting even if nothing like so interesting, and so virile, as the original from which he is diluted. Zweig turns the whole action into a rather pointless practical joke which he rescues from the painful through the charm of his characters. The result of Zweig's work and Strauss's music is an appealing comic opera, but Jonson's central dramatic situation has been perverted and its moral purpose gutted. One should not complain. *Die Schweigsame Frau* is a music-drama, not a play, and it is German.

Jonson, and the disparity between them is not tectonic but moral. This is what defines the true nature of Jonson's play: his moral position is lucid, Middleton's confused and dark. From the beginning of *A Trick To Catch the Old One* Witgood's sins have been more than venial; he has betrayed a young woman and reduced her to whoredom; now he tricks Walkadine Hoard into marrying her. He uses everybody he knows to improve his own financial state. All things considered, he is an unlovely specimen, and though he takes an oath at the end of the play to repent, he does not convince us that he has changed. His uncle, Pecunius Lucre, is no better; he has used the young man outrageously. He has seized Witgood's property though his mortgages were much less than the value of the lands; and when he returns the land, he does so only because there seems to be more money in forgiving than in withholding forgiveness. Witgood and Pecunius Lucre live in a hard and irrational world.

Jonson's world is not easy, but it is orderly. Dauphine and Morose belong to a different order of characterization from Witgood and Lucre, for they are representations of ideas, like the dramatis personae of the morality drama. Where we are intrigued by the psychology of Middleton's people, we pay our attention in Jonson to the ideas to which his characters give rise. Morally Middleton's play is unresolved. We never can make up our minds how we are supposed to react to the persons and situations, because Middleton himself has apparently not made up his own mind: he asks us to accept as honorable what a moment later he condemns. Jonson's play, on the other hand, is built on bedrock. There is never any doubt what he thinks is right and wrong. He might admire a rogue and be amused by a scoundrel, but he never attempts to tell us that a rogue is not a scoundrel. While his plays are more ordered and more thoughtful than many earlier English comedies, they are not unique in these respects; such Jacobean contemporaries as Middleton were often as orderly as he. His play may be a farce, its situations preposterous, its characters out of an artificial world; nevertheless, the fact remains that *The Silent Woman* rings true because it is consistent and reasonable and dramatizes a single ethical view. In it Jonson preaches a variety of Christian humanism whose roots extend into the classical past even while it flowers in English. Jonson may be at home in his Elizabethan-Jacobean world, but he is superior to it. This is a farce by a thoughtful man reaffirming conventional values, and it has its debt to religion.

2. *The Alchemist*

The Alchemist appeared in 1610, only a year after the first production of *The Silent Woman*; but *The Alchemist* was a dramatic success and it has retained its popularity ever since. In the eighteenth century Garrick played Abel Drugger, receiving such acclaim that the play passed into the folklore of the time. Later, Dickens considered playing Sir Epicure Mammon and conducted a couple of rehearsals. Lay readers, insofar as Jonson has lay readers, probably prefer *Volpone* to this play, and one can understand why. *The Alchemist*, the most Jonsonian of Jonson's plays, is pure drama in the sense that Bach is pure music and Velasquez is pure painting. One is interested in it at least at first because of its theatricality. Shakespeare has some rewards for every interest: characters, stories, poetry, philosophical speculation. Jonson offers the aesthetic rewards appropriate to drama. As a matter of curiosity, one wonders if the pleasure one takes in Jonson's plays is not an index of the pleasure one takes in drama as drama. If one does not enjoy *The Alchemist*, one is likely to be enjoying the theater for qualities not essentially of the theater. While one ought to take one's pleasure where it is to be found and be thankful, it seems only decorous to respond to a work of art, a picture or a string quartet or a play, according to its peculiar rather than its accidental excellences. If we are to understand *The Alchemist*, we need to regard it as an artifact, an object made from the materials of life which makes a comment on life but is not itself an imitation of life. This is an unrealistic play, in all but the most superficial respects. Parts of its full action may be extracted for easy analysis, but the play must be regarded as a unit, and as a drama, if we are to see its full brilliance.

It is well known that Coleridge listed *The Alchemist* with *Oedipus Tyrannos* and *Tom Jones* as the three most perfect plots in literature.[14] This is rather strange when we stop to think of it, for *The Alchemist* is really more an intrigue than a plot. Plot implies development, either of character or of idea or of both; intrigue suggests multiplicity of events rather than complication of theme. Like farces from *The Clouds* to *Charlie's Aunt*, *The Alchemist* is a series of redundant comic incidents. They are independent of one another in that they are not interrelated, each contributing a share to a central startling revelation. The play's theme is implicit in each episode, and each episode summarizes the whole. As a result, it is likely to seem more a collection than a development. It may even seem more miscellaneous than it is. Una Ellis-Fermor has understandably called it "one of the most complex group of plots in English comedy."[15] Because many persons rush on and off the stage in rapid

14. *The Complete Works of Samuel Taylor Coleridge*, W. G. T. Shedd, ed., (New York, 1854), VI, 426.

15. Una Ellis-Fermor, *The Jacobean Drama* (London: Methuen and Co., 1936, 1953), p. 115.

AN ELIZABETHAN BROTHEL

Showing rear garden and bower, moat and drawbridge, guard and madam. From the *Roxburghe Ballads*.

succession, the reader tends to confuse the various intrigues. But it is much easier to keep them straight when we see the play on the stage. The action is nowhere nearly so involved as it might at first appear, and in some respects it is much less complex than the romantic Elizabethan comedies which trouble nobody. The incidents here are arranged according to a simple pattern common in farces. Once we perceive it, the "complexity" disappears.

The play begins with a long first scene in which we see that Face and Subtle, aided by Dol Common, have set themselves up as confidence men. There are two important story points in this first scene: first, the game is played in the house of Face's master while he is away in the country; and, second, the alliance between the scoundrels is very precarious. We know from the beginning that they will turn on each other at the first opportunity, and during the course of the action we are reminded from time to time of the precarious yoking. With this necessary exposition out of the way—the scene is given dramatic tension by the quarrels among the principals—the play whirls immediately into a merry-go-round of activity. We are introduced in successive scenes to Dapper (I.ii), who aspires to be a gambler; to Drugger (I.iii), who wants to be shown how to get rich quick; to Sir Epicure Mammon (I.iv), who is accompanied by Surly and who wants to be richer than God. In Act Two the parade of gulls continues with Ananias (II.iv), the Anabaptist who wants the property of his church turned to gold. Only one other set of characters is introduced after this parade: Kastril (III.iv), who wants to be taught to be a Roaring Boy. Kastril is accompanied by his sister, the rich widow Dame Pliant. All of these persons come to Subtle and Face as clients. All of them except Kastril want to make money more quickly than can be managed legitimately.

Jonson's dramatic technique is obvious: it is duplication. As in fairy stories and nursery tales, a single kind of dramatic conflict is reiterated with variable characters. In the story of the Three Pigs, for example, three times the Wolf has occasion to cry, "I'll huff and I'll puff and I'll blow your house in." In Billy Goat Gruff, the Troll says repeatedly, "Who is that trip-trip-tripping on my bridge?" and in The Three Bears, somebody is always asking, "Who has been sitting in my chair?—eating my porridge?—sleeping in my bed?" Similarly Face and Subtle are approached five times with five similar requests. In The Alchemist our interest is with the scoundrels rather than with the victims, as is the case generally in the nursery stories, but the pattern of action is the same. Altogether the plotting of The Alchemist is hardly "complex"; it consists of a number of duplications of a single nursery situation. Compared to this, *A Midsummer Night's Dream*, with its cross allegiances and complicated identities, is a labyrinthine confusion.

The difference in the duplicated stories is not in the variation of the basic pattern of action but in the degree of gravity of the problem. As each new situation is introduced, its protagonist appears more corrupt than those previously introduced, and he introduces a more profound moral problem. We meet the various gulls in a descending order of moral depravity. Dapper, the first applicant for Face's illicit assistance, wants to win at gambling, but no worthy man is hurt thereby. Drugger, client number two, wants to attract customers by trickery; gullible but relatively innocent customers are the losers. Sir Epicure Mammon, client number three, by aspiring to unlimited power promises to corrupt the world and all its people. Ananias and Tribulation Wholesome, in bringing the property of the orphans to be transformed to gold, are already corrupted; they are hypocrites and sophists.

In all their appearances, each of the five groups of characters is kept artfully and marvelously separated from all the others; if these situations were historical rather than dramatic, Ananias, Sir Epicure, Drugger, and Dapper could not be kept from meeting. The situations dealing with Dapper, Drugger, Sir Epicure Mammon, and Ananias are each handled separately and reach their climaxes independently. Our interest alternates among them. Dapper, who wants to gamble, after Act I, scene ii appears again in Act III, scene v; then he is bound and gagged and "laid aside" for the rest of the play. Even in Act III, scene v he is only momentarily our exclusive concern. Our experience with Drugger, the tobacconist, is similar. After this introduction, he reappears alone only in Act II, scene vi, promising to bring Kastril and Dame Pliant to the gullers; thereafter he never holds the center of the stage. He is, in effect, dropped. Sir Epicure, after his spectacular entrance (II.i,ii,iii) repeats his Godlike aspirations only once, in Act IV, scene i; and then in Act IV, scene v he is gulled and dismissed. The fifth group of characters also appears only a few times. After a lengthy introduction of the Puritans (II.iv,v) we see them again in Act III, scenes i and ii (only one scene separates these two appearances) and then we are through with them until their brief appearance at the end of the fourth act. Kastril, the only remaining character, after his delayed introduction (III.iv), appears only twice in Act IV; Dame Pliant is completely passive and is more a piece of furniture than an actor. Jonson uses a single technique throughout: first an introduction, then an interval of neglect, finally the gulling. This duplication of action is a triumph of dramatic artifice; but it is not complicated. A simple situation is repeated five times. One must not mistake quantity for complexity.

There are two plot elements which I have passed over because they seem rather unlike the five situations which I have been discussing. One deals with Surly and the other with Lovewit. Surly alone sees through the rogues' pretensions. Introduced in the company of Sir Epicure, his sullen matter-of-factness only heightens his companion's flights of fancy. After this introduction, like the others we see him only once more, in Act IV, scenes iii and iv, when he attempts to gull the gullers. Surly's part differs from the other five in that whatever crossplotting the play contains comes through him. He tries the disparate elements together. And yet even when he tries to expose Subtle and Face to the others (in IV.vii), the five plot lines are separated. Surly deals first with Dame Pliant and Kastril, one at a time, and then the scene reintroduces independently and successively Drugger, Ananias, and, in the last act, Lovewit. Right down to the end of the fourth act Jonson juggles his five plots, never allowing their actions to become tangled, scarcely allowing them to intersect. Surly does not confuse the various lines, and his part in the play duplicates the parts played by the other five.

Lovewit is the only remaining character not accounted for. He appears exclusively in Act V. When it begins, the confidence men have been successful: they have driven out Surly, gulled Sir Epicure, swindled the Puritans, reduced Drugger to messenger service, taken in Kastril, arranged to marry the Widow Pliant to one of themselves, and disposed of and forgotten Dapper. They have every expectation of total success. At this point Lovewit, the owner of the house, returns. Now the dramatic conflict shifts. During the first four acts, Face, aided by Dol and Subtle, has attempted to take in five successive groups of gulls. The principal conflict has been Face versus the gullible. Now Face at last is in conflict with Lovewit, and he is on the defensive. The first two scenes of the last act outline the new antagonism; the third resolves it by forcing Face to throw himself on his master's mercy. During these first three scenes the earlier conflict of rascals versus gulls has been momentarily set aside. Now in Act V, scene iv the old conflict is reintroduced and for a moment Face is once again on the offensive. Dapper is cozened, just as the others have been; the scene restates the principal earlier conflict of the play. It ends with a sharpening of the implicit antagonism between Face and Subtle which has existed from the very first.

Thus by the end of Act V, scene iv, Face must complete the swindling of the hostile crowd of Sir Epicure, Ananias, Surly, and Kastril; he must hoodwink Dol and Subtle; and he must reconcile Lovewit. The conflict, which was single, is now triple. First, Face disposes of Dol and Subtle by threatening them with the police. This is easy. Next he turns to the gulls. Suddenly they all appear on stage simultaneously, for the only time in the play. Even now, however, they are a collection, not a group. In a brilliant maneuver Face recovers from their attacks and, thanks to Lovewit, comes off scotfree. But though the avaricious fools are thus finally losers, in Lovewit Face has met his match. And yet we leave the play unconvinced that Face will suffer much or for long; Lovewit had best watch his step. Given a chance, Face will play Mosca to Lovewit's Volpone.

For all the multitude of detail, the play has no development; each character and each action remains at the end substantially what it was at the beginning. Interestingly enough, Subtle, Face, and Dol change costume for each of the six intrigues. Subtle appears as a fortune teller to Drugger, as a "priest of Faery" to Dapper, in the gown of an "innocent father" to Sir Epicure, in street clothing to the Puritans. Dol dresses as a Great Lady for Sir Epicure, as the Queen of Faery for Dapper. Face is "Captain" to Dapper, Drugger, and Surly, is Lungs or *Ulen* to Sir Epicure, is a servant to Ananias and Kastril, is Jeremy the butler to Lovewit. These costumes separate the intrigues from one another and help the audience to keep them straight.

The Alchemist needs to be read as a play, not as a narrative. We need to visualize it on a stage. Our interest is kept up by Jonson's manipulation of his material even more than by the material itself. The action does not develop; it constantly accelerates, and this increasing speed fascinates. (The Cambridge *History* says, "What most discourages the reader of Jonson is the absence of charm."[16]) The pace of acceleration is uniform.[17] Each new incident calls for faster thinking on the part of the cony catchers, comes closer on the heels of its predecessors. It is like watching an expert juggler who tosses up a couple of balls, then three, then four, then snatches up the bowl that held them, then the table on which the bowl rested, then the rug on which the table stood, keeping all the collection in the air at once, whistling a bit of three-part dissonance from a Bartok quartet, his eyes, all the while, closed. There is an element of stunt in *The Alchemist*, and Jonson's stunt depends on its redundancy.

Since the formal arrangement of *The Alchemist* is repetition and its characters are uncomplicated, one is tempted to think the play a kind of elaborate syllogism. This view seems justifiable when we look at it dramaturgically, for the play has an admirable, rational clarity in outline. But a play is more than its architecture. Face's world is not nearly so

---

16. Ashley H. Thorndike, "Ben Jonson," *Cambridge History of English Literature*, A. W. Ward and A. R. Waller, eds. (New York: University Press, 1910) VI, 30.

17. Cf. Ellis-Fermor, pp. 45–46.

crepuscular as Prospero's perhaps, but it has its relationship to the half world of suggestion. In 1610, some months before producing *The Alchemist*, Jonson wrote to Prince Henry, his scholarly young patron: "... a *Writer* should always trust somewhat to the capacity of the *Spectator*."[18] One will recall that Jonson had said in the Prologue to *The Silent Woman* (1609) that

> Our wishes, like to those (make publique feasts)
> Are not to please the cookes tastes, but the guests. (8-9)

His views had been tempered since the days of the satirical comedies; he was now convinced that the clever writer exploits the prejudices of his audience. He goes to them before he can expect them to come to him. The remarks to Prince Henry continue: "... a *Writer* should always trust somewhat to the capacity of the *Spectator*, especially at these *Spectacles* [i.e. court masques]; Where Men, beside inquiring eyes, are vnderstood to bring quick eares, and not those sluggish ones of Porters, and Mechanicks, that must be bor'd through, at euery act, with Narrations." The assumptions of Jonson's day being different from our own, what "capacity" could Jonson "trust" to? One may properly ask, How should the attitudes of Porters and Princes to the occult and to alchemy influence their understanding of *The Alchemist*?

The Alchemist is a satire of the gullible and the sharks who take the gullible in; it uses alchemy, and the occult generally, as the means of exposing them, but Jonson does not attack the occult in itself. He may or may not have thought it possible to turn base metals into gold; his masque *Mercury Vindicated from the Alchemists at Court* (1616) is evidence that he did not, but he satirized Subtle for pretending knowledge which he does not possess. He attacks the scheming, not alchemy.[19] We come from the play exclaiming, How clever Subtle is! not, How false alchemy is! Indeed Jonson "trusts" in the "capacity" of his *Spectators* to give the validity of alchemy some credibility. The effect of the play depends on their belief—or half belief at least—in the occult.

For Jonson's contemporaries the diameter of knowledge was small, and the imagination was free to furnish a vastness with possibilities. Travelers from new worlds could describe fantastic beasts, and others could search for fountains of youth. The winter lives of summer birds

---

18. *The Masqve of Qveenes*, ll. 105 ff.; Herford and Simpson, VII, 287.

19. Cf. Bertil Johansson, *Religion and Superstition in the Plays of Ben Jonson and Thomas Middleton* (Essays and Studies in English Language and Literature, ed. S. B. Liljegren, VII, 1950), 251 and passim, and Edgar Hill Duncan, "Jonson's *Alchemist* and the Literature of Alchemy," *PMLA*, LXI (1946), 699–710.

AN ELIZABETHAN LABORATORY

Woodcut in Conrad Gesner, *The newe iewell of health*, translated by George Baker (1576), fol. 39.

"There are virtues in things, which belong not to any element. They are called hidden properties, because their causes are hidden so that man's understanding is not able in any wise to find them out. Wherefore the philosophers have attained to a very great part of them by long experience more than by the search of reason." *Batman vppon Bartholome* (1582), fol. 169v.

and the name Achilles took when he hid himself among women were, to Sir Thomas Browne, equally unknown. The violence of storms could not be explained, nor the sudden madness of domestic beasts. When the old man in *Macbeth* finds storms portentous of unnatural evil, he is not "poetical": his very air was alive with significances not realized, now lost. "Of all the common and familiar subjects of conversation that are entered upon in company of things remote from nature and cut off from the sense," Pierre LeLoyer wrote in 1586, "there is none so ready to hand, none so usual, as that of visions and Spirits, and whether what is said of them is true. It is the topic that people most readily discuss and on which they linger the longest because of the abundance of examples, the subject being fine and pleasing and the discussion the least tedious that can be found."[20] The Elizabethans and Jacobeans had not yet ruled out the possibilities of spiritual influence on the physical world. Their world was both richer and more frightening than ours.

They lived, one might say, in a tiny clearing in a great ignorance. Witches were abroad. In nearby Scotland between 1590 and 1597 nests of creatures in league with the devil had been found out and destroyed. Rumors of occult activities on the continent must have reached the sluggish ears of Jonson's mechanics. Reginald Scot reported in 1582 that "great princes [on the continent] mainteine & give countenance to students in those magicall arts. . . ."[21] and it must have been common knowledge that in the province of Lorraine alone some nine hundred wretches were burned for witchcraft between 1580 and 1595.[22] The fever extended to England. Elizabeth's law of 1563 prescribed the death penalty for all who "use, practise, or exercise invocations or conjurations of evil and wicked spirits to or for any intention or purpose," and James's law of 1604 reaffirmed and to some degree stiffened the penalty for practicing sorcery. One of the chief historians of witchcraft in old and New England has said that "the last few years of Elizabeth's reign abounded in witch-prosecutions and were marked by intense popular excitement on the subject."[23]

20. Translated by Z. Jones in 1605. Quoted in "Introduction," Lewes Lavater, *Of Ghostes and Spirites Walking by Night* 1572, J. Dover Wilson, ed. (Oxford: Printed for the Shakespeare Association at the University Press, 1929), p. x.

21. Reginald Scot, *The Discoverie of Witchcraft* (1582) Montague Summers, ed. (London: J. Rodker, 1930), XIII, XIX, 178.

22. "Introduction," George Gifford, *A Dialogue Concerning Witches and Witchcrafte* (1593) Beatrice White, ed. (London: Published for the Shakespeare Association by H. Milford, Oxford University Press, 1931), p. v.

23. George Lyman Kittredge, *Witchcraft in Old and New England* (Cambridge: Harvard University Press, 1929), pp. 282, 283, 289.

To Jonson's porters the occult was not ludicrous, nor was it ludicrous to the authorities. It was dangerous. In 1603 the Convocation of the Church "passed a canon establishing that no minister, or ministers, should in future attempt to expel any devil or devils, without the license of his bishop."[24] The proscription against invocations of spirits suggests that they were fairly common. Only two years before the appearance of *The Alchemist* Dr. Simon Reade, a cunning medical practitioner of Southwark, was brought to trial for invoking the spirits of "Heavelon, Faternon, and Cleveton." Through their aid he hoped to locate the £37 10s. which had been stolen from one Toby Matthew (not apparently the recusant son of the Archbishop of York, though that Toby Matthew was perfectly capable of dealing in the occult). Jonson refers to the Reade affair in his play (I.ii.17ff). Reade was pardoned upon confession that his conjurations were an attempt to gull this poor Toby; but one can wonder if he thought, at the time of the conjuration, that his actions were the humbug he later claimed. The bishops, the people, and the exorcists all assumed that spirits were about.

And they had their authorities. Between 1566 and 1620 some fifty pamphlets and books dealing with witchcraft were published in England.[25] The most famous is of course King James's *Daemonologie* (1597; republished 1603), in which the King defends the belief in the existence of witches and describes occult conjurations, contracts, and practices. He gives an account of various kinds of conjurations and spirits, including the *Succubi* which are named in *The Alchemist* (I.ii.48). The King's book is important because it gives an official approval to discussions of witchcraft; the historian Gardiner says it echoes "opinions which were accepted freely by the multitude and were tacitly admitted without inquiry by the first intellectuals of the day."[26] But the skeptical Reginald Scot, against whom James directed his *Daemonologie*, delights the modern heart. In his encyclopedic attack on black magic, *The Discoverie of Witchcraft* (1584), Scot writes that "our jugglers . . . can make a more livelie shew of working miracles than anie inchantors can doo: for these practise to shew that in action, which witches doo in words and terms," and "he that can be persuaded that these things [witchcraft and sorcery] are true . . . may soone be brought to beleeve that the moone is made of

24. See, for example, in Walter Scott, *Letter on Demonology and Witchcraft* (London, 1830), p. 247.

25. Introduction, Thomas Potts, *The Trial of Lancaster Witches*, G. B. Harrison, ed. (London: Peter Davies, 1929), p. xxiv.

26. Samuel R. Gardiner, *History of England 1603–1642* (London, 1893–1895), VII, 322–333.

greene cheese."[27] From the first sentence of *The Discoverie* every rational reader feels at home with Scot, for here is a sensible man applying simple logic to what is passed off as mysterious. Great clouds of silly scholastic superstition evaporate when exposed to his common sense. It is a matter of more than passing importance that all discoverable copies of Scot's great book were publicly burned by the common hangman on James's order when he came to the English throne. Though Jonson makes no mention of it in his elaborate notes to the *Masque of Queens*, out of deference to the law and the King who had condemned it, he must have known the book. He may have been skeptical of witchcraft; but he does not say so openly. It was a bold man in those times—and in James's court—who would deny that spirits influenced the daily physical world. This common belief gives Jonson's play a dimension easily overlooked in a more scientific age: our different prejudices strip some of the suggestive implications from *The Alchemist*.

Like the belief in the spirit world, for Jonson's generation alchemy and astrology continued to be subjects of serious semi-religious inquiry. In some quarters such search was thought to be dangerously prideful, for it seemed to seek out God's secrets, but it flourished nonetheless. As James was interested in demons, the greater Elizabeth was interested in alchemy and astrology. The Queen was practical. If she could get hold of the philosopher's stone, she could ring all England round with brass; if she could turn base metals into gold, she could pay her creditors. Since the welfare of the state depended on her, she inquired into the working of the stars. The date of her coronation had been determined astrologically by Dr. John Dee, the "supreme scientific authority in England";[28] and when she considered marriage with the Duc d'Anjou in 1570, Burghley, her chief secretary, set the astrologers "to draw prognostics of what might be expected to ensue from such a marriage if it should take place."[29] Early in the reign Sir Thomas Smith, secretary of state to Elizabeth, persuaded both Lord Burghley and the Earl of Leicester to become members of a corporation devoted to experimentation in alchemy, the end of which was to turn iron into copper. Though this flier cost Burghley and Leicester each one hundred pounds earnest money and further

27. Summers ed. Book XIII, Chapter 21, 181; Book XV, Chapter V, 227. This edition, though handsome, omits the important concluding "Treatise upon the nature and substance of spirits and divils."

28. Francis R. Johnson, *Astronomical Thought in Renaissance England* (Baltimore: Johns Hopkins Press, 1937), p. 135.

29. Edward Nares, *Memoirs of William Cecil, Lord Burghley* (London, 1828), II, 534. See also John Strype, *Annals of the Reformation* (Oxford, 1824), II, 22.

"round sums" later,[30] its failure to produce results apparently did not kill Burghley's interest in alchemy. When he heard that Kelley, an English citizen in the service of Rudolph II in Prague, had succeeded in producing gold from base metal, he commissioned Dyer, the poet, to bring him home. In a rather pathetic letter to Kelley—who, incidentally, is referred to in *The Alchemist*—Burghley, now an old man, his strength expended in service of his Queen, wrote in 1591 that he wished that he "might enjoy some small receipt from you, that might comfort my spirits in mine age, rather than my coffers with any wealth: for I esteem health above wealth."[31] Edward Dyer was probably the member of the court most deeply committed to alchemy.[32]

Kelley was one of the supreme prestidigitators of all time.[33] He put off his return to England and never produced more than a touch of gold. Dr. Dee, that savant in an age of savants, had accompanied him to Central Europe; but he returned from the Emperor's court promptly on the Queen's request. On December 16, 1590 he received a visit at his home in Mortlake from Richard Cavendish, who assured him that he had royal permission "to do what I wold in philosophie and alchemie, and non shold chek, controll, or molest" him.[34] Dr. Dee was only one of Elizabeth's court alchemists. She seems to have supported one Cornelius de Alneta,

30. Strype, II, 523.
31. Strype, IV, 6.
32. "Sir Edward Dyer, a grave and wise gentleman, did much believe in Kelley, the alchymist; that he did indeed the work, and made gold: insomuch as he went himself into Germany, where Kelley then was, to inform himself fully thereof. After his return, he dined with my Lord of Canterbury, where at that time was at table Dr. Browne, the physician. They fell in talk of Kelley. Sir Edward Dyer, turning to the Archbishop, said: *I do assure your Grace, that that I shall tell you is truth. I am an eye-witness thereof, and if I had not seen it, I should not have believed it. I saw Master Kelley put of the base metal into the crucible, and after it was set a little upon the fire, and a very small quantity of the medicine put in, and stirred with a stick of wood, it came forth in great proportion perfect gold, to the touch, to the hammer, to the test.* Said the Bishop; *You had need take heed what you say, Sir Edward Dyer, for here is an infidel at the board.* Sir Edward Dyer said again pleasantly; *I would have looked for an infidel sooner in any place than at your Grace's table. What say you, Dr. Browne?* saith the Bishop. Dr. Browne answered, after his blunt and huddling manner, *The gentleman hath spoken enough for me. Why* (said the Bishop) *what hath he said? Marry,* (saith Dr. Browne) *he said he would not have believed it except he had seen it; and no more will I.*" Bacon caps the anecdote with a quotation: "Democritus said; *That truth did lie in profound pits, and when it was got, it needed much refining.*" *The Works of Francis Bacon,* James Spedding, R. L. Ellis, D. D. Heath, eds. (London, 1859), VII, Apophthegms New and Old, No. 262, 263; 162.
33. Ralph M. Sargent, *At the Court of Queen Elizabeth* (London and New York: Oxford University Press, 1935), p. 116.
34. Caroline Fell Smith, *John Dee (1527-1608)* (London, 1909), p. 224.

MAKING THE INSTRUMENTS

Woodcut in Conrad Gesner, *The newe iewell of health*, translated by George Baker (1576), fol. 115.

or de Lannoy, for a time early in her reign; and there is evidence that prominent members of the court dabbled in alchemy independently.[35] The Countess of Pembroke spent great sums on alchemy each year and even kept Adrian Gilbert, half brother of Walter Ralegh, as laborant for a time. The distinguished Oxford mathematician, Thomas Allen, was reported to be employed by Leicester as a kind of second Friar Bacon.[36] Francis Bacon's attitude toward alchemy and astrology was ambivalent. In *Sylva Sylvarus* (1627) Bacon says: "The world hath been much abused by the opinion of making of gold: the work itself I judge to be possible . . ." At another time he wrote (in *Historia Densi et Rari*): "The manufacture of gold, or the transmutation of metals into gold, is to be much doubted of." He rejected as idle superstition the doctrine of horoscopes while acknowledging that heavenly bodies influence the great cycles of history.[37] Bacon's king, James I, ruled in *Daemonologie* that *Astrologia* must not be used to foretell "what commonweales shall florish or decay: what persones shall be fortunate or vnfortunate: what side shall winne in anie battel . . ."[38]

The evidence shows that the most enlightened and powerful of Jonson's time respected alchemy and astrology and for the most part did not doubt the power of the occult. We may safely assume that the porters and mechanics for whom Jonson wrote also accepted them. "Both alchemy and astrology were associated in the popular consciousness with magic, and it was not for the layman to inquire too deeply into their mysterious procedures," Louis B. Wright has said. He continues: "Especially was alchemy a mystery subtly bound up with the smoke and soot of hell," just as astrology, he might have added, was associated with the glory and wisdom of heaven.[39] It is this mysterious, supernatural association of alchemy and the occult which casts long shadows over *The Alchemist*.

The play may be seen as a variety of forbidden fable, descending from Elizabethan progenitors. *The Alchemist* is both fabulous and Gothic, like *Friar Bacon and Friar Bungay*. It asks us to shiver in the face of the un-

35. Robert Steele, "Alchemy," *Shakespeare's England* (Oxford: Clarendon Press, 1917), I, 473.

36. *Leycesters Commonwealth* (1641), Frank J. Burgoyne, ed. (London, 1904), pp. 99–100; Smith, p. 53; Kittredge, p. 180.

37. *Bacon*, II, 448; V, 346–347; IV, 353.

38. King James I, *Daemonologie* (1597); *Newes from Scotland* (1591), G. B. Harrison, ed. (London and New York: Bodley Head Quartos, 1924), p. 13.

39. Louis B. Wright, *Middle Class Culture in Elizabethan England* (Chapel Hill: University of North Carolina Press, 1935), p. 593. See also Madeleine Doran, "On Elizabethan Credulity," *JHI*, I (1940), 151–176.

known, to shudder at the unleashing of goblins perhaps damned. Because
of science and our skeptical habits of mind, we have for the most part
grown away from a respect for the occult; we do not feel the tremor that
Jonson could count on, and it is easy, now, to think the corners of *The
Alchemist* more illuminated than they are. Both Faustus and Subtle are
ambitious in the face of a perilous unknown; and both bravely use religious
dialectic to further private passions. Each is a Prometheus who would
steal immortal fire for mortal use. The ultimate difference between
Jonson and Marlowe is that Jonson sees such high aspiration as ludicrous,
and Marlowe sees it as nearly noble. Faustus is tragic. In the last scene
of Marlowe's play, all nature gathers around Faustus. The heavens
cloud and the thunder breaks. At the conclusion of *The Alchemist* Subtle
clambers over the back fence accompanied by his whore. Faustus, for
all his medieval associations, is the product of a brain enamored with
humanistic possibilities of worldly accomplishment; Subtle, for all the
rational discipline of his drama, shows his maker's mind to be humble
and basically Christian. It is important to the theme of the play that Face
rather than Subtle should survive and prosper. Unlike Subtle, Face never
aspired to more than any clever operator could reasonably expect to
accomplish. He trimmed his sails to the wind and made no compact with
devils. And he comes through. Jonson the rationalist saw that some areas
of experience are proper for human activities; and some, if not forbidden,
give faint promise of reward. To mistake one's measure and assume oneself a god on earth is both sinful and silly; those things which are God's
should be left as God's. The human sphere was quite rich enough for
Jonson, and Prometheus held no secret charm.

But though Jonson was not himself notably religious, short as he was in
the sense of wonder and awe, he was quite capable of using religious
materials for his plays. And this is what he did in *The Alchemist*. It has
been said that this comedy is a gigantic attack on avarice, that underlying
all the actions of all the characters is an inordinate desire for gain: "Be
rich," Sir Epicure cries. The theme should not be so oversimplified. The
"meaning" is a good deal more complex. *The Alchemist* is a Christian
play: Jonson is concerned with showing how false gods may usurp the
very name and ritual of the true God. No less than *Volpone*, but in a
different way, this play deals with religious perversions. Ananias and
Tribulation Wholesome obviously hide irreligious acts under religious
cloaks. The scenes in which they speak in the accents of Old Testament
prophets accentuate their distance from the prophets and show their
meanness. To overlook the Biblical echoes in their speeches is to miss
half the fun of the satire and all of its point. The climactic scene with
Dapper also has its Christian significance; but it is not, I think, so

obvious. It depends for its ultimate success on reference to Christian ethics and rituals. In Act III scene v Face, Subtle, and Dol persuade Dapper that to earn the favor of "her Grace," the Queen of Faery—that is, to persuade her to respond to his prayerful petitions—he must "throw away all worldly pelfe" and "keepe nothing, that is transitorie" about him (III.v.17,30). The means to "grace," they tell Dapper, are the traditionally Christian humility, poverty, and obedience; but because Dapper puts these virtues to service of the wrong god they cease to be virtues and become ridiculous. The scene reads like a Tudor interlude, for here as in the morality plays the protagonist is bedevilled by demons attempting to force him into a decision. The joke is that the decision is "moral" only by a wild stretch of the imagination and that the "demons," far from being supernatural, are Dol, Face, and Subtle. The scene is a burlesque, almost a parody, of the old ritual drama.

The Ananias-Tribulation Wholesome scenes are an attack on sophistical religion; the scenes with Dapper are a burlesque of traditional beliefs turned to false purpose. The scenes with Sir Epicure Mammon also have their religious significance. Sir Epicure wants to correct that nature which is a manifestation of the Almighty; he wants to improve on God. When he cries to Surly, "Be rich," he echoes God's commandment that there be light. Subtle says of him:

> He will make
> Nature asham'd of her long sleepe: when art,
> Who's but a step-dame, shall doe more, then shee,
> In her best loue to man-kind, euer could.
> If his dreame last, hee'll turn the age, to gold.
>
> (I.iv.25–29)

Like Faustus he is drunk with the idea of power, and like Faustus the power to which he aspires is directed to no service but his appetite. Sir Epicure is not merely avaricious. In attempting to out-God God, he commits sacrilege. His is a mortal, not a venial, sin.[40]

Subtle, the alchemist, also aspires to the Godhead. He even conceives of himself as a kind of god already. Partially taken in by his own chicanery, he constantly suggests that he is more than a simple charlatan, and in the great scene of exposition (II.iii), drunk on his own pretensions, he is no longer able to distinguish between the real and the pretended. Though his philosopher's stone is a ruse, he thinks himself something of a man-

---

40. See L. C. Knights, *Drama and Society in the Age of Jonson* (London: Chatto and Windus, 1937, 1951), pp. 206–210.

maker. When he addresses Face, for instance, his words remind us of the Voice out of the Whirlwind, the incomprehensible Creator:

> Slaue, thou hadst had no name—[without me] . . .
> Neuer beene knowne, past *equi clibanum*,
> The heat of horse-dung, vnder ground, in cellars,
> Or an ale-house, darker than deafe John's: beene lost
> To all mankind, but laundresses, and tapsters,
> Had not I beene. (I.i.81,83–87)

Subtle, Sir Epicure, all the persons of the play suffer from this sin of pride. They want to turn the world to their purposes whereas they ought, in the Christian view, to seek to place themselves humbly in the service of this world's God.

So far I have simply pointed out religious overtones in some parts of *The Alchemist*. But in fact the whole play is a reworking of the Parable of the Talents: *There was a certain man who, going into the country, called his servant to him and delivered to him his house and his property which he was to keep against the master's return. With industry the servant made the property pay him great dividends; and when the master returned, he called him to an accounting. The servant in fear turned his profit over to the master, for the master reaps where he does not sow and gathers where he does not reap; and he received back his own with interest. The servant's unprofitable assistants were cast out of the house, and the profitable servant was received into the master's bosom.* This parable can be used and was used by persons like Tribulation Wholesome to defend all kinds of eccentric business practices. In the parable, the master does not inquire how the servant had increased the wealth; he does not even ask the rate of interest; he does not seem to notice the "interest" which was forbidden by traditional Christian (medieval) strictures against usury. The parable can be made to indicate that the master would have us all make money; in this view material prosperity is both a responsibility laid upon us all and a means to divine favor. The view that prosperity is *evidence* of divine favor is not dead even now. In this play Jonson gives a Puritan reading of the Bible to show up its shabbiness. Its relevance to modern times needs no comment.

The Alchemist deals with avarice, obviously; but it does so in the context of a full system of religious morality. This satire treats of more than men in their social relationships, and it is not primarily concerned with what man has made or can make of man. Jonson is not distressed that one person can and does cheat another, or that one group takes advantage of another. The rascals and the fools receive equally dispassionate handling here. What Jonson objects to is the excessive ambition which offends against God's ordering of things. Seen in this light, *The Alchemist* is a religious, not a social, tract, and it is directed against the impious rather than the antisocial. It is not, in the final analysis, a satire tied to the changing conditions of society. It comments on human aspirations and religious humility. This central religious significance is discoverable in every character and in every scene of the play. Jonson drives his point home by repetition, and it is this which organizes the plot and determines the characters. But the point is not more developed than the plot. It is stated and reiterated. Technically Jonson's great accomplishment is his economy. And when one becomes aware of it, one can get to the Christian heart of the play.

3. *Catiline his Conspiracy*

Except for a flurry of interest after the Restoration, *Catiline his Conspiracy* has never been popular on the stage, and it has never been much admired by the general reader. Playwrights in the Augustan period found inspiration in its rhetoric, and some modern critics have noted qualities in it which deserve praise; but for the most part the opinion of the first audience in 1611 has been sustained.[41] When it was first produced by Shakespeare's distinguished company, Acts I and II went well enough, Jonson tells us in a prefatory "To the Reader in Ordinairie." But the long oration in the fourth act, Cicero's attack on Catiline, did not; and the play was hooted off the stage. Never one to yield easily to popular opinion, Jonson defended *Catiline* when it appeared in quarto shortly thereafter; and he continued to think highly of it all his life. It is the latest play contained in the 1616 Folio. Written at the peak of his powers at the very time he was producing masques for the Court and the brilliant successes in the popular theater, it poses genuine problems. This practical and experienced man of the theater must have intended something when he wrote this work, but what it was is easily passed over even now. We can best comprehend the meaning of this "tragic poem," as Jonson called it, if we consider it in the light of his dramatic and thematic habits. Since comedy and tragedy for Jonson differed in degree more than in kind, his comedies and tragedies are more alike than they are different, and *Catiline* is the natural fulfillment of some tendencies long developing.

Many of the differences between *Catiline* and Jonson's contemporaneous, successful comedies are obvious. One need hardly dwell on their

41. See Robert Gale Noyes, *Ben Jonson on the English Stage 1660–1776* (Cambridge: Harvard University Press, 1935), Chapter VIII.

greater agitation of plot, their more interesting pageant of figures, their amusing references to a recognizable world of affairs. One can pass over without comment the greater immediacy of the plays laid in contemporaneous London, and one need hardly speak of the grace beyond the reach of art which lifts them above the ordinary run of things. The similarities between *Catiline* and the comedies are perhaps more significant; and some of them are not so clear.

The tone of both *Sejanus* and *Catiline* is, compared to Shakespeare and the Greeks, singularly satiric; it is like the other Jonson plays. As usual Jonson attacks women. In the second act of *Catiline*, the scene of Fulvia in her dressing room is much like episodes attacking feminine vanity in *The Silent Woman*. The later scene in which she bargains her "virtue" with Curius for the satisfaction of her curiosity could as readily have gone into one of the satires as into this tragedy. Sempronia, the other prominent woman in the play, is not treated with greater respect than Fulvia. "A states anger," Cicero says, "Should not take knowledge eyther of fooles, or women" (IV.814–815); for women, like fools, have no nobility, nor have they the possibility of tragic dignity. The male figures in *Catiline* are not worthier. All of them have as little of the grandeur of tragic drama as the characters in the comedies. If in tragedy we normally see the human being stretching to his noblest height, we must conclude that *Catiline* is not tragic. Neither we the spectators nor they the protagonists are ennobled by the trials which they undergo. We do not come away from this "tragic poem" purged of pity and terror.

Rather we come away instructed, as we are instructed in the comedies. As Jonson sports with follies—and crimes—in his comedies, he sports with them here, too, and for the same purpose: to instruct us in the good life, in the rational life. The mirror he holds up to the world selects the details it reflects, but the resulting image is true to Jonson's view of natural law. Jonson is partisan, but he does not simplify his materials to produce his desired end. He recognizes the merits of the faults he anatomizes. Though Catiline is dangerous in the extreme, finally Jonson gives him a grudging admiration: he has courage, determination, resourcefulness. And the last we hear or see of him is praise: "Who had ere fallen greater?" (V.690) we are asked. *Catiline* and Jonson's other tragedy, *Sejanus*, arrive ultimately at a triumph of right, however great the cost of the journey. But Jonson assures us that the triumph is only temporary and that shortly even greater hazards will appear. Sejanus may have been deposed, but we can expect no better government from the "strangely-cruell Macro" who succeeds him; indeed we can expect worse. When Catiline disappears, we can anticipate little generosity from the Caesar and Crassus who stand threatening in the wings. Jonson's tragedies, unlike most of Shakespeare's, do not end in repose. Of Shakespeare's major plays only *Julius Caesar* ends on so despairing a note. Having agitated our emotions through the course of the play, Jonson sends us from the theater still distraught, ready to set about correcting the evils in society. We are urged to move quickly in the world of affairs, having been shown error and its consequences. *Catiline* and *Sejanus* are moral propaganda, constructed to encourage us to civic action. Jonson implies that the dangers presented dramatically are still abroad. When *The Alchemist* is concluded, Lovewit and Face continue the confidence game that Subtle has played; when *Volpone* ends, the avocatori continue to display the avarice that the fox has exemplified. *Catiline* is like these plays. Tentative conclusions are characteristic of both the comedies and tragedies. In purpose and temper the comedies and tragedies are similar.

Certain aspects of human life and the human situation which Jonson considers in the comedies are again examined in this tragedy; the only difference is that here they are more insistently presented. In all of the major plays Jonson contemplates the depths which lie on the other side of reason. In *Catiline* and the major comedies alike we find ourselves brought to the edge of civilization beyond which chaos lies. The action of them all is lighted by the flickering of aboriginal fires. Behind the aspirations of Sir Epicure Mammon and Subtle, we see willful ignorance and terror—and reason turned to diabolism. In both *The Alchemist* and *Volpone*, men use their highest abilities to fight their way back, unashamed, into greed, violence, superstition, and death. Their action is played out before half-recognized vistas of destruction. We tremble in their presence not, as is sometimes said, because of Jonson's lack of human warmth, but because in them we see that a civilization whose hallmarks are gentleness, moderation, good sense, and love is imperiled by a perversion of what ought to secure it: reason and a benevolent human will. Jonson's world is only partially safe, because the snake of violence in it has been scotched, not killed:

> This mischiefe is not like those common facts,
> Which, when they are done, the lawes may prosequute.
> But this, if you prouide not, ere it happen,
> When it is happen'd, will not wait for iudgement.
>
> (V.522–525)

The gaiety of Jonson's comedies is achieved against threatening odds. His laughter rises in the face of an enemy wielding fire and war.

In the tragedies we catch more than a glimpse of the beast which walks in darkness. *Catiline* is not a play about history; Jonson is not writing a play for historians, nor is he attempting to correct our mistaken views of the past. He loves Rome, but London better; and what wisdom he finds among the artifacts of antiquity he pillages for home consumption.[42] He is asking us to consider the nature of statecraft, so that we may correct the errors in our own society. He does not ask us to speculate for speculation's sake. Both historical fact and political theory require our attention, but these questions transcend history and politics. They deal with the limits of human knowledge. *Catiline*, like the comedies, asks teleological questions. This play is of ideas and the subject matter is chosen to illustrate general truth.[43] Jonson's satisfaction with it must have been based on his conviction of the validity of its central wisdom. A tragic poem for Jonson was one which had the widest and profoundest philosophical importance, not one cut to a dramaturgical formula.

Critics like to point out that there are more than thirty speaking parts in this play. Though his dramatis personae are types and can be easily distinguished from one another, we do not become much involved with any of them. They are too many. Clearly labeled, each serves his function. Catiline conveniently lists some of them:

> ... dull, stupide Lentvlus,
> My stale, with whom I stalke; the rash Cethegvs,
> My executioner; and fat Longivs,
> Statilivs, Cvrivs, Ceparivs, Cimber,
> My labourers, pioners, and incendiaries. . . . (III.722–726)

Each of the thirty is supplied enough lines to give a clever actor room to move about, but motives and characteristics cannot be long anatomized in these scenes. The minor figures are variant representatives of a main idea, and our attention quickly turns from them back to the philosophical conception of which they are a part. This play contains a rhetorical, a forensic, conflict rather than a histrionic one, and its characters represent a variety of points of view surrounding a main issue. In this tragedy some of Jonson's views which have been only partially expressed in other plays get a considerably more expanded statement.

The issue of *Catiline his Conspiracy* is nothing less than the survival of civilization itself. Catiline stands for uncontrolled, superhuman ambition; Cicero represents the humbler, human virtues of prudence and moderation. Catiline would destroy what the generations have carefully built; Cicero

42. See Joseph Allen Bryant, Jr., "*Catiline* and the Nature of Jonson's Tragic Fable," *PMLA*, LXIX (1954), 265–277.
43. See Ralph Nash, "Ben Jonson's Tragic Poems," *SP*, LV (1958), 164–186.

would sustain it. At first glance Cicero strikes us as smug and self-consciously virtuous, but we quickly see that he is not a "man" so much as a collection of intellectual qualities assembled for contemplation. Through him Jonson shows us how the enemies of rationality may be resisted. From him we learn that we must call up all our reserves if we are to withstand the demonic attacks of the ambitious. Though some of these reserves are less than glorious, being human we cannot boggle; we must employ what we can. Cicero does not hesitate to exploit the vanity of silly women for worthy ends, and he knows that in the interests of the general welfare statesmen must sometimes stoop to duplicity. He knows, and we come to see, that all politics are to some degree Machiavellian, because power is by its nature corrupting. In the character of Cicero we have a dissertation on the sordid, necessary business of statecraft. Prudence must be, for statesmen, a chief virtue; because the interest of the state requires that they not attempt more than they can support. Cicero says:

> . . . we must so prouide,
> That, while we take one head, from this foule *Hydra*,
> There spring not twentie more. (IV.531–533)

Cato is Cicero's alter ego, his sounding board. A man of ferocious conscience, even he sees clearly that craftiness is necessary to successful political action: he is no sophomore. From him we learn that in a just cause there may be a legitimate occasion even for violence. Being human, we can only choose among evils, hoping that good will flourish if the worst evils be put down. Through Cicero and Cato, Jonson shows himself to be a political realist; some might call him a cynic. The difference between the good statesman and the bad, he tells us, is not the tools he uses; it is the ends which he seeks. Cato in his epitaph over Catiline points up the difference. He says:

> . . . A braue bad death.
> Had this beene honest now, and for his countrey,
> As 'twas against it, who had euer fallen greater?
> (V.688–690)

Cicero and Jonson know that we must compromise with a moderate evil if we are to eliminate a greater; that politics, however unattractive to the single-minded idealist, is a chief defense against nihilism.

Catiline, unlike Cicero, is concerned exclusively with private ambition: "By publique ruine, priuate spirits must rise" (II.362). His ambitions are violent and terrible. Worse than a Machiavelli, he gives his allegiance to nothing. His pride is unlimited and the contemplation of revolution gives him sensual pleasure. He is an arrogant sadist:

> The cruelty, I meane to act, I wish
> Should be call'd mine, and tarry in my name;
> Whil'st, after-ages doe toile out themselues,
> In thinking for the like, but doe it lesse:
> And, were the power of all the fiends let loose,
> With fate to boot, it should be, still, example.
>
> (III. 746–751)

Like Milton's Satan, he is the representation of self-assertion. Cicero maneuvers, temporizes, comes to terms with the lesser in order to avoid the greater danger. Catiline will not compromise. He wants all the world. His aspirations are inhuman and grow like great Lucifer's:

> That I could reach the axell, where the pinnes are,
> Which bolt this frame; that I might pull 'hem out,
> And pluck all into *chaos*, with my self. . . .
> Who would not fall with all the world about him?
>
> (III.175–177;179)

As Cato is Cicero's alter ego, so Cethegus is Catiline's "better Genius" (V.565). His terrible rashness underscores the drama of ruin.

> Let me kill all the *Senate*, for my share,
> Ile doe it at next sitting. . . . I shall marre more.
>
> (IV.597–599)

Catiline, Cethegus, and all their company search for new worlds to destroy:

> *Curius:*   I would there were more *Romes* than one, to ruine.
> *Cethegus:* More *Romes*? More worlds.
> *Curius:*   Nay then, more gods, and natures,
> If they tooke part. (III.594–596)

This play is no realistic picture of a vicious man and his vicious followers.[44] It is a dramatic representation of the kind of degeneration we may expect when a society breaks loose from its moral moorings. Where self-expression becomes a sole ideal, Satanicism appears. When the bold man is undisciplined by morality, patriotism, or religion, nihilism wins. Catiline represents an idea, and he is a kind of symbol of all that civilization would restrain. He is demonic in attempting to destroy Rome, which itself has

44. K. M. Burton, "The Political Tragedies of Chapman and Ben Jonson," *Essays in Criticism*, II (1952), 397–412; see esp. p. 404.

"a symbolic significance: it stands for all that is good, holy, and ordained by the true gods."[45] *Catiline his Conspiracy* is about the eternally destructive element in human nature. A great and thorough humanist, Jonson saw in the historic figure of Catiline the universal, timeless forces of violence, darkness, and death.

Though he had hinted at it, Jonson had never before explicitly dealt with the fascination of destruction. *Sejanus His Fall* deals with a different problem. "Sejanus's ambition is to form a new Rome, himself as the builder," a poet, D. J. Enright, has written, "whereas Catiline's ambition is to destroy Rome, himself as destroyer."[46] Sejanus is a Machiavellian; he weighs not men nor men's words, and might for him makes right. But destruction for its own sake does not appeal to him; though he is evil, he is not demonic. Catiline is beyond Machiavellianism, and his descent is profound.

Jonson had touched on the diabolic in a comedy, *The Silent Woman*. The character of Morose is a comic treatment of the same inclination to destruction that is treated tragically in *Catiline his Conspiracy*. Morose and Catiline turn their backs on life and prefer death. In *The Silent Woman* the destruction is symbolic: Morose would exclude himself from human society; he would separate himself from normal relationships, both family and community; for him the perfect home is the grave: it is private, silent, and dark. Catiline's rejection of life is violent. He wants the community broken. He yearns for fire and storm. Compared to him and Morose, Volpone and Sir Epicure Mammon are health itself. Whatever else may be said of them, these two are avaricious of life. They cannot get enough of it. Volpone would live several lives at once: the invalid, the Venetian grandee, the mountebank, the lover. Sir Epicure has a vision of rich and sensual worlds awaiting his purchase. Both are creative, however misdirected. They have none of the urge to destruction which is a prime force in Morose and Catiline.

The destructive elements in *The Silent Woman* are latent; one might never have noticed them without the promptings of *Catiline*. Perhaps Jonson himself did not. But as we look back from 1611 we can see a gathering magnitude in Jonson's dramatic themes. Both *Volpone* (1605) and *The Silent Woman* (1609) are concerned with the morality of the individual man, but in *The Silent Woman* the implications are larger than at first they seem. The questions raised in *The Alchemist* (1610) are related to metaphysical and theological problems: what are the limits of man's

45. D. J. Enright, "Crime and Punishment in Ben Jonson," *Scrutiny* IX (1940), 247.

46. *Ibid.*, p. 246.

knowledge? *Catiline his Conspiracy* has yet wider implications than these three plays.

The tragedy has an important and unrecognized place in the literature of the English Renaissance. Only a few decades earlier, in his overpowering *Tamburlaine* (1587?) Christopher Marlowe had dramatized the eternal appeal of the destructive. Marlowe speaks, as Kocher says, "like a prior incarnation of Nietzsche"; his is a "desire for power, unchecked by morality."⁴⁷ He is a heroic Catiline. Marlowe's thirst for revolt is not confined to *Tamburlaine*; it runs through all his plays, for his "relish for destruction is something deeper-seated than a blind juvenile infatuation: we feel it like a hot passion in *Tamburlaine*, like a cold, gloating lust in *The Jew of Malta* . . . while the very choice of a subject like the *Massacre at Paris* is no less symptomatic than that of *Edward II*," Mario Praz has written. In Marlowe, he says, one constantly finds dramatized "the revolt of reason against the shackles of custom."⁴⁸ This is precisely what Jonson discusses in his play: the revolt of reason against its own product, civilization. Where Marlowe is attracted to the violent, where he writes in the mood of the Götterdämmerung, gazing longingly back into the obscurity of passion, Jonson is rational. Destruction does not charm him, and passion uncontrolled by judgment earns no praise. *Catiline* answers *Tamburlaine*, for it presents the same psychic phenomenon, the will to destruction. But Jonson's play warns us, urges us, into another, temperate, world.

Milton no more than Jonson was charmed by destruction, though he too deals with the destructive element in human life. Lucifer, the fallen angel, like Tamburlaine, is in love with power. "Better to reign in Hell, than serve in Heav'n" (P,L.,I.263), he cries from his burning pyre. "Evil be thou my Good" (IV.110). Like both Tamburlaine and Catiline, he possesses strength of body, determination, intelligence, energy, all virtues when turned to virtuous purpose. Indeed Milton apostrophizes the devil as the true *principium individuationis*. It is paradoxical that Renaissance man in his aspiration and his confidence should end by attempting to pull down the heavens, and the earth with it, as demonstration of his strength. It is paradoxical, I say, that self-assertion should end in self-destruction, and it may be that the recent admiration for Satan tells us more about modern readers than it does about *Paradise Lost*. Marlowe's Gargantuan mind "is not content with the mere display of either gruesome or magnificent scenes; it tries to surpass itself in the evocation of the distant dream, but in vain: behind power and wealth and

47. Paul H. Kocher, *Christopher Marlowe: A Study of His Thought, Learning, and Character* (Chapel Hill: University of North Carolina Press, 1946), pp. 72, 71.

48. Mario Praz, "Christopher Marlowe," *English Studies*, XIII (1931), 213, 218.

delight it feels the grip of the infinite, the hollowness of the universe."[49]
The universe is too small to contain these Nietzschean creatures. Lucifer,
like Tamburlaine, like Catiline, would obliterate all simply to assert
himself.

Catiline his Conspiracy links *Tamburlaine* to *Paradise Lost*. All of them
deal with the attractively diabolical and the fascination of destruction.
Perhaps Kocher is right and Tamburlaine's philosophy is a new idea
under the sun:

> Nature that framed us of four elements,
> Warring within our breast for regiment,
> Doth teach us all to have aspiring minds: (II.vii.18–20)

Perhaps this particular form of rationalization is "obviously completely
outside the whole Christian development, patristic and medieval as well
as Renaissance."[50] The spirit it gives voice to is not new. Marlowe did
not invent the Satanic; its origin is coeval with man's and it is with us yet,
being a human, not an inhuman, quality and the fiercest manifestation
of passion and pride. When Calvin describes Satan, surely he describes
Tamburlaine, Catiline, and Lucifer, if indeed he does not describe an
element in us all: " . . . there doth continually approch vpon vs an
enimie, yea, an enimie that is in courage most hardie, in strength most
mightie, in policies most suttle, in diligence and celeritie vnwearieable,
with all sortes of engins plentiously furnished, in skill of warre most
readie . . ." And he continues: "For he assaileth the truth of God with
lies, obscureth the light with darknesse, entangleth the mindes of men
with errors, raiseth vp hatreds, kindleth contentions and strifes, doth all
things to this end to ouerthrow the kingdome of God, and drowne men
with himselfe in eternal destruction. Whereby appeereth, that he is of
nature frowarde, spitefull and malicious."[51]

Marlowe's novelty lies in his admiration for what all Christendom
loathed, in his entertainment of what Christian humanism sought to
expel. And he found an ally in Bacon, that godfather of the modern

49. *Ibid.*, 217; see also Mario Praz, *The Romantic Agony*, trans. Angus Davidson
(Oxford: Oxford University Press, 1933), Chapter II. See also Helen Gardner,
"Milton's 'Satan' and the Theme of Damnation in Elizabethan Tragedy," *English
Studies*, I (1948), 46–66.

50. Kocher, p. 72.

51. John Calvin, *The Institution of Christian Religion . . .* translated into English . . .
by Thomas Norton (London, 1599), I, xiv, 13, 15. See also B. Rajan, "*Paradise Lost*"
and the Seventeenth Century Reader (New York: Oxford University Press, 1948),
"The Problem of Satan," pp. 93–107. Some observations of Leo Kirschbaum's (in his
introduction to *The Plays of Christopher Marlowe* [Cleveland and New York: Meridian

world. Until Renaissance times, "knowledge was virtue"; this belief was a heritage of Greek and Judaic worlds. Until the Renaissance, men sought the truth confident that the truth would make them free—that is, free of error—and therefore good. Bacon substituted *power* for *virtue*: "Knowledge is virtue" became "Knowledge is power." The unlimited search for knowledge is justified to this day on the grounds that it makes us lords of earth and sky. Jonson and Milton acknowledge the fascination of power, but they reject it. The demonic remains the demonic for them, however "hardie, mightie, suttle or skillful in warre" it might be.

Something in all of us cries with Ezra Pound, "Pull down, I say pull down," but rational men resist. *Catiline his Conspiracy* deals with an unhappily contemporary problem. The events of the past three decades have forced us to recognize that the impulse to destruction is constant, and Dr. Harris's view that Catiline "is cruel to the limits of credibility"[52] has come to seem rather naïve. But the destructive element may be controlled, Jonson tells us, by reasonable support of principles long agreed upon. According to him we must conserve; we must

> . . . retain what our great ancestors,
> With all their labours, counsells, arts, and actions,
> For vs, were purchasing so many yeeres. (V.8–10)

In this "tragic poem" Jonson dramatizes some of the dangers against which we even now build our fortress. If the play is too rhetorical to be stageworthy, as an intellectual document it deserves respect. As a political document, it deserves study.

Books, World Publishing Company, 1962]) are relevant: "It was Luther who above all emphasized the matter of *calling*. God had appointed each Christian to a certain duty in this world. This was his calling, and he was to pursue it with might and main. One can easily see that as soon as this justification was added to economic exploitation, the birth of the modern robber baron, as full of piety as of predatory energy, would occur" (p. 32).

52. Ben Jonson, *Catiline His Conspiracy*, Lynn Harold Harris, ed., Yale Studies in English, LIII (1916), xlviii.

CHAPTER VI

Bartholomew Fair, The Devil is an Ass, and The Staple of News

IN ALL HIS PLAYS written after those included in the *Works* (1616), Jonson makes explicit use of indigenous form and substance which he had drawn on casually before. His full intellectual vigor shows itself in three of these plays, those written before his 1628 illness; but only *Bartholomew Fair* is a major accomplishment. After that Jonson became cavalier toward dramatic craft. He no longer decorated his native inspiration with marvelous festoons of baroque extravagance, and he seemed bored with tricking out his sermons in stage costume. *The Devil is an Ass* (1616) makes use of that antique morality which he had earlier turned to stealthily —or unconsciously. *The Staple of News* (1625), with its allegorical personages, harks back to the old forms too; and it contains some of the baldest statements of his conservative ethic. These plays may be failures as stage pieces, but they are in no sense dotages; Jonson dramatizes major ideas in them and they therefore reward close attention. The last plays, *The New Inn* (1629), *The Magnetic Lady* (1632), and the fragmentary *The Sad Shepherd*—this last discovered among his posthumous papers— require special consideration: they are the work of a crippled master, deep in years.

1. Bartholomew Fair

Bartholomew Fair was not included in the celebrated 1616 Folio presumably because arrangements for the Folio had been completed much earlier, in 1612 or 1613.[1] We must regret this exclusion, because it and his next two plays were full of textual blunders, some of them serious, when they were printed in 1631; it was finally offered for sale in

---

1. See Herford and Simpson, IX, 14–15. The play has recently been edited for The Revels Plays by E. A. Horsman (Cambridge: Harvard University Press, 1961); for the *Yale Ben Jonson* by Eugene M. Waith (New Haven: Yale University Press, 1963); and for the Regents Renaissance Drama Series by Edward B. Partridge (Lincoln: University of Nebraska Press, 1964).

1640. *Bartholomew Fair* was first acted on October 31, 1614. After the flat failure of Jonson's learned tragedy, *Catiline his Conspiracy*, in 1611, its great success must have been particularly welcome. The Lanthorne's comments on the puppet theater at the Fair have a relevance to Jonson's own view of the contemporaneous drama: "Your home-borne proiects proue euer the best, they are so easie, and familiar, they put too much learning i' their things now o' days" (V.i.14–16). Jonson's mild disparagement of his "home-borne proiect" is a defense of his tragedy; but the fact is, Jonson was generally most successful when he stuck closest to home: London and the native English drama.

The crowd cheered the first performance of *Bartholomew Fair* and called out "O rare Ben Jonson," the words which were to appear more than twenty years later on his tombstone in Westminster Abbey. Except for a presentation at Court the next day, the play evidently was given few if any additional performances until the Restoration. It was "so satyricall against Puritanism, they durst not [show it] till now," Pepys wrote in 1661.[2] This may or may not be true. The Puritan Milton judged it on a level with *Volpone* and *The Alchemist*, a judgment shared by Dryden. Hazlitt thought the comedy "amusing to read once,"[3] but Swinburne said *Bartholomew Fair* "must be admitted to ensure its place for ever among the minor and coarser masterpieces of comic art."[4]

Over the years the comedy has been praised as journalism whatever its reputation as drama, and social historians who give accounts of markets and public spectacles draw on it generously. As early as 1641 the anonymous author of *Bartholomew Faire or Variety of Fancies, where you may find a faire of wares, and all to please your mind* enriched his account by borrowing from Jonson; and the modern, standard *Oxford Companion to English Literature* (1932, 1946) cites it as a source too. The Fair was held annually within the churchyard of the priory of St. Bartholomew, West Smithfield, on St. Bartholomew's Day (August 24, O.S.) from the twelfth century. In Jonson's lifetime it lasted two weeks and was opened by the Lord Mayor of London. During its earlier history it was a national market, primarily for cloth; but it early became a notorious pleasure-fair as well. A court of pie-powders—that is, a local, civil judiciary—was held in it daily, as we learn from the play, in order to keep some semblance of

2. Herford and Simpson, IX, 246.

3. William Hazlitt, "Lecture II, on Shakspeare and Ben Jonson," *Lectures on the Comic Writers* (1819) in *The Complete Works of William Hazlitt*, P. P. Howe, ed. (London: J. M. Dent and Sons, 1931), VI, 45.

4. Algernon Charles Swinburne, *A Study of Ben Jonson*, in *The Complete Works of Algernon Charles Swinburne*, Edmund Gosse and Thomas James Wise, eds. (London: W. Heinemann, Ltd., 1926), XII, 43.

order. Taking it all in all, Jonson's detailed description of the goings-on in the Fair is so vivid that many readers are tempted to agree with Herford that this comedy is "of an age, and not for all time."[5]

But others disagree rather sharply. In the past two decades *Bartholomew Fair* has received extended critical attention and praise. Freda Townsend and others, seeing it as the culmination of Jonson's dramatic art, have read the other plays as preparatory to it.[6] Disagreeing with those who think "there is no hero, no dominant character, no well-defined unity of plot" in it,[7] these recent critics have tried to find an implicit thematic unity in the play. Heffner, for example, says: "The central theme is the problem of what 'warrant' men have or pretend to have for their actions," and he concludes that "the emphasis in *Bartholomew Fair* is thus on the narrow range of motives that actually govern men's actions in contrast to the wide variety of warrants which they pretend to have."[8] "Warrant for behavior" does not, as Heffner himself acknowledges, account for all the elements in the play. When we regard *Bartholomew Fair* as a sophisticated morality play, we can see that its theme is the vanity of human wishes. It is an urbane comment on various kinds of folly into which men are likely to fall. When we come from reading or seeing it, we have been reminded:

> Surely men of low degree are vanity, and men of high degree
>   are a lie;
> In the balances they will go up;
> They are together lighter than vanity. (Psalm 62,9)

It is vain, according to this play, for men to assume that by taking thought they can add one cubit to their stature or that by their own efforts they can perceive the Providential ways of this inscrutable world.

i

The plot of *Bartholomew Fair* is slight, but the play is rich in incident. On St. Bartholomew's Day the Puritan John Littlewit and his pregnant

---

5. Herford and Simpson, II, 145. For a similar opinion, see George Gregory Smith, *Ben Jonson* (London: Macmillan and Co., 1919), p. 117. For a full account of the fair itself see Henry Morley, *Memoirs of Bartholomew Fair* (London, 1859).

6. For example, John J. Enck writes (*Jonson and the Comic Truth* [Madison: University of Wisconsin Press, 1957]): "*Bartholomew Fair* stands alone in English literature, perhaps in world literature, and is purely Jonsonian" (p. 189). See also Freda L. Townsend, *Apologie for Bartholmew Fayre* (New York: Modern Language Association of America, 1947), passim.

7. Herford and Simpson, II, 137.

8. Ray Heffner, Jr., "Unifying Symbols in the Comedy of Ben Jonson," *English Stage Comedy* (English Institute Essays, 1954), W. K. Wimsatt, Jr., ed. (New York: Columbia University Press, 1955), pp. 89, 95.

wife, Win-the-Fight, accompanied by Dame Purecraft—his mother-in-law—and Rabbi Zeal-of-the-Land Busy—her suitor and their reverend elder—persuade themselves that they may righteously visit the worldly Fair. Once there they meet all variety of cut-purse, rogue, confidence man, and rascal; and they meet other visitors like themselves. Adam Overdo, the naïve Justice of the Peace who has come to discover "enormities," ends in the stocks, punished for his arrogance; and Bartholomew Cokes, the heir from Harrow o' the Hill who will buy anything offered him, is robbed and made sport of. For two hours we are treated to side-shows and byplay. The action is so various that it cannot be easily summarized; but within this variety, the play has Jonson's customary symmetry.

Bartholomew Fair might at first glance appear to be a new kind of thing among Jonson's plays, since it emphasizes multiplicity rather than neatness and is humanely warm as well as witty. But our fascination with its vivid detail obscures its rational orderliness. The play is notable for the new maneuverings of old situations and for its bravura, not for originality. There are four central intrigues, each dealing with one kind of vanity. The first, the story of Adam Overdo's vain search for justice, is the most important because it is concerned with the largest issue. The second might be called Bartholomew Cokes and the Vanity of Appetite; the third, Littlewit and the Vanity of Human Wit; and the fourth, Zeal-of-the-Land Busy and the Vanity of Religious Certainty. The story of Quarlous and Winwife and their search for rich wives constitutes a minor plot, but these two personages are almost as much choric characters as they are participants in the action. Variants of the five plots have appeared before in Jonson's plays; an intellectual before he was a dramatist, Jonson had a critical rather than a creative imagination.

His use of the chorus shows his lack of originality. Such commentators as Quarlous and Winwife have appeared in other Jonson plays, *Every Man Out of his Humour*, for example. Jonson tried in that play to give a panoramic view of society like that he gives in *Bartholomew Fair*, and Cordatus, who "has the place of a Moderator," and Mitis, who "is a person of no action" to whom Cordatus talks, explained the action; their presence was evidence that Jonson was unsure that his critical point could be made clear through drama alone. Similar choric characters appear in *Cynthia's Revels* and *Poetaster*, but in these later plays they are variously integrated into the intrigues. Like Cordatus and Mitis they comment, but unlike them they participate. Quarlous and Winwife both scheme and judge the schemers: the two of them plot to marry Grace Wellborne, ward of Adam Overdo, or Dame Purecraft, the rich widow;

GAMING IN A BROTHEL

From the *Roxburghe Ballads*.

"Who would imagine that in a kingdom so fertile in all sorts of wholesome discipline there should grow up such rank and such pestilent beds of hemlock—that in the very heart of a state so rarely governed and dieted by good laws there should breed such loathsome and such ulcerous impostumes—that in a city so politic, so civil and so severe, such ugly, base and bold impieties dare show their faces? What an army of insufferable abuses, detestable vices, most damnable villainies, abominable pollutions, inexplicable mischiefs, sordid inquinations, horrible and hell-hound-like-perpetrated flagitious enormities have been here mustered together!" Thomas Dekker, *The belman of London* (1608), sig. I 1 r.

but they identify themselves as observers too (II.v). The sensible Grace Wellborne says: "you are reasonable creatures, you have vnderstanding, and discourse" (IV.iii.35–36). Throughout the play they guide our judgments. Like a proper chorus, they tell us that Zeal-of-the-Land Busy is a "notable hypocritical vermine" (I.iii.135–136), but they also tell us that we are not to think harshly of Cokes. In the conclusion Quarlous points the general moral: "remember you are but *Adam*, Flesh, and blood! you haue your frailty . . ." (V.vi.96–97).

Quarlous and Winwife are thus commentators of a familiar type, but they have some additional dramatic purposes to which similar choric figures had not yet been put. They help to communicate a sense of the multifarious nature of experience. Adjacent lives, though occasionally touching and even interacting, follow independent lines of action; but Quarlous and Winwife, by their almost accidental relationship to the affairs of Littlewit, Overdo, Bartholomew Cokes, and the others, show us how diverse are the strands which make up any event, and how loosely and casually connected. Further they give the play a breadth of social reference because they are of better birth, of wider experience, and somewhat deeper learning than the others. Previously the choric figure—Crites, for example, in *Cynthia's Revels*—has added intellectual implications. This chorus gives social scope as well.

Winwife and Quarlous are not the only choric characters in the play; they are only the most important ones. At one time or another most of the principal actors act as dispassionate observers of the rest. Employing a technique he has used to good effect in all the comedies, Jonson brings three or four independent groups on stage at once, where they comment on one another. These comments can be heard only by the audience. Jonson presents action, and opinions of the action, simultaneously; also and more important he again conveys a sense of the multiplicity of experience. In Act III, scene ii, for example, Quarlous and Winwife first deal with Whit the bawd; then Zeal-of-the-Land Busy appears with Dame Purecraft and the Littlewits; then Knockem introduces a bit of byplay with the ladies; then Mooncalf and Ursla, assisted by Whit, introduce another intrigue; and in the following short scene Overdo adds yet another range of experience. All of this is accomplished within some two hundred lines. In the last act (V.iii,iv) Overdo observes Grace and Winwife, who observe Cokes, who observes the puppets; in the meantime, Overdo sees the Fair people (Filch, Knockem, Edgworth, and Whit) involved with Win Littlewit and Mistress Overdo, and these two observe Waspe and Filch, who are observing Winwife and Grace. The play is constructed like a Chinese puzzle: mirror beside mirror beside mirror. In a typical scene the various groups merge and separate without communicating. The play has no conversation, because nobody listens to anybody else. Disguises are easy: people do not look at each other either. The inhabitants of this world are people isolated by their excessive concern for their own feelings —that is, by their vanity. Littlewit dotes on his young wife Win; but in his delight in his own emotion, in his sentimentality, he is oblivious to her emotion. Justice Overdo, pleased with his own shrewdness and sense of responsibility, is blind to much surrounding him that needs correction and ends in the stocks. The Rabbi in satisfying his appetites loses Dame Purecraft, the rich widow. Each is defeated by his own vanity.

The handling of the multiple intrigues of *Bartholomew Fair* is surely one of Jonson's great accomplishments. We have seen how in *The Alchemist* he introduced each intrigue independently; how, after allowing it to hold the stage for a moment, he withdrew it. Each action comes to an independent climax; and only in the final scenes are the lines of action assembled. One has throughout the play the sense of puppets manipulated by a master puppeteer; and the very arbitrariness of their movement is part of the fun. Like the action of *The Alchemist*, the intrigues of *Bartholomew Fair* come to independent climaxes, each separated from the others. Overdo's search for justice has very little to do with Littlewit's desire to see the puppets; Cokes's delight in the toys is fairly independent of Winwife's desire to marry Dame Purecraft. Each is introduced separately after careful preparation, as Dryden long ago observed. But unlike the actions of *The Alchemist*, the intrigues of *Bartholomew Fair* once introduced are not withdrawn. The stage becomes increasingly crowded as more and more persons are brought on, necessarily increasing in proximity to one another. But in spite of the numbers, the actions and the relationships remain marvelously lucid.

The lucidity of the earlier plays was achieved by isolating the various actions; the lucidity of this play is achieved by dramatic subordination. In *Volpone* Corbaccio, Corvino, and Voltore are of equal importance and are a great deal alike. They are not "flat," because their behavior is so extraordinary: no man who cuckolds himself is "simple." We see them serially and so do not confuse their slightly varying qualities. In *The Alchemist* the dramatis personae are more distinguishable, but they too blur in our memories. Drugger, Dapper, even Face and Subtle, do not survive the play as vivid individuals. The figures of *Bartholomew Fair*, however, stick tenaciously in our minds—and this is the more remarkable because we see them so briefly. Stage mannekins, they interest us because of their violent primary colors. Each figure has one or two big scenes in which he outshines everybody and then he fades into the background.

There is no need to remember what other characters participate in Ursla's scene with the hot water; she drives everybody else from our awareness. Lanthorne Leatherhead sells his toys to the simpleton Cokes; when he reappears, he is a puppeteer. Nightingale, the ballad singer, in his turn helps with the picking of Cokes's pocket, then he too withdraws. Joan Trash passes through the Fair with her gingerbread men. Each takes his turn in the spotlight and then retires, some to reappear briefly for another turn, some to remain obscure except in our memories.

Bartholomew Fair is a brilliant employment of some of Jonson's usual dramatic subject matter. Doting husbands like Littlewit appeared in the "comicall satyres"; gentlemen out for rich wives like Quarlous and Winwife can be found in *The Alchemist*; rich parvenus are everywhere, and so are eager widows and clever servant-guardians. Humphrey Waspe, the scheming servant; Knockem Jordan, the captain of the bullies; and Captain Whit, the bawd, all have their prototypes in Jonson's earlier plays. Their actions are manipulated with a confidence unmatched in English comedy. But Jonson has used both the subject matter and this scheme of organization before.

ii

The old morality plays were concerned with one theme, human salvation. Allegorically they represented the individual, as Dover Wilson says, "on its road between birth and death, beset with the snares of the World or the wiles of the Evil One."[9] In addition to being a fascinating portrait of a particular place in a particular time, *Bartholomew Fair* is also the World complete with its snares. It is Vanity Fair. When Zeal-of-the-Land Busy says, "the whole Fayre is the shope of Satan!" he tells us what we know to be true: the Fair is more than it seems to be. Here, in John Bunyan's words, "at this Fair are all such Merchandize sold, as Houses, Land, Trades, Places, Honors, Preferments, Titles, Contraries; Kingdoms, Lusts, Pleasures, and Delights of all sorts, as Whores, Bawds, Wives, Husbands, Children, Masters, Servants, Lives, Blood, Bodies, Souls, Silver, Gold, Pearls, Precious Stones and what not?"[10] If we would escape it, we must "needs go out of the *World*." Thackeray, two centuries and more later, saw the world as a fair too. Remark, he says, "the richly dressed figure of the Wicked Nobleman, on which no expense has been spared, and which Old Nick will fetch away at the end of this

9. John Dover Wilson, *The Fortunes of Falstaff* (Cambridge: University Press; New York: Macmillan Co., 1945), p. 17.

10. John Bunyan, *The Pilgrim's Progress*, James B. Wharey, ed. (Oxford: Clarendon Press, 1928), pp. 94–95.

DRINKING IN AN ELIZABETHAN TAVERN, MORALIZED
From the *Roxburghe Ballads.*

singular performance,"[11] even as the Devil carried away the Vice in the old days and Waspe threatened to carry away Cokes in our play. To Thackeray and Bunyan and Jonson, the fair was a reflection of the great, vain world. It gives us "a human world in an eternal situation, not a series of abstractions in a contrived predicament."[12] The play has nevertheless a metaphorical meaning.

From one point of view *Bartholomew Fair* is a journalistic report of contemporaneous times; from another, like the outmoded didactic drama, it is a symbolic drama of moral ideas. What those moral ideas are can be seen if the play is read in the light of a tract on moral conduct which Jonson must have known, *The Passions of the Mind in Generall* by Thomas Wright. Father Wright was probably the priest who converted Jonson to Roman Catholicism while they were both in prison in 1598,[13] and his book was written to ingratiate its author with the Anglican authorities. On its completion in 1598 it was sent off to the Bishop of London, with the assurance that it contained nothing "either against this state or present religions."[14] In Elizabethan days psychology had not yet been separated from morality, and all of Wright's analyses come at last to show that "the inordinate motions of Passions . . . are thornie briars sprung from the infected root of original sinne. . . ." His purpose was to set forth "the inordinate motions of Passions, their prevention of reason, their rebellion to virtue."[15] A Papist in a Protestant country, he examines moral behavior conventionally, carefully citing the most uncontroversial doctors of both the Anglican and Roman churches: Basil, Augustine, Paul, Jerome, Aquinas, as well as Aristotle. The book was pirated in 1601 and' subsequently reissued in 1604, with Father Wright's approval, carrying a commendatory sonnet by Jonson—the single work of prose to which Jonson contributed prefatory verse. In the next twenty-five years the book went through five editions.

The Passions of the Mind in Generall is the only treatise on moral philosophy that we can be sure Jonson read; he was generally hostile to

11. William Makepeace Thackeray, *Vanity Fair* (1847), "Before the Curtain."

12. For a contrary, conventional opinion, see Nevill Coghill, "Comic Form in *Measure for Measure*," *Shakespeare Survey*, VIII (1955), 18.

13. Theodore A. Stroud, "Ben Jonson and Father Thomas Wright," *ELH*, XIV (1947), 274–282. My quotations are from the 1604 edition of Father Wright's book; this edition carried Jonson's sonnet.

14. P. 2. See Louis B. Wright, *Middle Class Culture in Elizabethan England* (Chapel Hill: University of North Carolina Press, 1935), p. 589.

15. See also Stroud's essay, "Father Thomas Wright: A Case of Toleration," *Biographical Studies 1534–1829*, A. F. Allison, D. M. Rogers, eds. (Bognor Regis, 1951), pp. 189–219. The *DNB* is unreliable.

moral and theological tracts.[16] We know this, for he said in *Discoveries*: "Some *Controverters* in Divinity are like Swaggerers in a Taverne, that catch that which stands next them, the candlesticke, or pots; turne every thing into a weapon: oft-time they fight blind-fold; and both beate the Ayre. The one milkes a Hee-goat, the other holds under a Sive. . . . These Fencers in Religion, I like not" (ll. 1046–1050,1057).[17] Yet it was his business as a poet, Jonson wrote, to have "the exact knowledge of all vertues, and their Contraries" (*Discoveries*, ll. 1039–1040), and Father Wright's book is just such a volume as one would expect to interest him. It attempts to steer clear of the controversial issues separating the sects and churches. Professor Madeleine Doran has said that his "*ex tempore* conception of the passions was reinforced by, indeed partly grounded in, ethical tradition," which had "particular dramatic expression in the morality play. In that convention, men are viewed in general with regard more to particular passions or particular virtues and vices than to individual 'character.' The emphasis is on common humanity, all alike subject to the old Adam, or law of the flesh."[18]

If the Fair itself is representation in small of the great vain world, both the individuals who go to the Fair and those who are part of it are in one degree or another representations of aspects of Vanity, their dramatic relationships in the play dictated by the relationships of the qualities they suggest. Bartholomew Cokes, for example, passes through the world a bit like the pilgrims in Bunyan, appraising the world's offerings, yielding to the frivolous and the tawdry. He is a comic representation of the young man tried on the road to salvation; or, if this phrasing seems too theological, he is the young man whose power of discrimination is tested on the road to wisdom. In one sense or another he is in danger of losing his soul, as some of his associates in the Fair recognize:

Nightingale: His soule is halfe way out on 's body, at the game. . . .
Edgworth: . . . Talke of him to haue a soule? 'heart, if hee haue any more then a thing giuen him in stead of salt, onely to keepe him from stinking, I'le be hang'd afore my time, presently: . . .
(IV.ii.45;54–56)

16. See Herford and Simpson, I, 151. In his poem "An Execration upon Vulcan" (1625?) Jonson says he lost a valuable theological library in the fire that destroyed his books. His library reassembled after the fire apparently contained no important works of divinity. If he had been deeply read in the Fathers, scattered references would surely have turned up in his plays and poems, but in fact very few are to be found there.

17. Herford and Simpson, VIII, 595–596.

18. Madeleine Doran, *Endeavors of Art: A Study of Form in Elizabethan Drama* (Madison: University of Wisconsin Press, 1954), p. 238.

The wily ones claim that Cokes has no "soul," but we do not in the end dismiss him easily. Perhaps we find this young fool who is "for ever wantoning on the verge of imbecility"[19] sympathetic because he is innocent and without malice (IV.ii.76–78). His transport of delight at the puppet show makes us laugh as adults laugh before a child's Christmas. To the last lines of the play the carnival of the world amuses him, and we sympathize, for we are amused both at his delight and at the carnival.

Our pleasure in Cokes is heightened, I think, by his difference from Waspe, his companion-guardian. Though he is not a Puritan, Waspe possesses many of the unattractive qualities of that repressive philosophy. His pleasures are not carnal; they are worse. They are the pleasures of power masquerading as righteous responsibility; for Waspe is the kind of man who derives almost sensual delight from authority. He will injure anyone who comes near him, those of inferior station first, for they do not sting back. He is irascible because, determined to rule, he is often necessarily frustrated. While the spectacle of the foolish young man and his put-upon guardian has precedents in Jonson's plays, in Roman drama, and in native comedy, it has particular moral significance in *Bartholomew Fair*. Cokes as a simple materialist suffers from concupiscence—that is, from a passion for the world's goods. Waspe suffers from a different form of the same appetite. Waspe and Cokes are two aspects of a single fleshly weakness. Father Wright says, "It is necessary to permitte a common division of our sensuall appetite found out by experience, allowed of by Philosophers, and approved by Divines; that is, in *concupiscibile*, which in English may be termed, Coveting, Desiring, Wishing; and *irascibile*, that is, Anger, Invading, or Impugning (for so I think it might better be called). These coveting and invading appetites, are not two faculties or powers of the soule, but one onely power and facultie, which hath two inclinations" (p. 19). Cokes and Waspe are complementary. If they bore Latin names—Concupiscence and Irascibility—we would recognize them as derived from the allegorical drama. Though they are portraits of people to be seen at the Fair—or, rather, Jonson persuades us that they are—they are also representations of ideas. They are at home in the world of the flesh and in the world of ideas.

Waspe and Cokes are necessary to each other for both dramatic and intellectual reasons. Similarly what at first glance appear to be arbitrary turns of plot are actually a logical progression, relating parts of a whole. The actions are very nearly allegorical. Win-the-Fight Littlewit, for example, is drawn to the Fair by a desire to eat pig—by gluttony—and

19. W. Gifford, ed.; enlarged by F. Cunningham, *The Works of Ben Jonson* (London, 1875), IV, 509.

before she has left it, she yields to lechery, thus moving from one corporeal sin to another. "Great feasters and gullars cannot but be subiect to many vices," Wright says. "First, leacheries springeth from gluttonie, because, as their seats are neere by scituations, so they are subordinat in operation; gluttonie is the forechamber of lust, and lust the inner rooms of gluttonie; therefore all disorders and tumults raised in the former, presently are perceived in the latter."[20] Win illustrates the connection of gluttony and lechery. The relationship is even more clearly exhibited in Ursla, the "pigge-woman." But Ursla is more. She represents the triumph of the flesh. Busy identifies her: "But the fleshly woman, (which you call *Vrsla*) is aboue all to be auoyded, hauing the marks vpon her, of the three enemies of Man, the World, as being in the *Faire*; the Deuill, as being in the fire; and the Flesh, as being her selfe" (III.vi.33–37). From our first meeting with her, she seems to be extra-natural. By allying and contrasting herself constantly to hell and its demons, she invites us to see her in symbolic perspective. "I am all fire, and fat, *Nightingale*," she says, "I shall e'en melt away to the first woman, a ribbe againe, I am afraid. I doe water the ground in knots, as I goe, like a great Garden-pot, you may follow me by the S.S. s. I make." (II.ii.50–53). As Cleopatra is "all fire and air," Ursla is "all fire, and Fat . . .," and as Falstaff lards the green earth as he walks along, Ursla waters it. More explicitly than Falstaff, Ursla is the comic representation of Vanity. When she says, "I that haue dealt so long in the fire . . .," we understand doubly and are reminded of the bonfires to which she and her kind lead us. Indeed her activities recall the ancient Vice, that Vicar of Hell. Her language is abusive, she beats Mooncalf and others, she comes bearing flaming brands and smoking water. She is a "*Piller* of the *Fayre*" and gathers to herself all the qualities variously parceled out to the others: lechery, gluttony, thievery, duplicity, wantonness. It is only proper that she should sit in her chair as on a throne: "Pray thee take thy chayre againe, and keepe state" (II.iii.57–58), Knockem the horse trader tells her. She rules the Fair and us too: for her world, the world of the flesh, seduces us all.

20. Father Wright has some remarks about "passionate appetites" in pregnant women: "It is wonderfull what passionate appetites raigne in women when they be with childe; I have heard it credibly reported, that there was a woman in *Spaine*, which longed almost till death, to have a mouth full of flesh out of an extreame fatte mans necke . . . most of these appetites proceeded from women extreamely addicted to follow their own desires, and of such a froward disposition, as in very deede, if they were crossed of their willes, their Passions were so strong, as they undoubtedly wold miscarry of their children; for vehement Passions alter vehemently the temper and constitution of the body, which can not but greatly preiudice the tender infant lying in the womb" (pp. 74–75).

In Ursla we see the Flesh and the Devil, and in Adam Overdo, her counterpart, Justice and Reason. As in the morality plays, virtues are balanced against vices. Justice Overdo is one more in a whole literature of disguised benevolent magistrates who search their purviews of responsibilities for sin and error—"enormities," Overdo calls them—in order to restore the rule of right. It was Hazlitt who first noted that in a number of Elizabethan plays a disguised magistrate visits the society for which he is responsible to ferret out its sin and disorder. *Measure for Measure* is on his list, and other critics and scholars have added to it.[21] In their various ways Malevole in *The Malcontent* (1604), Hercules in *The Fawn* (1602), and somewhat differently Felice in *Antonio and Mellida* (1599) are magistrates of Hazlitt's definition, and so are the Duke in Day's *Law Tricks* (1604) and the son of the aging Duke in Middleton's *The Phoenix* (printed 1607). The young prince in *The Phoenix* defines the magistrate's action and purpose: "I hold it a safer stern, upon this lucky adventage . . . to look into the heart and bowels of this dukedom, and, in disguise, mark all abuses ready for reformation or punishment."[22] Like the other magistrates, Justice Overdo looks into the heart and bowels of his Smithfield and marks all abuses for reformation or punishment.

Stories of disguised and snooping magistrates are to be found in folk tales and sophisticated fiction alike. There is even one in Wright's book.[23] Overdo's position as judge makes him a "man of power upon whose sole jurisdiction not King James himself may intrude."[24] He sees himself as absolute, and as such he is semi-symbolic, semi-allegorical. "Cloud-like," he says, "I will breake out in raine, and haile, lightning, and thunder, vpon the head of enormity" (V.ii.5–6). On another occasion he says, "And as I began, so I'll end" (II.i.48), recalling the Biblical "I am Alpha and Omega, the beginning and end" (Rev. 21, 6). Overdo claims divine authority for himself in the manner of Justice Shallow and other Elizabethan and Jacobean justices.

From the very first, we recognize Overdo as a morality figure. While Ursla suffers from the sins of the flesh, Overdo suffers from the sins of the spirit. His is the father sin, the sin of pride. Quarlous, who would deflate his self-importance, adjures him in his final address, "Remember you

21. See Oscar James Campbell, *Shakespeare's Satire* (New York: Oxford University Press, 1943), p. 127.

22. A. H. Bullen, ed. (London, 1881), I, 107.

23. See p. 55. See also *A Mirour For Magistrates of Cyties. Representing the ordinaunces, Policies, and Diligence of The Noble Emperour, Alexander (surnamed) Severus, to suppresse and chastise the notorious Vices noorished in Rome . . .* by George Whetstones, Gent. (London, 1584), esp. Sig. B3v.

24. Morley, pp. 96–97.

are but *Adam*, Flesh, and blood! you haue your frailty, forget your other name of *Ouerdoo*, and inuite vs all to supper" (V.vi.96–98). According to Wright, the "old *Adam* [is] the law of the flesh, sensualitie, the enemy of God, the spring of vice, the roote of impietie, the bane of godly conversation, the obiect of mortification, the sinke of sinne, over craving, never content, tyrannizing over the greatest, and overthrowing the least."[25] In the end, Adam Overdo finds, like Waspe, that "He that will correct another, must want fault in himselfe" (V.iv.99–100). Though Overdo strives for justice in contrast to Ursla, who encourages all that he wants to correct, he is as guilty of "enormities" as the others. He is the fool in whose clothes he dresses—the premier exemplar of the theme of vanity.

Zeal-of-the-Land Busy is no less foolish, no less mad, than Overdo. He too oversimplifies human experience and trusts too fully in himself. Like Ananias Wholesome, he hates tradition; tradition, being the natural growth of old time, reduces the vanity of a single generation (see I.ii. 142–148). Busy would recover from vainglory if he could see how little he is likely to contribute to the whole store of world knowledge. He is not a simple hypocrite who pretends to be what he is not, like Dame Purecraft; Busy actually believes he is what he says he is. He is a sentimentalist posturing before the mirror of himself. At heart he suffers from what Father Wright calls "the naughty will," and he is more nearly a lost soul than Dame Purecraft. The naughty will, Wright says, "commandeth the witte to employ all the power and force, to find out reasons and persuasions that all the appetite demaundeth, standeth with reason and is lawfull; the which collusion, I take to be one of the rootes of all mischiefes, that nowe cover the face of the world, that is, a wicked will commanding the wit, to find out reasons to please for Passions." (pp. 53–54). Busy is more vicious than Overdo, for his "original ignorance" is positive whereas Overdo's ignorance is only accidental. In Wright's language Overdo suffers from Ignorance but Busy suffers from Error: "All the defects of our wit may be reduced to two, Ignorance, and Errour; by Ignorance we know not things necessary; by Errour we know them falsely: Ignorance is a privation, Errour a positive action: all ignorance cannot be prevented; many errours, but all cannot be escapted; from ignorance floweth vice,

25. Father Wright's definition of *Adam* is in accord with the Anglican *Book of Homilies: Appointed to be Read in Churches*, 1547–1623, John Griffiths, ed. (Oxford, 1859, p. 17): "the Holy Ghost, in writing the holy Scripture, is in nothing more diligent than to pull down man's vainglory and pride; which of all vices is most universally grafted in all mankind, even from the first infection of our father Adam, and therefore we read in many places of Scripture many notable lessons against this old rooted vice, to teach us the most commendable virtue of humility, how to know ourselves, and to remember what we be of ourselves."

and from errour heresie" (p. 295). Zeal-of-the-Land Busy is not a simple allegorical figure representing the Corrupted Will. He is, first, a typical Puritan. But in the community of this play, where Overdo and Ursla and the Fair itself bring their morality associations, Busy is Error become Heresy.

The story of Littlewit and his artistic aspirations, though one more variation on the general theme of vanity, is less indebted to the morality play than the other elements I have been discussing. And yet Littlewit's actions too have their ethical overtones. A competent law clerk who is not taken in by the pretensions of the Puritans nor the activities of the Fair, for all his native shrewdness, Littlewit is unreasonable. His passions direct his relationship with his wife and his sensuality directs the construct of the play he writes, "The ancient modern history of *Hero*, and *Leander*, otherwise called *The Touchstone of True Love*." Wright has explained how "reason once beeing entred into league with passions and sense, becommeth a better friend to sensualitie than the passions were before: for reason straightwaies inventeth tenne thousand sorts of new delights, which the passions never could have imagined" (p. 10). Littlewit's intellectual powers are thus misdirected. The senses and the passions have their rational place in the scheme of things, but Littlewit's are unbridled: "It hath been declared (I think) sufficiently, howe most men inordinately followe the unbrideled appetite of their sensual passions; yet no doubt but they may, by vertue be guided, and many good men so moderate and mortifie them, that they rather serve them for instruments of vertue, than foments of vice, and as an occasion of victory, than a cause of foyle" (p. 15).

The puppet show that Littlewit writes is a microcosm of a microcosm.[26] As the whole world is contained in the Fair, so the Fair is contained in the puppet play. If a player is the "Page of *Pride*, and the waiting woman of *vanity*" (V.v.81–82) the Tire-women, the feather-makers, the dealers in wigs and fans and ornaments are no less so. We tread dangerous ground when we single out one group as more puffed up with vanity than another. "I speak by inspiration, as well as he" the Puppet tells Busy. "I haue as little to doe with learning as he; and doe scorne her helps as much as he" (V.v.112). Busy is "converted" when he sees that we are all tarred with the same stick, that no profession has a monopoly on corruption. The form of Busy's conversion is important, for it is repeated twice over in the next and concluding scene of the play. Lanthorne says to Busy: "Be conuerted, I pray you, and let the Play goe on!" and Busy replies: "Let it goe on. For I am changed, and will become a beholder

26. See Jonas A. Barish, "'Bartholomew Fair' and Its Puppets," *MLQ* XX (1959), 3–17.

with you!" (V.v.115–117). "Converted" from the insularity of his private view, he becomes a spectator of life. Rather than refusing (or pretending to refuse) the world's delights, he now embraces them. Adam Overdo's conversion parallels Busy's . When he learns that the "enormities" for which he searches are ubiquitous, when he finds that all men, even himself, suffer from vanity, he declares, "this pleasant conceited Gentlemen hath wrought vpon my iudgement, and preuail'd: I pray you take care of your sicke friend, Mistresse *Alice*, and my good friends all— . . . I inuite you home,with mee to my house, to supper . . ." (V.vi.106–108, 110). In the future he promises "*Ad correctionem, non ad destructionem; Ad aedificandum, non ad diruendum:* so lead on." He will mend, not destroy; build, not demolish. No less than Busy, he perceives that life is to be embraced, not rejected; that the world for all its vanities, the people for all their ignorance and error, are to be accepted. And it is on this note of affirmation that *Bartholomew Fair* ends. Cokes, who has "lost all i' the *Fayre*, and all my acquaintance too," nevertheless invites the whole company to dinner. "Yes," he says, "and bring the *Actors* along, wee'll ha' the rest o' the *Play* at home" (V.vi.114–115).

In *Bartholomew Fair* Jonson comes close to the Shakespeare of *Twelfth Night*. If Malvolio is not so outright a Puritan as Zeal-of-the-Land Busy, both of them can be reproved with Toby Belch's celebrated rebuke: "Dost thou think, because thou art virtuous, there shall be no more cakes and ale?" (II.iii.124–126). This play is like Shakespeare because it is not doctrinaire: it is catholic in its generosity. Jonson forgives his rogues, and he bludgeons no hypocrites. The lawgivers, Overdo and Busy, repent their presumption and see at last that they cannot order the world to their understanding. The persons whom they had sought to correct remain as they were: lively, simple, clever. To deny them a place in one's world, Jonson suggests, is to condemn oneself to the cloister or to death. Winwife and Quarlous earn Jonson's highest admiration, for they are rational; they turn circumstances to their advantage without injury to innocent bystanders. When Grace becomes Winwife's spouse, she is perhaps not so well off as she might wish; she is yet better off than without him. The world being the soiled place it is, she may be grateful. And although Quarlous in marrying Dame Purecraft for her money gives no assurance that he will not continue fleecing the gullible, he will at least help his "bride" cut through the sham of her life. Quarlous and Winwife are prudent; and prudence is, after all, a virtue too.

Viewed from all its aspects, this play which owes so much to the indigenous dramatic traditions illustrates an urbane, humanistic doctrine: the senses inspire the passions, which only the reason can control. The senses, the passions, the mind, each has its proper areas of responsibility; trouble comes when they invade one another's territory. And yet to be doctrinaire, to expect too much reason from essentially irrational creatures, is itself irrational. Most human pursuits are vain, but too zealous an endeavor to correct them is vain too. You—we—live in a Vanity Fair whose streets must sometimes be swept. But oh! what a spectacle the place is! How delightful the sounds, how delicious the food! How much there is to see! You may have to live among thieves; but how clever their roguery! Your play may be populated only with puppets, but how lively they are, and how pretty! You may serve your turn in the stocks, and you may suffer the outrage of bawds, but you can at least "drowne the memory of all enormity in your bigg'st bowle at home" (V.vi.99–100). Yes, and as Cokes says, "wee'll ha' the rest o' the *Play*" there (V.vi.114–115).[27]

2. *The Devil is an Ass*

Though *The Devil is an Ass* was acted in 1616, only two years after the brilliant *Bartholomew Fair*, in the opinion of most critics it is much

27. Henry Morley's comment on the relation of Jonson's play to the native dramatic traditions is worthy of extensive quotation: "From its birthplace by the church, and in the fair, the English drama had departed, growing into independent life in the wide world, but leaving in the old home many recollections of its childhood. From Mysteries and Miracle plays the drama, still in its childhood, had grown to Moralities, with personated virtues to teach morals, and a comic Vice to help the devil's work in raising laughter. The Moralities, as they grew older, learnt to enliven their more abstract dialogues or doctrine with examples illustrative of their theme, and so included monitory scenes from human history, such as the fortunes of Antony and Cleopatra, Damon and Pythias, or the Siege of Troy. The Vice put on the dress of the Elizabethan clown. All this was in the childhood of the drama, whereof memories clung to its birthplace long after it had gone out mature into the world, and had begotten sons equal in dignity with the best poets that have ever laid their spell upon mankind. The Fair, like an old Nurse who once carried the infant child of a great house upon her arms, and was not then too ignorant to be its oracle and guide, looks from a lowly hut upon the palace of her nursling, and croons over to herself the old ditties, tells over to herself the old stories that once satisfied the lord of the great house, who is so tall and stately, and so choice in mirth, and so far-reaching in knowledge.

"Once only that bright foster-son crossed the old woman's threshold in the days of his great wealth and honour, and sat chattering and laughing at her feet. She could afford then to be laughed at, for her house after all, though dirty and ruinous, was a good house. She was a most respectable shop-keeper, she had a wholesale trade, and no lack of custom as a retailer of toys and hardware. He was a wayward wilful lad in his swaddling-clothes, and in his handsome manhood he might laugh at his old nurse, and welcome. In the name, therefore, of Ben Jonson, English drama paid a visit to the Fair in Smithfield." (Morley, pp. 146–148.)

inferior. Dryden thought it a "dotage,"[28] and few later critics have failed to note in it either a "more than incipient decadence of constructive power"[29] or "irresolution."[30] "For once," John Palmer writes, Jonson "does not seem to have made up his mind exactly what he intended to do."[31] The play has not seen a production since its first one; and Jonson told Drummond in 1619 that because of the play he "was accused," that is, censured, and that "the King desyred him to conceal it."[32] Presumably Jonson withdrew the play as regulated. From this distance it is difficult to determine certainly what offended the mighty, but one rather imagines that Jonson's attack on the "projectors" in James's court did not please. James had fallen into the habit of allowing royal grants—that is, exclusive rights—not only for the manufacture and trade of certain articles of common utility, but for "projects" like the draining of the Fens of Lincolnshire. The royal monopolies were generally abused; according to one contemporary account, "The Projector pretend[s] the publicke good, when he intends nothing but to robbe the rich, and cheate the poore."[33] Jonson's is the earliest dramatic representation of the projector.

Perhaps to soften the implied criticism of James's policies, Jonson included a satire of witchcraft in the last act of his play. To his considerable credit the King had only recently, in August, 1616, exposed false dealings in some celebrated witch trials.[34] The King firmly believed in the existence of demons, but he could also admit that many claims of bewitching were specious. In such matters he prided himself on being able to tell a hawk from a handsaw, and this scene about witchcraft can be read as an allusion to the King's good sense. James died in 1625, and *The Devil* was printed in the 1631 Folio. By then Jonson was too enfeebled to correct proofs with his customary care; he had had a physical breakdown in 1628. Part of what appears to be early senility in *The Devil* may therefore be the result of his inadequate revising before publication; part may well be the result of his boredom with theatrical craft. After 1616 he could not seem to bring himself to make the exertion another

28. "Of Dramatic Poesie, An Essay," *Essays of John Dryden*, W. P. Ker, ed. (Oxford: Clarendon Press, 1899, 1926), I, 81; portions are conveniently quoted in Herford and Simpson, XI, 513–529, esp. p. 515.

29. Herford and Simpson, II, 165.

30. Enck, p. 210.

31. John Palmer, *Ben Jonson* (New York: Viking Press, 1934), p. 281.

32. *Conversations*, 409, 414–415 (Herford and Simpson, I, 144, 169).

33. Daniel Featley, *Clavis Mystica* (London, 1636), p. 477; the sermons contained in this volume date from 1610 to 1613.

34. See George Lyman Kittredge, "King James I and *The Devil is an Ass*," *MP*, IX (1911), 195–209.

WITCHES AND THEIR FAMILIARS

Woodcut from Matthew Hopkins, *The Discovery of Witches* (1647).
"Know you this by the way, that heretofore Robin Goodfellow and Hobgoblin were as terrible, and also as credible to the people, as hags and witches be now." Reginald Scot, *The discouerie of witchcraft* (1584).

Bartholomew Fair would require, and after the production of *The Devil is an Ass* Jonson withdrew from the commercial theater for some ten years, until driven back by economic necessity in 1626. He spent his energies on court masques, on literary friendships, even—in the spirit of derring-do—on walking to Scotland. *The Devil is an Ass* shows no failure of intellectual power, and its plot and characters, though persuasively conceived, are incompletely rather than falsely realized. By careful attention to the text one can make out what Jonson had in mind, however he bungled his job.

In *The Devil is an Ass* Jonson makes use of morality themes and techniques without disguise. Earlier he had so successfully represented the surface appearance of London life that he had obscured the nature of his drama: he was an allegorist.[35] Now his method of composition became more obvious. The old plays, like Jonson's, are both realistic and allegorical, and though the old plays no longer please anybody but the antiquarians, this is because their detail is incomplete and their ideas immature; their method is sound enough. Jonson offered his audience eternal truth wrapped in contemporary garb just as they did. He shared the conventional Renaissance view that the senses were given to instruct the mind.

In his early plays Jonson had drawn on the indigenous tradition because it was the only one he had, and he attempted to correct its nature according to what he took to be classical precepts. Now, in these last plays, he asks us to be totally aware of the native traditions of English drama. Satan in his own person opens this play, and he speaks the language long used in the moralities. At various points, Jonson refers to such celebrated allegories as *Lusty Juventus* (I.i.50), *Mundus et Infans* (I.iii), and Medwall's *Nature* (V.ii.11ff). *The Devil is an Ass* is supposed to be seen as the latest in a series of plays stretching back to early Elizabethan times. "Remember," Satan tells Pug the "lesse divill" in the first scene of the play,

> Remember,
> What number it is. *Six hundred* and *sixteene.*
> Had it but beene *fiue hundred*, though some *sixty*
> Aboue; that's *fifty* yeeres agone, and *six*,
> (When euery great man had his *Vice* stand by him,
> In his long coat, shaking his wooden dagger) . . .
>
>   (I.i.80–85)

35. I am in fundamental agreement with Edward B. Partridge, *The Broken Compass: A Study of the Major Comedies of Ben Jonson* (New York: Columbia University Press, 1958), p. 185.

then Vice and Iniquity could walk the stage undisguised: not now. In the Proem to *Volpone* Jonson had disparaged the "antique reliques of barbarisme," the fools and devils of the stage, even while he was employing them disguised (ll.74–81). Now he introduces them openly.

The Devil is an Ass tells how the Devil, on earth, discovers Hell the safer place. Plays about "The Devil Abroad" had often been represented on the Elizabethan stage, and Jonson refers to two of them in his Prologue. "Your deare delight, the *Diuell* of *Edmunton*" (Prologue, 22), a charming comedy produced in 1604, combines local color with a classical consideration of form, but its theme of youthful love and its uncraggy verse show that it belongs to the days of Elizabethan romance. It has no malice, no ill humor, no satire; and its story of Fabel, the merry devil, recalls the traditional morality mischief maker, Rafe. Like him, Fabel claims responsibility for the confusions of the plot (see for example V.ii.134–143). The second play is also Elizabethan and indigenous (Prologue, 26). *If This be not a Good Play, the Divell is in it*, by Thomas Dekker, printed in 1612, is even more a morality than the *Merry Devil of Edmunton*. Dekker's Shacklesoule is derived from the legendary Friar Rush, who traveled on earth disguised as a cook; in the Dekker version he and his two companion devils tempt and pervert the Court, a priory, and a merchant. Topical and very funny, it is not satiric. Dekker is addressing a different audience from Jonson's; moreover, he saw the playwright's function as that of a hired entertainer and nothing more. In alluding to *If This be not a Good Play*, Jonson asks us to compare his own play to Dekker's.

There were other well-known devil stories and plays which Jonson did not enumerate. Machiavelli had retold a medieval variation of "The Devil Abroad" in his celebrated *Belphagor*, and this story was popular in Elizabethan England.[36] One of its dramatic versions, *Grim the Collier of Croyden; or, The Evil and His Dame* (1600), was entertaining enough to deserve comparison to Greene's *Friar Bacon and Friar Bungay* (ca. 1589), another play containing devil elements. In *Grim the Collier*, which contains not only the devil but cuckolds, shrewish wives, and faked madness, the outdeviling of the devils becomes the conquest of vice by virtue. Barnabe Barnes's *The Devil's Charter* (1607) owes something to Marlowe's *Faustus* and contains a scene or two like the other devil plays, but for the most part it is quite different from them. Dealing with murder and treachery in the papal court, it lacks their simple charm.

At one and the same time Jonson uses and abuses the indigenous folk

36. Maximilian Rudwin, *The Devil in Legend and Literature* (Chicago: Open Court Publishing Co., 1931), pp. 241–242.

drama. From the first scene we are expected to laugh at the trappings of the ludicrous morality play, and yet the playwright utilizes the very devices he satirizes. He may be supercilious about *vetus comoedia*; but his play actually illustrates how the old forms could be put to use. Satan fired Jonson's imagination and became an impressive figure; and Pug, the lesser devil, is not so ridiculous as he was apparently intended to be. Jonson set out to disparage the old-fashioned play and was almost caught by it instead.

But *The Devil is an Ass* is only potentially a successful play, and one cannot agree with Freda Townsend that it shows "continued excellence in constructive power."[37] *Bartholomew Fair* gives an impressive panoramic view of society, and though this play attempts the same episodic techniques, the incidents are not subordinated to one another and the action is scattered. Its construction is at once similar in kind and inferior in quality to the great plays.

The first act begins in Hell, with Satan, Pug, and Iniquity "the Vice" in open controversy. Critics ever since Gifford have justly admired this scene, which takes its place with the celebrated opening of *The Alchemist*. Thereafter the three major actions of the play are duly introduced, one at a time; this is Jonson's usual method of introducing multifarious material. First we meet Fitzdottrel, the young squire of Norfolk who wants to be a man about town so badly that he trades his wife's favors to Wittipol, a young gallant, for a fine cloak to swagger in (I.ii,iv,vi); next we find Pug, out of Hell, searching for a master in London (I.iii); and finally we discover the "projectors", Ingine and Meercraft (I.vii,II.i), whom current slang would call "fast operators": they enrich themselves by making deals, either business or matrimonial or political, from which they get a cut. The second two actions are subordinated to the Fitzdottrel intrigue; this last is complicated even before the machinations of the projectors is introduced. From the easy handling of the multiple situation it is clear that an old hand is in complete if rather negligent control.

In the second act the intrigues move swiftly forward, but without confusion. The act begins with an elaboration of the projector's announced schemes. We discover that Meercraft is a minor Epicure Mammon, with an imagination able to call up a sensual future in full detail. Unlike Mammon, he disciplines his imagination for commercial use: he is a barker, a huckster, an entrepreneur who gets his percentage. Fitzdottrel cannot resist him when he is promised wealth and a dukedom. The other two actions—

---

37. Freda L. Townsend, *Apologie for Bartholmew Fayre* (New York: Modern Language Association of America, 1947), p. 82.

Pug, the Devil Abroad; and Wittipol, the gallant who would cuckold Fitzdottrel—become entangled in this act. Pug's rather naïve offer to help Mistress Fitzdottrel achieve a liaison with Wittipol shows both the lady's resourcefulness and Pug's simplicity, and it is an ironic comment on the devilishness of the world. Beside the Londoners, Pug looks like virtue itself; "they haue their *Vices*, there," Satan has warned Pug, "most like to *Vertues*" (I.i.121).

The multiple action of the play has proceeded in orderly fashion from introduction to complication, but in the last scene of the second act the plotting begins to break down. In order to fleece Fitzdottrel, Meercraft promises to introduce him into fashionable society. Now suddenly Jonson seems to become fatigued or bored; and rather than striving to resolve the play in its own terms, he resorts to tricks and situations which have been successful in earlier plays, disregarding their necessary relevance and propriety here. The play becomes increasingly a pastiche of former successes. We turn away from the established satire of money and what we would call status—Fitzdottrel and the Dukedom of Drown'd Lands— toward the satire of the law and courtly affectation, two of Jonson's usual targets. In Act III, in his account of the operation of an office of dependency, Jonson satirizes false gallantry rather than business. The present handling may have had a certain topicality, but it is not closely related to the general movement of the play. The court of dependencies and the project for draining bogs to produce the Drown'd Lands may both have a necessary relationship to other corruptions of James's court—but the relationship is not made clear. Both are seen as aspects of a single weakness: vanity allied to avarice. Jonson misses a chance to point a neat conclusion about contemporaneous corruption. He also misses a chance to draw a parallel between Guilthead's social aspirations for his son Plutarchus (III.i.iii) and Fitzdottrel's social climbing. The Guilthead-Plutarchus episodes which are now introduced thus seem to be dramatically irrelevant, however interesting in their own right.

An even more complete breakdown comes with Wittipol's reappearance in Act III, scene iv. In Acts I and II the butt of the satire has been Fitzdottrel; Wittipol has been the manager of the schemes that will abuse him into virtue. Now Wittipol stands aside and Meercraft becomes the protagonist. We note with amusement how Meercraft rescues himself from difficulties with Guilthead and Ingine and how he seems able to turn all occasions to his own advantage, but we cannot forget Wittipol's plans to seduce Mistress Fitzdottrel. Our interests are divided.

Act IV brings a satire of "ladies colleagiate" in scenes reminiscent of *The Silent Woman*, but they are not inevitably related to foregoing action and ideas. Fitzdottrel recedes into the relative background and even Meercraft, who manages these episodes, is subordinated. The affected ladies dominate. The collapse of the construction is complete when in Act IV, scene vii Fitzdottrel decides, urged by Meercraft, to sign over his property to the Spanish Lady—Wittipol masquerading as one of the Collegiate Ladies. Wittipol's sudden revelation of himself shortly thereafter does not create the dramatic sensation a similar revelation created in *The Silent Woman*; it is insufficiently prepared for. Altogether the fourth act of *The Devil* comes close to self-imitation, and it is so loosely tied to the first two acts as to be nearly irrelevant.

Nor is Wittipol's sudden conversion completely convincing. In place of cuckolding Fitzdottrel, his avowed purpose in the early acts of the play, Wittipol now suddenly rescues Mistress Fitzdottrel and awakens her husband to an awareness of his own foolishness. For consistency's sake, if for no other reason, Wittipol should have persisted in his plans: Fitzdottrel deserved cuckolding and his wife had earned a lover. The situation but not the tone reminds one of Machiavelli's *Mandragola*. In that celebrated comedy too the young wife is seduced by the young gallant, but that affair is conducted in high good humor without a hint of opprobrium. In English drama before the Restoration, ladies do not conduct themselves in this casual fashion; women of uneasy virtue belonged to the lower orders. Courtly love is one thing, wantonness is another; and the gallants know it. Wittipol's change of heart is unconvincing, inconsistent, and altogether English.

The last act of the play does not strike us as inevitable, as it ought to. Ambler, a "gentlman usher," whom we have heard spoken of through several scenes, is now introduced for the first time. By bringing him on stage at this point, Jonson may have intended to reverse the course of his action as he did in *The Alchemist* when he introduced Lovewit. But Ambler cannot command our attention. Though his inadvertent trouble with Pug returns Pug to Hell, it seems only accidental that Ambler has only now turned up; and the concluding action, in which Fitzdottrel pretends to be possessed by demons, also seems arbitrarily added to the play. Jonson unhappily backs away from his themes of cuckoldry and business avarice in these last scenes.

The play is further weakened by the feebleness of its characterization. The personages are not sharply drawn, and a good many are mere shadows. Manly, Wittipol's friend, is like the young gallants we have seen in Jonson's other plays, but here he does not make his presence felt. Everill and Ingine are not sharply drawn either. And the characters who are elaborately portrayed show unresolved inconsistencies. Fitzdottrel himself is given qualities—jealousy, vanity, avarice, credulity—which are never fully harmonized: Jonson's forte, generally, is simplicity rather than complication of motive. Only Meercraft comes alive. Jonson seems to have assigned each of his dramatis personae a function and then to have deserted him. If they were more brilliantly colored or decked out in the realistic foolery of the earlier plays, some of the confusions might disappear. But the characters no less than the plot lack focus; they are little more than intellectual ciphers indicating the direction of the play's thematic development. Bored perhaps with the re-creation of types which he has staged often before, Jonson has gone only half way in *The Devil*. Despite its entertaining individual episodes and its topical relevance— dueling, projection, social climbing, witchhunting and the like—this play is curiously etiolated.

The Devil is an Ass lacks dramatic unity, but the three contemporary social problems that it undertakes to anatomize are connected. Yet once more Jonson attacks courtly affectation by showing us persons attempting to rise hastily beyond their birth. Fitzdottrel wants to buy a dukedom, and his excessive concern for appearance is part and parcel of his desire to ascend the social ladder. He wants his wife to learn the tricks of noble conduct, apparently believing that nobility is nothing more than an elaborate etiquette. The same aspiration is reflected in Guilthead's relation to his son: the son must learn to act the gentleman. The first scene in which he and his son appear (III.i) spells out clearly what Jonson thinks nobility consists of; nowhere else is he so explicit. First, a gentleman is learned; one cannot be a gentleman without being something of a scholar (i.8). Next he is a countryman, supported naturally by his land; he is no "citizen" drawing interest from debtors (i.16–26). Finally he was born to gentility, which can be acquired neither by marriage nor by purchase (i.27–30). Guilthead, the citizen anxious for gentility, has named his son Plutarchus, because he says:

> ... I bought *Plutarch's* liues,
> And fell s[o]' in loue with the booke, as I call'd my sonne
> By'his name; In hope he should be like him:
> And write the liues of our great men! (III.ii.22–25)

Passing over Plutarch's high moral purpose, he finds the *Lives* to be Accounts of Successful Men I Have Known. No less than Fitzdottrel, Guilthead searches for short cuts: his son must learn how to act a part. He and Fitzdottrel mistake the trappings for the essentials. But perhaps Plutarchus has learned from his namesake; he knows better than his father.

Jonson is concerned not only with the ethics of the gentry; he also analyzes the ethics of the businessman. Meercraft is the first modern businessman to appear in English drama, perhaps in English literature. His name summarizes Jonson's opinion of him. The projector is concerned with *craft* as cunning as opposed to *craft* as skill. Meercraft is devoted to *mere-maneuvering*. He does not distinguish between the worthy and the insignificant, for he measures value in personal gain in money. As willing to deal in toothpicks as in draining of swamps, he is bound by neither social responsibility nor religious duty. Like Fitzdottrel and Guilthead, Meercraft is concerned with means, not ends. Historians have identified the early seventeenth century as the time of the rise of capitalism. At its very beginning Jonson observed that capitalism sometimes substitutes money for human—i.e. moral—values and is more interested in method than in merit. This is not the first time that Jonson has satirized the admiration for technique which drives out human values, but it is the first time he explicitly associates this admiration with the rising capitalism. One of his stock methods of attacking the admiration for technique is by the use of jargon. Wittipol's wonderful account of cosmetics (IV.iv) and Everill's discussion of dependencies (III.iii) recall Subtle's facility with the vocabulary of alchemy and Volpone preaching in St. Mark's Square. Jargon, as Jonson sees it, is language in which ignorance masquerades as erudition. Here it is also emblematic of the faults of the rising world, for it pretends a professional concern for general amelioration and is actually a means of exploiting the weak and the credulous.

In addition to the ethics of the gentry and the ethics of the businessman, *The Devil* is concerned with witchcraft. The projector and the false gentleman are charlatans, and witchcraft is shown to be often another, analogous, kind of charlatanism. Through it the gullible—those who do not search out motives and causes—are taken in. Discursive reason alone can show up the fakery of projects, of social aspiration, and of the occult; and it can protect us from the cheats. Reason may be turned to unworthy ends; Jonson's counterfeiters are not witless. But the counterfeiters are separated from the rational in that they use their wit for private gain and not for public good. Fitzdottrel tells Wittipol:

> Truly
> Your trauells may haue alter'd your complexion:
> But sure, your wit stood still.

and Wittipol replies

> It may well be, Sir.
> All heads ha' not like growth. (I.iv.62–65)

Though he has traveled, Wittipol's basic principles have been constant and he has remained reasonable.

The reasonable man is one whose mind is disciplined by a respect for the received opinions of mankind, one who reasons from assumptions held by the generations. When a witty man becomes a reasonable man, he becomes moral; he then puts himself in the service of accepted values. All the major themes and actions of *The Devil is an Ass* lead to this single thesis. By a consideration of manner rather than of matter, we lay ourselves open to counterfeiters and to cheats. Jonson's thesis is hardly new; he is firmly within the traditions of Christian humanism. His brilliance comes in perceiving its relation to diverse elements of his contemporary world. *The Devil is an Ass* is less competent dramaturgically than the great comedies, but intellectually it is not humbled by them. In this play one sees a masculine mind identifying some of the basic social and intellectual developments of the time, and—what is more remarkable— diagnosing the illnesses of the modern world scarcely before they had got started. Bored as he may have become with the theater, Jonson's mind remained alert and his understanding profound, and time was on the side of his judgments.

3. *The Staple of News* as Summary

The Staple of News appeared approximately ten years after *The Devil is an Ass*. Through it Jonson, who had been laureate to James, hoped to attract royal patronage; but he did not receive immediate favor from the new King. Entered in the Stationers' Register on April 14, 1626, the play must have been intended for prompt publication. The play has never received much critical attention and Dryden included it among the dotages, but Gifford said, "few of Jonson's dramatic works . . . exhibit stronger marks of his peculiar talents than this," and Swinburne called it the "last magnificent work of his maturest genius."[38] More recent scholars and critics like Madeleine Doran have found it "intolerably dull."[39] As before, Jonson clothes his ideas in plot; he does not discover them in his fiction: for him the generalization precedes the localization. Looked at as a document expounding a concept *The Staple of News* is summarizing: it contains a succinct statement of his ethics, the best, I think, to be found in his drama. For a student of Jonson the play is instructive, but even *The Devil is an Ass* is livelier, more imaginative, and more human.

The ideas differ from those of the earlier plays primarily in the baldness of their statement. When Peniboy Senior, the representation of

38. Gifford, ed. (London, 1875), V, 292. Swinburne, XII, 54.
39. Doran, 365.

"old *Couetousnesse . . . the Money-bawd*, who is flesh-bawd too, they say" (Second Intermeane [i.e. interlude] after the second act, 8–9), courts Lady Pecunia, he describes the depths to which he will descend for her favor. He is one who

> sells the acates are sent him,
> Fish, Fowle, and venison, and preserues himselfe,
> Like an old hoary Rat, with mouldy pye-crust.
> This I doe heare, reioycing, I can suffer
> This, and much more, for your good *Graces* sake. (II.i.16–20)

Pecunia replies:

> Cannot my *Grace* be gotten, and held too,
> Without your selfe-tormentings, and your watches,
> Your macerating of your body thus
> With cares, and scantings of your dyet, and rest?
>
> (II.i.22–25)

Peniboy Canter, acting as a chorus, points the moral. Nowadays, he says, men

> contemplate nothing
> But the vile sordid things of time, place, money,
> And let the noble, and the precious goe,
> Vertue and honesty; hang 'hem; poore thinne membranes
> Of honour; who respects them? O, the *Fates*!
> How hath all iust, true reputation fall'n,
> Since money, this base money 'gan to haue any!
>
> (III.ii.242–248)

Money has usurped the place of all other values, he says; men now think only of financial gain. They are unreasonable:

> . . . All things within, without 'hem,
> Moue, but their braine, and that stands still! mere monsters,
> Here, in a chamber, of most subtill feet! (IV.ii.136–138)

When men are rational, they reduce money to its proper place. They begin to be wise when they see that money is only one of the world's goods. Jonson does not preach poverty and mortification of the flesh, nor does he deny that money is desirable; he knows that "*Merit* will keepe no house, nor pay no house rent" (II.iv.62). He contends that one should neither prostrate oneself before the world, nor treat it with contempt; one must act between these extremes.

Jonson's teleological doctrine of moderation is presented dramatically in a number of actions. It is the burden of the story of Lady Pecunia,

from which we learn that money should neïther be hoarded nor wasted;
when used rationally it leads us to virtue. One's religious life is similar.
"Superstition," we are told, "Doth violate the Deity it worships:/No
less then scorne doth" (V.vi.23–25). The extremes of zeal and cynicism
are alike to be avoided. The life of the flesh must also be governed by
moderation: "Surfet, and fulnesse, haue kill'd more then *famine*"
(V.vi.27). In a pair of clever scenes (III.iii,iv), Jonson discusses the
accoutrements of life. The first is a satire of elaborate cooking; the second
is a satire of the penurious denial of the pleasure of the senses: "What
need hath Nature/Of siluer dishes?" Covetousness asks. "Hunger is not
ambitious," (III.iv.52–53,56). Unmodified covetousness and unrestrained
sensuousness are both wrong: the true way lies between excess and
niggardliness. It is the use to which the world's goods are put that determines their value, and values may be judged not according to their size
but to their purpose. " . . . And beleeue it, *brother*," Pennyboy Canter
says, "The vse of things is all, and not the *Store*" (V.vi.25–26). The world
is corrupt when its masters are corrupt, sound when used by healthy
men. Jonson's criticism of newsmongering, the subject of one of the two
major intrigues of the play, is consistent with his general theories. Jonson
attacks equally the exploitation of human curiosity by the contemporary
newspapers and the ordinary men and women who yield unreasonably
to their desire for gossip. The popular desire for news seems to him
irrational, because it is without purpose; sensible men seek to know only
what is demonstrably relevant to their lives.

These views of reasonable moderation have been Jonson's habitual
views. He has pitted the superstitious Celias against the scornful Cor-
vinos, the smug Surlys against the zealous Subtles, the enthusiastic
Puritans against the legalistic justices. In the earlier plays, after contrasting the extremes, he has allowed his audience to draw their own
conclusions. If we must err, I think that Jonson would prefer that we err
on the side of zeal. At least, he consistently makes the energetic and
imaginative man more attractive than his restrained and legalistic anta-
gonist: he was, after all, an Elizabethan, conscious that new worlds awaited
conquering. *The Staple of News* states clearly what formerly has been
implied.

The two plot lines of *The Staple of News* are rather arbitrarily connected, but they dramatize the ideal of moderation. The first, which
gives the play its title, is almost entirely topical. It is a satire of the first
public newspaper in England. Until 1620 or thereabouts the great lords
may have received newsletters from abroad, but the people heard only
word-of-mouth reporting. With the outbreak of the Thirty Years War in

1618, they began to take an unprecedented interest in foreign affairs, and shortly thereafter single folio newsheets called *corantos* began to appear in London. Modeled on Dutch and German (Frankfort) originals and in most cases simple translations of continental broadsides, they consisted of miscellaneous paragraphs, each with a place and date. The sheets appeared irregularly and unedited. Flatly written, their success shows the local hunger for information. Shortly they were replaced by "newsbooks" of between eight and twenty-four pages, quarto. These too appeared irregularly and under various titles, but almost from the beginning they were edited, their writing heightened, and their material arranged to make a continuous story. In the summer of 1622, some seventeen of them were issued within nineteen weeks. By the close of 1624 their greatest popularity was already over, and by 1632, though they had achieved a kind of "maturity of form," their continued publication was forbidden by Orders in Council.[40] The most important publishers involved with these newsbooks were undoubtedly Bourne, Archer, and Butter. Butter's name is constantly punned in *The Staple of News*.

Throughout the whole twenty-year period 1620–1640, the coranto and the coranto-coiner (a man who might correspond to our columnist— I suppose a seventeenth-century Drew Pearson, as it were) became subjects for satire. Donald Lupton wrote in 1622 that the authors wrote "all conceites ordinarily, which their owne idle braine, or busie fancies, upon the blockes in *Paules*, or in their Chambers invented."[41] Nine years later, in 1631, Richard Braithwait could claim that "the more intelligent merchants do jeere [the coranto-coiner], the vulgar doe admire him, holding his novels [news] oracular."[42] Judged from our point of view, much of this criticism was unjustified. Though the news was partial and slanted, according to a leading historian the authors "were not egregiously or deliberately unfair," nor did they "willingly or purposely propagate false news, though they frequently printed mere rumors, usually, however, with a statement of what they were . . ."[43] The Jacobean critic, in his inexperience, held the papers to a higher accuracy than was humanly possible. Some of the printed criticism of the corantos and newsbooks

---

40. See Laurence Hanson, "English News Book, 1620–1641," *The Library*, 4th Series, XVIII (1938), 355–384.

41. D[onald] Lupton, *London and the Countrey Carbonadoed and Quartred into severall characters* (London, 1622), p. 142.

42. [Clitus Alexandrinus, pseudo. Richard Braithwait] *The Whimzies; or A New Cast of Characters* (1631), James O. Hallwell, ed. (London, 1859), p. 20.

43. Matthias A. Shaaber, "The History of the First English Newspaper," *SP*, XXIX (1932), 551–587. For a full and recent history see Joseph Frank, *The Beginnings of the English Newspaper, 1620–1660* (Cambridge: Harvard University Press, 1961).

THE TRIUMPH OF PECUNIA

Bodleian Library, Oxford (Douce Collection), 142 (220). By Ph. Galle, 1563. See Chapter VI, footnote 49, in this volume.

was the result of a quite English reluctance to admit value in the new-fangled, and some was motivated no doubt by simple envy of a good thing. Jonson's criticism is leveled at the idle curiosity of the public. Like Henry David Thoreau, he thought that "for the philosopher all news is gossip, and they who edit and read it are old women over their tea." In his play, Jonson presents a specific local situation which never becomes representative of a type or a kind. The only pleasures it offers are antiquarian.

The allegorical second plot of *The Staple of News*, dealing with the courting and marrying of Lady Pecunia, contrasts with the topical first plot. The Lady Pecunia story aspires to general considerations with only incidental relevance to a local circumstance. The symbolic Pecunia is associated alternately with Peniboy Senior, who is a representation of Covetousness; and Peniboy "the Sonne, the heire and Suiter," who is Prodigality. In Pecunia's entourage are a number of allegorical figures, Mortgage, Statue, Band, Waxe, Lickfinger the cook, and others. Jonson's distinguished, if old-fashioned, editors say that "in this allegorical treatment of Wealth, Jonson clearly, and indeed inevitably, had in mind the satirical comedy in which Aristophanes so trenchantly exposed the naïve illusions of the plain man about riches, and extolled 'Poverty' as the nurse of arts and mother of invention."

One doubts the full validity of this opinion, for as they go on to say, "the points of contact with the *Plutus* in our play are neither very numerous nor very important."[44] Other scholars have thought Jonson drew on other contemporaneous comedies. Charles Crawford (1905) noted what he thought were stylistic similarities between this play and *The Bloody Brother* (printed 1639);[45] and Winter (also in 1905) thought *The London Prodigal* (1605) was Jonson's chief inspiration.[46] Like *The Staple*, it is a sophistication of the story of the prodigal son. A third suggested source emphasizes Jonson's affinities with the long tradition of native didactic drama.[47] *The Contention betweene liberalitie and Prodigalitie*, which was presented before Queen Elizabeth in 1602, was probably written years earlier, for it is a morality twenty years out of fashion. As in *The Staple*, money, personified as a woman, associates herself alternately with representations of prodigality and of niggardliness. The old play is very

44. Herford and Simpson, II, 182.

45. Charles Crawford, "Ben Jonson and 'The Bloody Brother,'" *Shakespeare Jahrbuch*, XLI (1905), 163–176.

46. Ben Jonson, *The Staple of News*, De Winter, ed., Yale Studies in English, XXVIII (1905), xxv.

47. Arthur Bivins Stonex, "The Sources of Jonson's 'The Staple of News,'" *PMLA*, XXX (1915), 821–830.

neatly organized, and its conventional pattern of action is so much like *The Staple of News* that it seems unnecessary to assume that Jonson's "formal structure [comes] from Latin comedy."[48]

Aside from obvious similarities in characters and situation, the plays are alike in other ways. The author of the old morality has, like Jonson, a greater interest in economic and moral conceptions than he has in representations of human beings. Ethically his opinions are congenial to Jonson: both plead for moderation. Though classical, this ideal seems made to order for the morality drama of contention, for moderation is the obvious solution to such debates. Jonson himself repeatedly directs our attention to the indigenous drama of this type. The allegorical representations of Mirth and Tatle and Expectation and Censure, who are also realistic Jacobean Gossips, complain as choric commentators that this play has no devil and no Vice. Through them Jonson announces that his play is a morality cleared of some of its more tiresome claptrap.

Jonson had precedents in the domestic drama for what might appear to be a singular combination of allegorical and dramatic figures. This combination has troubled the scholars. Jonson even had precedents in the domestic drama for linking local satire (of the newsbooks) and economic theory. In all the discussion of his sources, no one, I think, has noted how similar *The Staple of News* is to Robert Wilson's two plays, *The Three Ladies of London* (1584, second edition 1592) and *The Three Lords and Three Ladies of London* (1590). These plays continued to be well known long after their first production, and even so late as 1598 one can find casual references to them.[49] Jonson must have known them.

Jonson's late play and Wilson's two plays are similar in some rather important respects. All the plays combine moral and economic ideas, and all link local satire with general didacticism. All represent money

48. Doran, 165.

49. Edward Guilpin alludes to it in *Skialetheia, or A Shadow of Truth*, Satire I, (1598), G. B. Harrison, ed., (Shakespeare Association Facsimiles, No. 2, 1931). Cf. the illustration of Lady Pecunia in this volume (page 176). The Latin distich in the illustration may be rendered: "Deadly Peril and anxious Fear, yoked together in thy chariot, lead thee, O Queen Money. But because thou dost cloak Folly, Theft, and bloody Murder, therefore the strong hope of all these rests in thee." Pecunia rides in a chariot, and her triumphal progress is accompanied by Envy and Pandemia (*i. e.* All the People: Greek *Pandemos*), besides the allegorical figures named in the distich. Pecunia's cloaking of Latrocinium (robbery with violence) illustrates the relationship between metaphor and action so often seen in the interludes. Her costume, like that of Money in *Liberality and Prodigality*, and *All for Money*, is decorated with coins." T. W. Craik, *The Tudor Interlude, Stage, Costume, and Acting* (London: Leicester University Press, 1958), p. xii.

as a woman—a contemporary commonplace. Lady Lucre in *The Three Ladies* accepts Fraud, Usery, Symonie, and Dissimulation as servants rather as Lady Pecunia in *The Staple of News* accepts allegorical servants. The representation of Pecunia as feminine seems natural enough: "Pecunia [is properly] the title of a Woman, Both for the termination of the Word, and because (as Women are) shee is lov'd of men" Richard Barnfield said in his introduction to *The Encomion of Lady Pecunia* (London, 1598; A 3). Neither Wilson's plays nor Jonson's is sternly allegorical; in all, allegorical dramatis personae engage in activities largely independent of their signification. Wilson's inconstant feeling for allegory is replaced by an interest in the particular fact independent of its universal application. In his plays the story threatens to overpower the idea; and his natural, though primitive, inclination is toward narration. Jonson does not have so insistent a feeling for story; with him the idea threatens the action. He is much more firmly in control of his material than poor Wilson, but his play and Wilson's plays are of a kind: an inconsistent mixture of symbol and fact. If one must find a precedent for Jonson's play, here it is.

Jonson has dealt with the contentions of semi-allegorical figures before, and he has quite customarily combined allegory and genre types. The semi-allegorical Politic Would-Be and the Venetian magnificos are linked in *Volpone*, and semi-allegorical Mammon is joined to London types like Dapper in *The Alchemist*. In the great plays the allegorical characters are interesting independent of their abstract signification; and the type figures suggest such intellectual depths that they become almost symbolic. The plays surround themselves with an intellectual penumbra. *The Staple of News* differs in that here the allegorical abstractions mean little more than they are asserted to mean; and the non-allegorical figures are not provocative.

This summary play has one claim to high attainment: the quality of its diction is almost beyond praise. None of the characters have virtuoso speeches like Sir Epicure Mammon's or Volpone's, and dashing linguistic tricks like the elaboration of jargon (IV.iv) are unsustained in this play. But the elegance of the language is a constant delight. Each of Jonson's words falls into its place like a pebble in a pond. Each vowel is calculated, each line marches its predetermined length unfaltering, and each speech rises and falls like an aria from a Mozart opera. Jonson himself said in the Prologue: "Would you were come to heare, not see a Play" (l. 2). This is not the kind of verse to satisfy post-Augustan tastes—there are no huge cloudy symbols of high romance in it. This is language for those who admire skill for its own sake.

But alas, for all its excellence of language, the play deserves its neglect. It has sunniness of temper that earlier plays lack. Jonson treats his prodigal with an unusual generosity, and even the least sympathetic characters are dealt with gently. But the dramatic tricks are old. Jonson is bored with drama, and so he bores us.

CHAPTER VII

The Dotages

JONSON WAS no longer capable of the fierce satiric temper of the great comedies after his illness of 1628, and the plays that he wrote thereafter are marked by a gentleness unlike anything in his earlier work. The last plays are failures nevertheless. What he had written between 1614 and 1626—*Bartholomew Fair*, *The Devil is an Ass*, and *The Staple of News*—all had dramaturgical similarities to native morality drama; the last, sad dotages—*The New Inn* and *The Magnetic Lady*—suggest English folk tales; and the final, fragmentary play—*The Sad Shepherd*—is pastoral. Jonson discards the burden of satire in all of these comedies almost entirely. As different as he and Shakespeare generally are, at the last both wrote varieties of romance, plays whose judgments are softened by age, or wisdom, or fatigue.

1. *The New Inn*

There is considerable critical unanimity concerning *The New Inn* (1629). Its first production was such a disastrous fiasco that the audience did not even stay to see the conclusion, and its scheduled presentation at Court was never called for. Some of Jonson's friends, even his "sons," criticized it severely. Dryden in 1668 placed it among the dotages, and Swinburne in 1889 said that "the work shows portentous signs of mental decay, or at all events of temporary collapse in judgment and in sense."[1] John Palmer, among modern critics, thinks it is "a supreme example of a 'dotage' in construction," and F. S. Boas finds in it a "strangely different note from any hitherto sounded."[2] Students need to decide whether the failure is in the "judgment" or in the "construction" of the play, and they need to know how "strangely different" it actually is. Certainly the

1. Algernon Charles Swinburne, "A Study of Ben Jonson," *The Complete Works of Algernon Charles Swinburne*, Edmund Gosse and Thomas James Wise, eds. (London: W. Heinemann, Ltd., 1926), XII, 56.
2. John Palmer, *Ben Jonson* (New York: Viking Press, 1934), p. 289. Frederick S. Boas, *An Introduction to Stuart Drama* (Oxford: Oxford University Press, 1946), p. 128.

"palpable absurdities" of its romantic plot—those are Gifford's words—require some explanation.[3]

Jonson seems to have written *The New Inn* to re-establish his place in Court and city; it accomplished at least one of its ancillary purposes: favor with the new King, Charles. In its Prologue Jonson speaks with his old arrogance, perhaps because he knew his play was weak: "If any thing be set to a wrong taste," he wrote, "'Tis not the meat, there, but the mouth's displac'd" (ll.7-8). One recalls a complementary remark in the Prologue to *The Silent Woman*: "Our wishes . . . Are not to please the cookes tastes, but the guests" (ll.7-8). In his Epilogue Jonson is humbler, perhaps pathetic:

> If you expect more than you had to night,
>   The maker is sick, and sad. But doe him right,
> He meant to please you. . . . (ll.3-5)

It is like Jonson, as I say, to attempt a reconquest of the stage, for Jonson thought that he as a poet-playwright had a high calling. It was his duty to instruct mankind, and fame was his reward. He wrote in the Epilogue that though "all strength must yeeld . . . Yet iudgement would the last be, i' the field,/With a true Poet" (Epil. 11-13), and in the "Ode to Himself," written (1629) while he still smarted from the failure of *The New Inn*, he swears that "no palsey's in [my] braine" (50). Both duty and necessity caused him to write *The New Inn*.

Palsied or not, Jonson concocted a most absurd plot for his play. A summary is sufficient comment on the hair-raising demands it makes on our credulity. Some years before the play begins Lady Frampul bears her eccentric husband a second daughter. Feeling that he is indifferent to her, she leaves his house, taking the infant Laetitia with her. She disguises herself as a gypsy and finally comes to a hostel at Barnet called the Light Heart Inn; the innkeeper, Goodestock, is actually her husband in disguise. Smitten by conscience when his wife deserted him, Frampul wandered as a vagabond for years before settling here. The couple do not recognize each other, and Lady Frampul sells her husband a boy called Frank who is really their daughter Laetitia in disguise; she herself stays on at the Inn, now disguised as a drunken Irish servant. The elder daughter, in the meantime, has assumed the title Lady Frampul.

The action of the play begins when the new Lady Frampul comes to Light Heart Inn for amusement, unaware that her parents and sister are there. She discovers Lovel at the Inn; he is in love with her, but already

3. *The Works of Ben Jonson*, W. Gifford, ed.; enlarged by F. Cunningham (London, 1875), V., p. 413.

she is attended by two suitors, Lords Latimer and Beaufort. Taking a fancy to young Frank (Laetitia), for sport she dresses the supposed boy in female clothing. Shortly Lord Beaufort falls in love with the girl-boy-girl, and they are married in the barn. Latimer falls in love with Lady Frampul's maid-companion Prue, who acts as queen of a Court of Love.[4] On order of Queen Prue, Lovel makes eloquent protestations of love to Lady Frampul and wins her favor, and the play ends with the various Frampuls revealing their true identities. Though three of the four members of the family have lived under one roof for some years, they have not recognized one another until now. This elaborate, romantic plot accounts for only about half the action. The rest is taken up with the shenanigans of "mechanicks"—tradesmen and workmen—like Stuffe, the tailor, who dresses his wife in his patroness's clothes so that he may pretend she is a courtesan; Sir Glorious Tipto, a degenerate *miles gloriosus*; and low comedians like Peirce, Iordan, Jug, Peck, and Hodge: their jokes are conventional.

The New Inn and one kind of stage comedy then popular—the romance —are of a kind. Both contain a plethora of confused identities, disguisings, and love affairs. "In this play," Symonds wrote, "Jonson attempted something in the romantic style, suggested probably by Fletcher's handling of remote subjects."[5] Practicing playwrights were quick to see it as one of their own. Whoever wrote *Love's Pilgramage* (1635?) lifted some of it for inclusion in his new play; and the author of *The Widow* (printed in 1652 but written much earlier) used Jonson's concluding scenes for his own purposes. These unknown playwrights seemed to have recognized unexhausted possibilities.[6] But Jonson's play is not, however, a simple exercise in the style of the season. He was much too independent to write à la mode. And even if he had knuckled under to contemporaneous taste, he would not have imitated the Fletcher romance. This was the very kind of play which he had spent his life railing against. Ever since 1598 he had attacked the escapist comedy which amused without instructing, and he had set out then to write such plays as other plays should be in order to drive such trivia from the stage.

The relationship of *The New Inn* to the popular entertainment is not simple. This play was surely planned as a corrective to the recurring

4. See Rayburn S. Moore, "Some Notes on the 'Courtly Love' System in Jonson's *The New Inn*," *Essays in Honor of Walter Clyde Curry* (Nashville: Vanderbilt University Press, 1954), pp. 133–142.

5. John Addington Symonds, *Ben Jonson* (London, 1888), p. 177.

6. See Herford and Simpson, II, 198–200; X, 338–340; Gerald E. Bentley, *The Jacobean and Caroline Stage* (Oxford: Clarendon Press, 1941–1956), III, 368; IV, 900–903.

abuses of the theater, and it fails because its satiric edge is dull. Jonson's intentions were what they had always been, but he no longer had the necessary vigor and acuity to achieve them. John Palmer noted that in this play "we seem to be dealing with a travesty."[7] He is nearly right. *The New Inn* follows the style of the romance and exaggerates its peculiarities, but it lacks corrective purpose. In this case travesty is incomplete satire. Jonson is not severe enough in judging Goodestocke and the other characters; he sympathizes with them. He cannot hold himself to the hard dispassion that his satire required. Something rather like this failure of nerve had threatened *Volpone*, one will remember. In that play Jonson became so fascinated by his old fox that the fox nearly turned the play into a comic celebration of malicious cleverness rather than an attack on unnatural avarice. By 1629 Jonson's tenacity of execution, not his judgment and not his integrity, failed him. Wanting to set the stage aright once more, he could not. He was too old: "the maker [was] sick, and sad."

Jonson clearly intended to attack even larger objects than the corrupted stage. The Platonic posturing of the Carolinian court was attracting general attention at this time, because it threatened the public weal: as the Court acted, so did society. Henrietta Maria, the young French wife of Charles I, had brought to England not only a French entourage but French tastes for display and pageantry. In large part because of her, the old traditions of the Courts of Love were revived and practiced in a hot-house society. She and her followers seemed determined to live life according to D'Urfé's *Astrée*, a pastoral romance of wide vogue which spelled out the circumstances of such courts and such behavior. These pseudo-Platonic theories had become fashionable on the continent—*Astrée* had appeared in France between 1607 and 1619—and were just less fashionable in England, where the novel was translated in 1620.[8]

A shallow woman, not altogether dissimilar to Marie Antoinette, Henrietta Maria tended to confuse art and life. Because of her romantic ideals of courtship and marriage, literary matters became of public importance. As Professor Sensabaugh says, "ideals which in earlier ages had seemed remote from everyday life now become problems of common concern."[9] Sensabaugh defines the characteristics of this "new" code: Since beauty and goodness are one and the same, beautiful women are

7. Palmer, p. 288.

8. See Kathleen M. Lynch, *The Social Mode of Restoration Comedy*, University of Michigan Publications, Language and Literature III (New York: Macmillan Co., 1926), esp. Chapter III.

9. G. F. Sensabaugh, *The Tragic Muse of John Ford* (Stanford: Stanford University Press, 1944), p. 105.

A KITCHEN-MAID AND JOHN OF LEYDEN

Drawings by Inigo Jones for costumes for Antimasques in Sir William Davenant's
"Britannia Rules," 1638. Reproduced by courtesy of His Grace the Duke of Devonshire.

saints to be worshipped; love is divine and omnipotent, not physical and human; true love is not only more important than marriage, it is the sole guide to virtue; love allows any liberty of action and thought. The whole code was out of touch with the ordinary realities of human psychology; the Queen seemed to have had neither a passionate nor an intellectual nature. Because she was interested in the theater and especially the masque, the code of courtly love appeared frequently in Court entertainments.

The relation of *The New Inn* to these Platonic ideals is not at all obscure. In the play the young Lady Frampul is a member of a coterie devoted to their principle and practice, and Lovel's attachment to her appears to be Platonic. For her sport, Lady Frampul establishes a Court of Love at the Light Heart Inn, and "by the dexterity, and wit of the *Soueraigne* of the *Sports, Prudence*" (Argument, 66–67) requires Lovel to discourse on the nature of love. This long discourse in the third act explicitly raises the problem of courtly love. Throughout the play Jonson asks how far romantic love may dictate total behavior, and Lovel in one scene proposes a Platonic answer: all values are subordinate to this spiritual yearning after absolute beauty. Jonson arranges the scene to undercut his views. While Lovel defends the Platonic ideal, on the opposite side of the stage Beaufort makes contrasting comments. Embracing his lady, he says:

> I relish not these *philosophicall* feasts;
> Giue me a banquet o' sense, like that of *Ovid*:
>
> (III.ii.125–126)

By juxtaposing the Platonic argument with the sensual performance, Jonson contrasts Lovel's banquet of ideas with Beaufort's banquet of sense. He endorses neither.

Ironically, Lady Frampul is ravished by Lovel's arguments, or by his charm, and upon the completion of his address she shows that she has not understood him, if she has even listened. Lovel has argued for a non-corporeal, intellectual love:

> The bodyes loue is fraile, subiect to change,
> And alter[s] still, with it: The mindes is firme,
> One, and the same, proceedeth first, from weighing,
> And well examining, what is faire, and good;
> Then, what is like in reason, fit in manners;
> That breeds good will: good will desire of vnion. . . .
> And where it starts or steps aside from this,
> It is a mere degenerous appetite,

A lost, oblique, deprau'd affection,
And beares no marke, or character of Loue.
(III.ii.159–164;167–170)

The lady replies in a different temper. Her reaction is "of the sense":

O speake, and speake for euer! let min[e] eare
Be feasted still, and filled with this banquet!
No sense can euer surfet on such truth!
It is the marrow of all louers tenents! (III.ii.201–204)

She then cites the sources on which she thinks Lovel has drawn for his learning about love: "*Plato, Heliodore*, or *Tatius,/Sydney, D'Vrfé*, or all Loues *Fathers*" (III.ii.205–206). A strange mixture of philosophers, poets and rather subliterary novelists, this list shows us Jonson's low opinion of the current Platonism. One remembers that he had never praised Petrarch, Spenser, and the whole troop of courtly love-Platonists; and even *Astrophel and Stella* and the *Arcadia* did not earn his commendations.[10] We are, in short, supposed to recognize the essential ludicrousness of Lovel's thesis however elegantly he puts his case. Indeed, though Lovel sues for one kind of love, he gets another. At the end of the play, when he receives Lady Frampul's hand in marriage, he shows that Platonic love even for him was hardly what he wanted. The doctrine of intellectual love is shown to be an affectation which cannot withstand the appearance of genuine emotion or a real human situation.

As well as showing that this kind of Platonic love is an affectation, Jonson is satirizing the complementary lust, which the relationship between Lord Beaufort and Frank suggests. Beaufort has fallen into passionate embrace with Frank, who is disguised as a girl (and who is actually a girl, but enough of that!) and has married her. He disowns his match upon the discovery that he has married a beggar's child. His o'er hasty marriage was exceedingly rash; but his withdrawal from it was equally rash. When Frank turns out to be the daughter of Lord Frampul, he accepts her once again: "Giue me my wife, I owne her now, and will haue her" (V.v.81). The play gives us two sets of lovers, then, both of whom neglect an aspect of love: Lovel and Lady Frampul are silly because they strive, or think they strive, for a non-physical love, and Beaufort is ludicrous or worse for yielding too hastily to passion. Neither is reasonable. Seen in this light, *The New Inn*, far from being "strangely different" from Jonson's other plays, is actually a further attempt to preach the wisdom of temperance; and Jonson is maintaining here what he has always maintained, that men are neither beasts nor angels, but

10. Herford and Simpson, I, 10.

creatures of the middle span; that the wise man does not bruise body to pleasure soul, nor does he deny the claims of the spirit to satisfy the flesh. *The New Inn* differs from Jonson's great plays in the imperfection of its construction, not in its judgment. Jonson was quite right. When he wrote this play there was no palsy in his brain: the palsy was in his craftsman's hand.

Lovel's second speech, in the fourth act, deals with valor. Like the discussion of love, this speech too is made in the Court of Love. Lovel is now charged with defining "what true valour is,/Which oft begets true loue" (IV.iv.27–28). He proposes straight classical—that is, Stoic—doctrine: valor proceeds from judgment, not passion. Lovel says:

> The things true valour is exercis'd about,
> Are pouerty, restraint, capitiuity,
> Banishment, losse of children, long disease:
> The least is death. (IV.iv.105–108)

One hears Jonson's aged voice through Lovel's. As before, the young Lady Frampul does not understand. Though Lovel preaches reason, the young woman yields herself to a quivering delight in his presence. "Who would not hang vpon those lips for euer!" (IV.iv.141) she says. She is seduced by his eloquence. As before, Jonson satirizes man's pretense that he is capable of living a life which is fully spiritual. Jonson knows that we are more complicated than this, and he is too old to think us able to attain our aspirations.

In his speech about valor, Lovel attacks some further affectations of the Court: the ridiculous quarrels, the vanities, the false reports. The truly valiant man rises above such pettiness, because he is concerned with the matter more than the manner of courtesy. Lovel explicitly contrasts such a man with the low comedians in the play: they are filled with bravado, not with bravery. Vain and unthinking, they are less than men:

> For me now to be angry with *Hodge Huffle*,
> Or *Burst* (his broken charge) if he be sawcy,
> Or our owne type of *Spanish* valour, Tipto . . .
> Were just to make my selfe, such a vaine *Animal*
> As one of them. (IV.iv.193–195,198–199)

Hodge, Burst, and Tipto are related to Lovel's hero rather as Beaufort and Frank are related to Lovel's ideal lover: they complement him. Tipto represents the false valor that comes from anger uncontrolled by reason. Huffle, Burst, and Tipto, being undisciplined and therefore irrational, are "vaine Animals." They are not the only foils in this scene, however.

Beaufort and Latimer, in disputing with Lovel, show themselves mis-
guided; they represent a different kind of false value. If the "mechanicks"
mistake the trappings for the heart, these two young men about town
overvalue that bubble, reputation. Beaufort pleads for

> the ignorant valour
> That knowes not why it undertakes, but doth it
> T[o]'escape the infamy merely—(IV.iv.100–102)

This kind of valor, Lovel maintains, "Deserues the name of daring,
not of valour" (IV.iv.119). The valiant man "vndertakes with reason,
not by chance" (IV.iv.128). Beaufort and Latimer are not so seriously
in error as Tipto, for they can be corrected; they are nevertheless mistaken.
In this scene, then, Lovel's views are contrasted with two kinds of false
valor. As usual, Jonson seeks the middle way, and instructs men in the
reasonable life.

In this discussion of love, Jonson attacks the codes of love found in such
pastoral romances as D'Urfé's *Astrée*. In his discussion of valor, he attacks
the codes found in such chivalric romances as *Amadís of Gaul* and
Palmerin de Oliva. These long, overplotted novels had originated in
Spain a century earlier, and were the genesis of *Don Quixote*. Though
never widely popular in England as they had been in France, Spain, and
Portugal,[11] for a time the drama was full of the honor these romances
celebrated. Beaumont and Fletcher burlesqued it in *The Knight of the
Burning Pestle*, which reappeared in two quartos in 1635. Honor was one
of Ford's staple subjects, and it was prominent in the plays of Massinger
and Shirley. Jonson had glanced at the "Spanish" conception of honor
in *The Silent Woman* and *The Alchemist*, and his satire of chivalric ideals
in *Every Man Out of his Humour* owes something to *Amadís of Gaul*.

Jonson saw that fashionable "love" and "valor" were parodies of
true love and true valor, and both his humanistic sympathies and his
common sense found the courtly ideals ridiculous. But his satire of them
failed because he was simply past caring enough. With all the ingredients
of the successful plays, this is satire without the sting and correction
without the whip. *Bartholomew Fair* had been almost Shakespearean in
its breadth of sympathy, and *The Devil is an Ass* and *The Staple of News*
were not so sharp as the earlier, greater comedies. Now, in his weakness
and age, Jonson could plot a satire, populate it with fools, plan elucidation
of the usual vices; but he could not execute it. By temperament an
Elizabethan, he was a satirist and a classicist by stern determination. In

11. See Henry Thomas, "The Romances of Amadís of Gaul," *Transactions of the
Bibliographical Society*, XI (1909–1911), 251–297; and "The Palmerin Romances,"
Transactions of the Bibliographical Society, XIII (1913–1915), 97–144.

his old age, the determination being weakened with the body, he relaxed into an Elizabethan temper. Only the vestigial elements of the intended satire remain.

2. *The Magnetic Lady*

The Magnetic Lady and *The New Inn* are companion pieces in that they are plays of Jonson's decline. Though Swinburne and a few others have found qualities in it to admire, generally the contemporaneous opinion of James Howell is the opinion of its few readers: "You were mad," he wrote to Jonson, "when you writ your *Fox*, and madder when you writ your *Alchemist*; [but] when you writ your *Epigrams* and the *Magnetic Lady* you were not so mad...."[12] Most critics agree that many of the Jonson clichés are repeated in it with a minimum of illuminating novelty. Still, one is tempted to say of this play what might be said of much of Jonson's minor work: if this play were by any hand but Jonson's, it would not be neglected; it has its merits and its charms. Jonson's best drives out his good.

The plan of *The Magnetic Lady* does not differ from the basic plan of the great plays. The title character, Lady Loadstone, serves as a magnet attracting a collection of persons suitable for satire. Jonson has used a magnetic figure to draw gulls to one place before: indeed, this is his standard technique. Lady Loadstone is in this respect a feminine Subtle or Volpone. And Compass is to Lady Loadstone as Face is to Subtle, and Mosca to Volpone. Compass, Face, and Mosca are all three ushers, or perhaps confidence men, who bring in the fools for fleecing, or correction, or both.[13] In the great plays the magnetic center fascinates us ·by his audacity. In this play Lady Loadstone is incompletely realized. In place of passionate intensity and acrobatic wit, she is a shadow. More than that, as one of its editors has complained, "the play lacks the unifying force of a central satiric motive."[14] All the persons who are drawn to the magnetic lady are materialists, but their motives are too disparate to be dramatized under a single heading. Sir Moth Interest speculates with the property of others; Sir Diaphanous Silkworm searches for a wife; Doctor Rut is a quack; Parson Palate is more concerned with physical than spiritual satisfaction. All of them want to get whatever reward the world offers, as who doesn't? The satire lacks direction.

The second part of the play, which deals with the marriage of Placentia, Lady Loadstone's niece and ward, is fresher. Placentia, an heiress, is

12. Herford and Simpson, II, 203.

13. *Ibid.*, 205.

14. Ben Jonson, *The Magnetic Lady, or Humors Reconciled*, Harvey Whitefield Peck, ed., Yale Studies in English XLVII (1914), p. xii.

about to be married by her uncle, Sir Moth, and her aunt, Lady Loadstone, to a person of their selection. During the course of the play we
discover that Placentia and Pleasance, her waiting woman, were exchanged
in the nursery by Placentia's mother, Polish, Lady Loadstone's "gossip."
The true heiress is thus the waiting woman, and the seeming heiress is the
daughter of the "she-parasite." This exchange is discovered by the
audience only in the fourth act, after the false heiress has borne a baby
out of wedlock in the third act. These sections of the play are relatively
exciting: lost heirs, recovered fortunes, knowing but secretive midwives,
and mothers who falsify records for the benefit of their daughters.

Less satirical than the rest of the play, this part is romantic, in the
manner of Elizabethan comedy. It interests us as the folk tales from which
it springs interest us, because it has suspense, it is ingeniously concocted,
and it is filled with dramatic irony. This is not of course the initial appearance of the folk story in Jonson; as we have seen, it appears in
Volpone, The Silent Woman, The New Inn. In *The Magnetic Lady* Jonson's
satiric flame had nearly burned itself out, or is at least no longer bright
enough to inspire him to high achievement even while the Elizabethan
romance comes alive under his hand. The successful characters are not
satiric portraits but Elizabethan individuals. Polish, the mother of
Placentia and companion of Lady Loadstone, is the premier accomplishment of this play; all things considered she is the fullest female creation
of Jonson's career. When she is on stage, even Compass, who otherwise
intrigues us, loses some of his brilliance. In Polish Jonson extends himself
to a full portrait of a woman, and in her alone is there no evidence of a
diminution of his power.

Compass, the Mosca of the piece and the other convincing character
of *The Magnetic Lady*, is not sharply motivated, and his actions are not
delineated with precision. He says he is involved in this "for sport;/For
nothing else" (I.i.51–52), but from the first he seems to have some scheme
for private advantage. He appears to be enamored of Pleasance even
before he discovers that she is herself the true heiress. Since romantic
love independent of prudence hardly exists in Jonson's world, one wonders
if we are to understand that Compass has had some prior inkling of the
confusion of Pleasance and Placentia. Ultimately Compass marries the
heiress—Jonson awards him the prize—and his "brother," Captain
Ironside, marries the rich widow, Lady Loadstone. One cannot be sure
that Compass has not plotted for this conclusion from the beginning. In
this play Jonson seems more interested in moving his characters about the
stage than in giving them rational motives.

The remainder of the figures are more sketchily drawn than Compass, in spite of the fact that they are on stage for considerable periods. They bore us, not only because they are not newly imitated from nature, but because they are around too much. Jonson is not circumspect. He holds our interest in the great plays by showing us each of his cardboard manni-kins for a moment only. They form a parade, appearing in sequence, in *The Alchemist* and *Bartholomew Fair*. In *The Magnetic Lady* they appear in groups, and once introduced stick with us. Even in the first act, where Jonson attempts his old parade, he gives us a series of static portraits rather than a sequence of shifting vignettes. The sketches have their brilliance, as Swinburne long ago observed;[15] but they are not dramatic. Jonson also misuses another technique which had been successful earlier. When more than two of his characters are on stage in the great plays, they comment on one another; sometimes there are as many as three and four groups simultaneously observing and criticizing, and the effect is a five-ring circus: independent but related actions wherever one looks. In *The Magnetic Lady* the actions and the observations are not isolated; indeed they intrude on one another.

Jonson recognized his failing power. He says in the first Chorus that he is "finding himselfe now neare the close, or shutting up of his Circle" (104-105). Afraid that the play could not stand to be judged on its own merits, he attempted to prop it with Choruses defending its lack of action, explaining its argument, and asserting its unity. But even here at the end of his dramatic career Jonson's old arrogance reasserts itself. The judge, he says with his familiar flourish, not the play, is on trial. He was to live for five more years after *The Magnetic Lady*, until 1637; but he completed no more plays. We cannot regret it. His genius had burned out.

3. The Sad Shepherd

The Sad Shepherd is a fragment. Discovered among Jonson's papers after his death, it consists of two and a half acts of pastoral romance which appears to be in finished form. Scholars and critics have not agreed on the date of its composition. J. A. Symonds among others has suggested that this splendid little play—the critics have been uniformly delighted with it[16]—is the slight reworking of an earlier, lost play.[17] When Jonson was in Scotland in 1618, he told Drummond that he had written a pastoral called *The May Lord*, and some think this fragment is that play.[18] The

15. Swinburne, XII, 57.
16. See Swinburne, for example, XII, 62.
17. Symonds, pp. 191-192.
18. *Conversations*, 393-398 (Herford and Simpson, I, 143).

two have a similarity in kind, and two names apparently in *The May Lord* turn up in *The Sad Shepherd*. No additional fact links them, but some negative evidence does. Critics have not thought that Jonson in his last years was capable of the high imagination this play shows, that in his dotage he could write so well.

The weight of evidence points to a late date for this play. In the Prologue Jonson says it was composed while he was confined to bed, forty years after his initial appearance on the stage. This would place it in the mid-1630's. Lord Falkland (Lucius Cary) seems to speak of it in the volume of memorial verse called *Jonsonus Virbius* (1638):

> Not long before his *Death*, our *Woods* he meant
> To *visit*, and descend from *Thames* to *Trent* (pp. 257–258).[19]

These references do not preclude the possibility that this play might be a revised version of an earlier work; but for internal reasons we can reject this hypothesis too. *The Sad Shepherd* differs from the major portion of Jonson's work in being gentle. It does not sport with follies or with crimes, either for correction or for entertainment; and it does not set out to expose the evils of the age. It even contains a character identified as "the Reconciler"—there were no "reconcilers" in *The Alchemist* or *The Silent Woman*. It does contain a number of topical references: Jonson could not stop living in the great world even though bedridden. But these references are only incidentally critical. Early in the play, when Robin Hood and his company defend their woodland frolicking from "The Sowrer sort/Of Shepherds [who] now disclaime in all such sport" (I.iv.18–19), Jonson seems to allude to a favorite target, the Puritans. A moment later he glances at the Puritans again:

> They call ours, *Pagan* pastimes, that infect
> Our blood with ease, our youth with all neglect,
> Our tongues with wantonnesse, our thoughts with lust;
> And what they censure ill, all others must. (I.iv.36–39)

But *The Sad Shepherd* is not generally caustic.

Even so *The Sad Shepherd* does not stand apart from the rest of Jonson's work.[20] For some years, as we have seen, his satiric strength had been waning. In both *The New Inn* and *The Magnetic Lady* it was the romantic materials which struck creative fire in him; the critical possibilities had received scant attention. The lyrical tone of this last play was fore-shadowed by the relative tenderness of these two romances. Here in his

19. Quoted entire in Herford and Simpson, XI, 430–437.
20. George Gregory Smith, *Ben Jonson* (London: Macmillan and Co., 1919), p. 207.

final effort Jonson gives us Robin Hood, Maid Marian, and all those gay outlaws of Sherwood Forest. Here, too, are goblins; Maudlin, the witch of Papplewick; and Puck-Hairy, her "hine" with magical powers. Captivated by these creatures, Jonson bestowed a special vitality on them. In their debt to the folk tale, they recall some of the figures in the other last plays.

The Sad Shepherd is evidence of Jonson's growing disinclination toward corrective drama and of his sympathy for the folk. No longer attempting to set things right, he had returned to something like the drama he had written before he found his high didactic calling in *The Case is Altered*. The plain experience of the country is now sophisticated by two generations of reading and two generations of service to the theater and to the Court. He had come to the "close, or shutting up of his Circle," and his railing tongue was at last quiet.

APPENDIX A

The "Seeling" in *Sejanus*:
A Note on Staging

IN THE CONTINUING controversy concerning the original productions of
Elizabethan and Jacobean plays, all scraps of evidence dealing with the
"study," the "chamber," and the "hut" must be examined with care.
In Jonson's *Sejanus* (1603) is a passage of interest to persons concerned
with the inner and upper stages. Latiaris, an agent of the evil Sejanus,
instructs his henchmen, Rufus and Opsius, to hide themselves until he
has trapped Sabinus into an expression of treason. He says:

> Here place your selues, betweene the roofe, and seeling,
> And when I bring him to his wordes of danger,
> Reueale your selues, and take him. (IV.95–97)

A moment later Rufus says, "List,/I heare them come"; and Opsius
replies, "Shift to our holes, with silence." (IV.113–114). When Sabinus
finally speaks out, Opsius cries, "Treason to Caesar." Rufus continues:
"Lay hands vpon the traytor, Latiaris,/Or take the name thy selfe."
Latiaris: "I am for Caesar" (IV.217–219). And Sabinus is taken.

Though scenes of eavesdropping are not at all unusual in the drama of
the time, the staging of this one has long been a problem. Herford and
Simpson suggest in their monumental edition of Jonson (IX.621):
"Probably the whole was played on the upper stage. The 'holes' of line
114—Sir E. K. Chambers queries if this was a misprint for 'hole'—must
be 'betweene the roofe, and seeling' (95). At line 114 the spies mount a
rope ladder into the 'hut' above and draw it up after them; they drop it
again at line 217 and descend." Professor Allan Gilbert (*MLN* 69 [1954],
164–166) has brought a number of arguments against this suggested
staging. He notes that the text makes no provision for a rope ladder and
that the third-story "hut" could be out of view of the audience. He finds
that Tacitus, Jonson's source for the passage, says the conspirators
conferred in a "chamber" and that they "applied their ears to holes and
cracks." He concludes that Latiaris met his assistants on the upper stage,

went below to meet Sabinus while Opsius and Rufus listened to what went on below through cracks in the floor. Although Gilbert's solution has the merit of disposing of Simpson's rope ladder and of bringing the action down from the "hut" into the audience's line of vision, it is not entirely satisfactory.

Jonson provides some seventeen lines (from 98 to 115) for an interval in which Latiaris can fetch Sabinus, but he provides no similar passage of time in which Rufus and Opsius can descend to the platform stage to join them. As Opsius cries "Treason" and Rufus shouts "Lay hands . . ." presumably they could rush down from above to take custody of the unfortunate Sabinus. If they talked while moving down, their words would very likely be lost, and their climbing, by rope ladder or other means, would cause considerable extraneous commotion on the stage. It is worth noting that when Sabinus greets the eavesdroppers, he calls attention to their advanced years:

> Spies of this head! so white! so full of yeeres!
> Well, my most reuerend monsters, you may liue
> To see your selues thus snar'd. (IV.221–223)

These old men could no doubt climb up and down ladders with the dexterity required by the speed of the passage, but they are not likely to. Such activity by old men would call attention to itself and be dramatically self-defeating. One doubts if the stage-wise Jonson would risk the ludicrous or the difficult at this point in his play. Few modern directors would.

Fundamentally Simpson's proposal grows out of a misunderstanding of the meaning of the word *seeling*: "Place your selues, betweene the roofe, and seeling . . ." Latiaris says. Both Gilbert and Simpson take the word seeling (ceiling) to refer to "the undercover of a roof or floor, concealing the timbers; the plaster of the top of a room." While the *OED* recognizes the word in this sense as early as 1535, *ceiling* in Jonson's day frequently had a different and now obsolete meaning. Until the middle of the seventeenth century, a ceiling was also "a screen of a tapestry, a curtain," and the *OED* cites Hall's *Chronicle* (1548) in its definition: "The Frenche kyng . . . caused the lord of Countay . . . with the lord of Argenton . . . to stande secretly behynd a selyng or a hangyng in his chamber . . . so that what soever were purposed to hym, they standyng behind the clothe, might easily se, and facile heare the same." Since a ceiling could be a tapestry, it seems unnecessary to hypothesize a rope ladder, an upper stage, or elaborate movements. The spies simply hid behind the arras, like Polonius, and jumped out to seize their victim at the appropriate moment. The "holes" which trouble Chambers and Gilbert were surely only lacunae in the weaving through which they peeped, like children in amateur theatricals. Jonson says on the title page of both the 1616 and 1640 Folios that *Sejanus* was first acted in 1603. Chambers suggests (*Eliz. Stage* III 367) that it was first produced at Court, for the theaters were closed from Elizabeth's death until March, 1604. Shakespeare's company, which acted it, would have found staging simple in a Great Hall at Court if they understood *seeling* to mean arras. When they got to the Globe in the spring after the plague, there they would have had a tapestry at the rear of their stage behind which to hide. If it screened off an inner stage, the "roofe" of line 95 would refer to the roof of the "chamber." One wonders how often hypothetical antique stagings depend on similar misreadings of Elizabethan English.

Jonson's "Unclean Birds":
A Note on Meaning

IN *The Alchemist* Ananias twice alludes to "unclean birds" (IV.vii.
51–55; V.iii.46–77). Both passages are rather cryptic. No one has been
able to say with any certainty what the birds are, what makes them unclean, and what relevance they have to the play. Their identity may now
be clarified. Hathaway suggested long ago that "the unclean birds are
more like to be vultures, &c., in some popular superstition. *Unclean*
carries a suggestion of scriptural origin like scorpions" (Yale Studies on
English, XVII [1903], 333). Unlike Herford and Simpson, who cite the
Bible, Hathaway does not seem aware of the possible reference in the
line to *Revelation*, 18.2: "And he cried mightily with a strong voice,
saying, Babylon the great is fallen, is fallen, and is become the habitation
of devils, and the hold of every foul spirit, and a cage of every unclean
and hateful bird." Professor M. A. Shaaber more recently has suggested
that Jonson is referring to "an established form of credulity" (*MLN*,
LXV [1950], 108). Though neither he nor Hathaway could identify the
particular bit of folklore to which Jonson refers, both are on the right
track.

In *Poetaster* (1601) when Jonson speaks of "unclean birds," he more
clearly identifies what he means than he does in *The Alchemist*. In the
Apologeticall Dialogue with which the play ends, the Author calls his
enemies:

> . . . these vile *Ibides*, these vncleane birds,
> That make their mouthes their clysters, and still purge
> From their hot entrailes. (219–222)

In their footnote in *Poetaster*, Herford and Simpson refer to Holland's
translation of Pliny to illuminate these lines. Holland (and Pliny) wrote:

> The . . . device . . . of clystres, we learned first of a foule in . . . Ægypt,
> called Ibis (or the blacke Storke.) This bird having a crooked and hooked
> bill, vseth it in steed of a syringe or pipe, to squirt water into that

part, whereby it is most kind and holsome to void the doung and excrements of meat, and so purgeth and cleanseth her bodie. (1601 ed., VIII, xxvii)

Herford and Simpson do not connect this passage in *Poetaster* either with *The Alchemist* or with Holland's Pliny.

In many medieval and Renaissance natural histories the ibis has a symbolic significance which is relevant to *The Alchemist*. According to the bestiaries, the ibis "is typical of Carnal Man, who goes in for dead dealings as if they were good spiritual food—by which his miserable soul gets nourished for punishment" (*The Book of Beasts*, ed. T. H. White, London, 1954, 120). Ananias (and Jonson) use the epithet with accuracy; Lovewit's house under Face and Subtle has become a haven for carnal men who hypocritically substitute the carrion of material wealth for spiritual nourishment, and, in Ananias's view, risk their immortal souls. The character of Ananias and our respect for the precision of the allusions in Jonson's mature work are increased by our recognition of the archaic symbolism of the birds. The emblematic significance of the ibis is not relevant to *Poetaster*; the Author in this Apologeticall Dialogue is doing little more than calling a name without further meaning.

Acknowledgments

Many persons directly and indirectly have helped me with this study, and I want to thank them all. Through the generosity of the Woods Charitable Fund, Inc. I was able to spend a year as a Woods Fellow at the British Museum and the Warburg Institute, London. The manuscript was prepared through money made available by the Research Council of the University of Nebraska; the Council also awarded me a summer fellowship so that I might complete a final draft of my manuscript. My personal debts are large: to all the staff at the Warburg where I met nothing but kindness; to Edward B. Partridge, who read the manuscript with care and made helpful suggestions; to Bernard Kreissman, who cheerfully examined sections and offered good advice; to William B. Coley III, who listened and criticized; to Frederick L. Gwynn, who published part of one chapter in *College English* when he was editor; to Richard Hosley, who asked me to read a part of two chapters at the Central Renaissance Conference before he had seen one word of the manuscript; and to Dr. A. L. Rowse, who encouraged me when I needed it. Most of all I have been helped by alert and stimulating colleagues at the University of Nebraska, who have quizzed and corrected me over the years. Of my last great debt, I am forbidden to speak; but I am grateful nonetheless.

R.E.K.

Index

INDEX

Page references in italics indicate major entries.